EXPLORATIONS IN SOCIAL PSYCHOLOGY

READINGS AND RESEARCH

EDITED BY

Steve L. Ellyson
Youngstown State University

Amy G. Halberstadt
North Carolina State University

McGRAW-HILL, INC.

New York   St. Louis   San Francisco   Auckland   Bogotá
Caracas   Lisbon   London   Madrid   Mexico City   Milan
Montreal   New Delhi   San Juan   Singapore   Sydney   Tokyo   Toronto

This book was set in Times Roman by TC Systems, Inc.
The editors were Jane Vaicunas, Laura Lynch, and Fred H. Burns;
the production supervisor was Richard A. Ausburn.
The cover was designed by Rafael Hernandez.
R. R. Donnelley & Sons Company was printer and binder.

Cover photo: Jean-Marc Giboux/Gamma Liaison

EXPLORATIONS IN SOCIAL PSYCHOLOGY
Readings and Research

 This book is printed on recycled, acid-free paper
containing 10% postconsumer waste.

1 2 3 4 5 6 7 8 9 0   DOC   DOC   9 0 9 8 7 6 5 4

ISBN 0-07-020200-1

Library of Congress Cataloging-in-Publication Data

Explorations in social psychology: readings and research / edited by
   Steve L. Ellyson and Amy G. Halberstadt.
      p.   cm.
   Includes bibliographical references and indexes.
   ISBN 0-07-020200-1
   1. Social psychology.   I. Ellyson, Steve L.   II. Halberstadt, Amy
G.
HM251.E95   1995
302—dc20   94-22115

ABOUT
THE EDITORS

STEVE L. ELLYSON, a 1974 Ph.D. from the University of Delaware, is presently a professor of psychology at Youngstown State University in Ohio, where he received the 1989, 1990, and 1992 Distinguished Professor Award for his teaching and research. AMY G. HALBERSTADT, a 1981 Ph.D. from The Johns Hopkins University, is presently an associate professor of psychology at North Carolina State University. Both are members of the American Psychological Association, the American Psychological Society, and the Society for Experimental Social Psychology. Both have experience teaching in a variety of institutions; Professor Ellyson has taught at Beaver College, Linfield College, and the University of California, Davis, and Professor Halberstadt has taught at Vassar College. Dr. Ellyson's research interests include examination of human nonverbal behavior, gender issues, altruism, person perception, and attitudes. Dr. Halberstadt's research interests include emotional experience and expression, socialization processes, gender issues, nonverbal communication, and parent-child relations.

Dr. Ellyson referees college and high school basketball games during the winter and plays baseball and softball in the summer, while Dr. Halberstadt has coached women's fencing at the intercollegiate level and was a nationally ranked foil fencer.

To Chris Anna Olson (1946–1976)
and
Krista Blake (1972–1994)

and all others who live and
die without compromising
their ideals

CONTENTS

LIST OF CONTRIBUTORS

ANTONIA ABBEY
ELLIOT ARONSON
ROBERT M. BELL
LISA M. BOSSIO
SHARON S. BREHM
JERRY M. BURGER
LINDA BURNS
HADLEY CANTRIL
ROBERT B. CIALDINI
LESLIE M. DOWNING
PHYLLIS L. ELLICKSON
STEVE L. ELLYSON
EVA FOGELMAN
SIGMUND FREUD
JANICE T. GIBSON
JOHN GLIEDMAN
LISA GOULD
AMY G. HALBERSTADT
GARRETT HARDIN
MIKA HARITOS-FATOUROS

ALBERT H. HASTORF
GREGORY M. HEREK
DIANNE F. HERMAN
ROBERT D. JOHNSON
ELLEN J. LANGER
RICHARD T. LaPIERE
MARK R. LEARY
MICHAEL R. LEIPPE
DARWYN LINDER
MICHAEL B. MAZIS
CHRISTOPHER PETERSON
DEAN G. PRUITT
JUDITH RODIN
D. L. ROSENHAN
MARK L. SNYDER
HARRY C. TRIANDIS
NORMAN TRIPLETT
COLIN M. TURNBULL
VALERIE LEWIS WIENER
PHILIP G. ZIMBARDO

PREFACE

Social psychology is still a relatively young science that did not exist a mere hundred years ago. The first attempt to apply experimental methods to social behavior was made by Norman Triplett, in an Indiana University lab in 1898. Since then social psychology has evolved into a dynamic and eclectic discipline probing the hows and whys of human social behavior.

Those of us who teach undergraduate social psychology are continually challenged with the task of presenting a meaningful picture of this field in the 10- to 15-week format of most introductory social psychology courses. Moreover, we want our students to be more incisive and careful thinkers. We have struggled with these problems for some time. Over a number of years of teaching social psychology at different colleges and universities, we have developed different sets of readings that aim to achieve these goals. We now hope that other instructors and students will find this book of readings helpful in understanding this exciting and impressive field.

Each reading is preceded by a short introduction. These were written to facilitate reading the original work of so many talented authors and highlight the interconnections between the specific readings and the larger themes represented in social psychology. While this reader was developed to be a companion to David Myers' *Exploring Social Psychology* (1994), we believe it can be easily adapted as a valuable supplement to any of the many excellent social psychology texts currently available. We will make direct reference to Myers's "modules" in our introductions and attempt to expand and elaborate on many of the ideas presented there. Often a reading accompanying a certain module section will lead into the next module as well. We recommend reading the general overview in the text first, and then turning to the material in the reader using a "general to specific" reading strategy.

The book is organized into four sections, an introductory section followed by Social Thinking, Social Influence, and Social Relations. The last three sections are constructed around a central issue in human social behavior, and each of these sections is further divided into readings that reflect that area's major issues. Instead of relegating a separate section on applied social psychology to the back of the book, we have integrated political, health-related, business-related, law-related, and developmental applications within the major sections. In addition, issues raised in one area are often important in other areas as well, thus we have tried to highlight the interrelationships across the area sections.

These thirty readings from the social psychology literature span nearly 100 years. But this book should not be mistaken for a history reader. Nearly half of the readings have appeared in the last ten years. Although we do not claim to have exhaustively covered all possible areas in social psychology, we have tried to provide a representative and readable sampling of the field.

Providing a comprehensive and cogent overview of nearly 100 years of research has been a stimulating and rewarding enterprise. The selection process was lengthy. Not a few minor and major disputes arose between the editors during this process. It would have been far easier to produce a readings book with four times this number of readings, and we have not been able to include many excellent readings. Also, several of the longer articles we did include are excerpted, and many other articles are edited slightly. Although professors may choose to assign only some of these readings, we anticipate that students will want to explore many of these topics on their own. Our aim has been to create a reader with many enticing choices for both the social psychology instructor and social psychology student. In short, we hope that this will be a reader that is *read*.

SPECIAL NOTE ABOUT EDITING

Some of the readings contained in this book are excerpted and abridged from their original published forms. As researchers, as well as editors, we were quite hesitant to alter the work of others. However, in attempting to cover as many issues in social psychology as possible and to be responsive to the needs of our audience, cuts were sometimes necessary. When faced with the choice of judicious trimming of long selections or total omission, we often chose the former option. Although we have attempted to keep such alterations at a minimum, all decisions made in this process are fully our responsibility.

The designation "abridged from" means that deletions are made. For the most part, these deletions are minor and involve author notes, lengthy or less essential footnotes, or somewhat redundant information. The designation "excerpted from" means that only a portion of a larger work, such as a book or book chapter, has been selected for inclusion, and that fairly major editing may have been necessary.

Readers are directed to the source data at the bottom of each reading's first page for information about the editing status of an individual work. In the case of abridged or excerpted works, readers seeking expansion of certain points or related information are strongly encouraged to consult the original publication.

Readers wishing to contact authors are directed to the *American Psychological Association Membership Register* for their current addresses. This book is available in most college and university libraries or departments of psychology and contains information about the majority of the living authors.

ACKNOWLEDGMENTS

We are first and foremost grateful to the authors of the selections included in this volume for their permission to reprint their work.

We would also like to thank the fine editorial and production staff at McGraw-Hill, specifically Jane Vaicunas, Fred H. Burns, Laura Lynch, Michael Clark, Ann Irons, and Katy Redmond for their competence throughout all phases of the production of this book.

The editors are also indebted to a number of our students who aided us in our selection and editing process. They are Christine Carson, Kim Colaluca, Pamela Condoleon, Christina A. D'Angelo, Cynthia L. DeBlasio, Elizabeth Popovich, and Greg Thurik.

In addition, we express our appreciation to our friends and colleagues, who are, in many ways, an extended family. They are Sandra Carpenter, John F. Dovidio, Samuel L. Gaertner, Judith A. Hall, Albert A. Harrison, James Morrison, Ulrike Steinbach, Christopher J. Sweeney, and Midge Wilson. Their contributions, in many ways, allowed this project to reach completion. Sadly, the work on this book coincided with the death of Steve Ellyson's "academic father" Ralph V. Exline and "academic uncle" Bernard Mausner. Both these teachers and scholars will be remembered for their thinking and for their work but mostly they will be missed for their excellence as human beings. Amy Halberstadt would also like to welcome Molly Amelia who was born into her family during the creation of this book.

Finally, we would like to thank our immediate families for their love, which we cherish.

Steve L. Ellyson
Amy G. Halberstadt

INTRODUCING SOCIAL PSYCHOLOGY

1

ON READING
THE READINGS

Steve L. Ellyson and Amy G. Halberstadt (1994)

Welcome to your world. You are a human being. Among other activities, you think, you laugh, you cry. Because humans are among the most social of all creatures on the earth, most of what you think about, laugh about, and cry about involves other people. You have before you a book of readings that in one way or another explores you and your social world.

Some of the readings contained in this book come from books or magazines presenting the work of social psychologists to broad audiences. You will find these relatively easy to read because they are written in a style with which you are familiar. But we have also included quite a few readings taken straight from various social psychological journals, including original research. You may ask—why did you folks do this? Good question. And here's our answer.

First, reading actual articles allows you to get a better understanding of the complexity and richness of the questions social psychologists ask and the answers that they obtain. Textbook authors must provide comprehensive coverage of many topics, so they can only briefly summarize the numerous studies that they describe. This strategy necessarily precludes an in-depth analysis of any one idea or of examples of how research studies investigate a particular topic or theory. This reader, by contrast, includes reviews, theoretical discussions, and research studies that explore a variety of important and interesting topics. You will also see how social psychology has developed over the last 100 years.

Second, by reading the original sources, you experience the research as directly as anyone can without actually participating in that particular study. We think that first-hand encounters with the actual foundations of social psychology enhance one's understanding of the field. Instead of reading someone else's very brief summaries, you can explore the research on your own.

Third, because no one has predigested the material, you will find yourself organizing the material for yourself. This is an advantage! You may remember from your introductory psychology course that learning is promoted by active processing and organizing of material. You will certainly be doing this as you read and reread these classic and contemporary articles.

A word of caution: These readings are not designed to provide you with final answers. Rather, they are intended to further engage your curiosity about social phenomena. Coming to understand social psychology is a process. It involves questioning assumptions, developing tentative ideas, analyzing those ideas and their underlying assumptions, reworking new tentative hypotheses in association with close examination of data and theory, and analyzing the hypotheses all over again. Thus, these readings are designed to stimulate further questioning, to help clarify your own assumptions, and to assist you in developing careful, thoughtful models of social behavior.

We encourage you to be an active participant as you encounter the articles in this book. As you read and reread these articles, try to imagine yourself as one of the subjects who took part in the study. What do you think you would have done in this study as a subject, or even as an experimenter? Ask yourself questions. Are the results what you would have guessed? (But beware of hindsight bias; see Reading 2.) Do they fit your social reality? If so, do the authors' explanations also make sense? What other explanations are possible? If the results don't fit your social experience, can you think of reasons that both the authors' results and your own experience might be right (or wrong)? Could your social reality be influenced by something special about you or by your own hidden assumptions? Or could the population sample studied be sufficiently different to account for different results? Or are these results counter-intuitive, yet reasonable in retrospect?

Because each of the following articles addresses human social behavior, apply your own knowledge and add to it. Natural curiosity about yourself and other people makes the material interesting. Original research reports reveal what lies behind those one- or two-sentence references found throughout your textbooks. Reading the primary research literature takes you backstage at the play, to the sidelines for the sporting event, to a more revealing angle from which to observe the magician. Reading the original report allows a much greater appreciation of exactly what a study did and what the study found. Even though the vocabulary in an article may send you to your dictionary or to your instructor, and the statistics may seem like they are part of some obscure foreign language, don't be dismayed. Tenacity on your part will pay off with an appreciation of how social psychologists look for meaningful answers to meaningful questions.

One other point is important. It is often difficult to recognize our own perspective as we try to understand the perspectives of other people. Bem and Bem (1970) suggest that some of our assumptions (what they refer to as "nonconscious ideologies") are so much a part of our culture that we are completely unaware of them. Referring to how an individual comes to have such hidden ground rules, the Bems ask:

What happens when all reference groups agree, when religion, family, peers, teachers, and the mass media all disseminate the same message? The consequence is a nonconscious ideology, a set of beliefs and attitudes which [we] accept implicitly but which remains outside [our] awareness because alternative conceptions of the world remain unimagined. As we noted earlier, only a very unparochial and intellectual fish is aware that [its] environment is wet. After all, what else could it be? Such is the nature of a nonconscious ideology (p. 89).

We all have underlying perspectives that influence how we come to understand new material. When you read about different cultures or even our own culture at an earlier time (for instance, Readings 12, 14, 17, 18, 30), you will become more aware than usual about others' underlying assumptions. As you explore these readings, try to apply this heightened awareness to your own assumptions and basic belief structures.

WHAT YOU WILL ENCOUNTER IN JOURNAL ARTICLES

Many of the readings that follow originally appeared in journals that report social psychology research. Journal studies are, however, written in a different style than the traditional textbook. The goal of the authors who write these articles is to present information clearly, and sometimes to persuade. This kind of writing requires a bit of getting accustomed to, and the following should help you to get the most out of these readings.

The American Psychological Association has issued a *Publication Manual* (1983) with writing guidelines that most journal articles follow. Familiarity with this standardized format helps both beginners and veterans to understand an article's content.

What should you expect to find in a scientific research report? Reports of empirical studies typically include an *abstract,* an *introduction, methods, results, discussion* or *conclusions,* and a listing of *references,* although theoretical and review articles often vary somewhat from this format. It is appropriate at this point to give you a preview of what you are likely to find in each section of a typical journal article.

The Title

The title is usually a brief summary of the main idea of the article. It should, on its own, convey the fundamental issues addressed in the study.

The Abstract

The abstract is a brief overview of the entire article. The abstract presents the research in a nutshell and includes the research goal, the subjects and method, the results, and the conclusions, all in about 150 words or less. Because many readers skim the abstract to decide whether to read the full article, abstracts are usually well-written and informative, although they can also be intimidating by virtue of having packed so much information into such a small space. However, if you find yourself getting bogged down in a particular article, a quick review of the abstract is sometimes an effective way to get back on track.

The Introduction

In the introduction the author describes the reasons for doing the research, what has been done before, and how this is a new question or a novel and/or useful way to address the problem at hand. By carefully positioning the research in a historical context and selectively discussing previous work, a link is established between the research effort and the existing body of literature. Broad theoretical issues are often discussed early in the introduction, followed by an increasingly specific focus.

Consider the following analogy. Your best friend has moved across the country and you embark on a car trip to visit her. You will probably first consult regional maps, then a state map, then a city map, and finally a neighborhood map as you try to locate your friend. The author of an article is also providing maps to readers. The directions become increasingly detailed, the research area more clearly focused. The single house you are looking for is much like the research question addressed by the report. A well-written introduction will allow you to make the trip from general questions to specific hypotheses without too much difficulty.

One thing you are sure to notice in most articles is that there are many references or citations to previously published research. Do not be intimidated by the presence of so many names and dates. Prior research provides much of the rationale for the current study. These citations are evidence that the author has been diligent in surveying the existing literature. The author's collecting and making sense of these citations can also be a time saver if you decide to continue exploring the topic on your own.

In addition to stating the general problem, the introduction describes the particular research strategy the author will use and proposes the specific hypotheses that will be tested. These hypotheses typically link "independent" variables (variables that the experimenter believes will affect subject behavior) with "dependent" variables (the specific subject behaviors, which hopefully are influenced by or "depend" on the independent variable; see the following statistical primer). You should search for these statements of what is expected to be found, and be clear in your mind as to exactly how the hypotheses will be tested.

Remember that it is the author's purpose in this section to plead a case for the importance of the research contained in the article. You should be able to follow the logic of the study and understand precisely what the author is examining. Just as your cross-country trip to your friend's house brought you closer and closer to your final destination, so too should the introduction section of a research article guide you to the author's destination, the hypotheses proposed. These are often summarized at the end of the introduction. Thus, the final paragraphs of the introduction are often another good place to turn to if you get bogged down in an article. Now that the author has identified why the research is important and what the research questions are, the next logical step is to find out how those questions will be answered. That is the function of the method section.

The Method Section

The method section is simply a detailed description of the way the study was conducted. Sometimes complex studies will begin with an *overview,* which summarizes the method. Detailed sections about the subjects and procedure then follow.

Subjects   This section is usually a factual account of who the subjects were and how many of them there were. Additional demographic data such as age, sex, race, and institutional affiliation are often included as well. This information allows you to determine the generalizability of the sample (how applicable the results may be for other populations). The way the subjects were selected is often included as well as any inducements or payments the subjects received to take part in the study. Look for and identify any specific differences between groups or subdivisions of subjects. Do the subjects bring any differences to the study, such as their sex or personality differences, that might influence their behavior?

Materials   If original questionnaires are used or a particular apparatus is employed, the author may provide a full description of these. The specific questions asked of the subjects are sometimes included in the text, or the questions may be appended at the very end of the article.

Procedure   This section should describe what happened to subjects and what was asked of them. Through a step-by-step account of the exact procedures, along with specific instructions given subjects, you should have sufficient detail so that, given the resources, you could come very close to replicating (repeating) the study. The procedure section is also important in that it allows the reader to get the feel of what it would be like to be a subject in the study.

Variables

Pay particular attention to the author's attempts to isolate or rule out alternative explanations or reasons (other than the hypothesized ones) for the behavior tested. These attempts at keeping other variables from affecting the behavior of subjects and contaminating the study are as important in a research effort as the need for a sterile environment in the surgery room.

Continue to be an active reader and seek answers to questions. What are the independent variables or predictor variables to be tested? And what dependent (subject) behaviors will be used to test the hypotheses? How does the author try to prevent or minimize other variables from providing explanations for subject behavior that would interfere with the independent variables? You should be able to answer these questions after having read this section of the report.

Finally, you will want to compare the procedure with the stated intentions in the introduction. Given the questions identified in the introduction, and the rationale for the study, is the author appropriately measuring the variables of interest? That is, does the procedure allow for meaningful answers to the questions posed in the introduction?

While experimental research may sometimes seem overly complicated, the logic behind it is remarkably simple. Experimenters manipulate and record variables (quite literally, things that can vary between or among people, such as what happens to them and how they respond) to determine if the manipulated variables are in any way responsible for variation in subject behavior. Just as you might prepare a sauce once with butter and once with margarine, and then note differences in taste, smell, or appearance, or change brands of cat food and note differences in your cat's eating behavior, so too do experimenters look for differences. Hence, a typical experiment may entail something happening to one group of subjects that does not happen to another group. If that "something" (the independent variable) is important enough, then the behavior of the two groups (the dependent variable) should differ, assuming that the two groups were comparable to begin with. For example, in preparing the sauce above, you'd make sure that all other ingredients were the same and that the two sauces differed only by the butter/margarine variable. So the presence or absence of that "something" is the focus of an experiment. In a very real sense, the question asked is "does the difference make a difference?" The sauce made with butter may be superior in taste to the one made with margarine. And then again, it may not be. Your cat may be particularly enamored with one particular type of cat food (S. L. E.'s cat, Carmen Miranda, will only eat Friskies Buffet's turkey and giblets) or it may make absolutely no difference as your cat will eat anything put before it (like A. G. H.'s cat, Ananda, the epitome of an omnivore). Differences exist or can be created. You can't know whether there really is a difference until you meaningfully test the question. And that, in a nutshell, is the logic behind experimentation.

The Results Section

This is the "how it turned out" section, in which experimenters quantitatively test their hypotheses based on the behavior of the subjects. The author should describe the results in such a way that unexpected as well as expected findings are shown. Not all hypotheses are supported; the unexpected may be as important as the expected. The numbers generated by measuring the subjects' behavior are summarized and analyzed in this section. Tables and figures often are employed to organize these numbers and the statistics generated from them, making the data easier to understand. Carefully examine all tables and figures. Read the titles of the tables or figures. Pay close attention to the column and row titles and the labels presented on figures. If you are unclear about what you are looking at, refer to the text of the results section and determine where the reference to the table or figure is made (such as "see Table 1" or "as shown in Figure 2"). Even though you may not understand the intricacies of specific statistics, you should be able to spot the patterns that emerge from the numbers and figures reported. A rudimentary understanding of statistics will enhance your understanding and ability to evaluate the results, but a good results section will be understandable even to the reader without any statistical knowledge.

An Aside About Statistics

Many students are unnerved by the statistics employed in research; students of social psychology are no exception. You will encounter an impressive arsenal of statistical

techniques and shorthand symbols if you spend any time reading the primary literature. Do not let these techniques and symbols throw you. The basic purpose of statistics is twofold. First, statistics are used to summarize large amounts of data in concise,
manageable terms. Second, statistical techniques allow authors to determine, within
certain parameters, if the results they obtained are sufficiently unlikely to have occurred by chance alone. Statistical techniques never allow us to completely rule out
the possibility that a finding is merely due to chance. We can only say how unlikely it
is that we have found a difference that does not, in reality, exist.

Your introductory psychology book may be a good source for the logic and meaning of statistics. If your introductory text does not have a chapter on experimental design and statistics, look for an appendix at the end of the book. Also, a brief statistical
primer at the end of this chapter will help you make sense of the most frequently used
terms and shorthand. In any case, no matter how exotic or mind-boggling the "number
crunching" you encounter, remember that statistics are used for the two basic purposes
we discussed in the last paragraph: (1) to simplify a quantity of numbers into more
manageable and understandable form, and (2) to measure how likely it is that chance,
or something other than what is hypothesized, can account for any differences obtained.

The Discussion or Conclusions Section

This is the "what this all means" section in which the results are interpreted by the author and the research is placed in perspective in light of previous findings. This section
usually begins with a brief restatement of the hypotheses and the results that either
support or do not support them. Be aware that the same data can be interpreted in different ways. Be skeptical. Authors usually, although not always, consider reasonable
alternative explanations for their results. Even if they do not, you should.

Whereas the procedure and results section are usually straightforward and com-
pactly written, the discussion section typically allows a bit more expansiveness on the
part of the writer. Now that the data are generated and the specific research questions
have been answered to some degree, you, as a reader, are also less restrained. Don't be
afraid to consider alternatives that the author has neglected. Critical thinking may also
lead you to the conclusion that the author has overstated the significance of the findings. You are free to agree or disagree with the author's suggestions of "what this all
means"; just be clear about your reasons and be prepared to support your own claims.

Many research reports conclude with the author's suggestions for further research
or implications for theoretical positions. Examine these and determine whether they
make sense to you. If you were the author, what would be your next research question?

References

The final section of most articles is composed of complete reference information for
all the cited work contained in the article. It provides easy access to any of the articles
the authors have used, and is very helpful if you would like to know more about a specific study mentioned in the article.

When psychologists discuss research, they usually refer to articles by the author or authors and year published. This convention allows credit to be given where it is due and functions as a "shorthand" way to readily convey information.

In an effort to make this book of readings more useful, we have listed each article's citations in one master reference section at the end of the book. Each reference appears in its entirety followed by cross-referencing to all the articles within this reader that cite it.

A READING STRATEGY

There is no one strategy for reading research reports that will work for everyone. Some people read an article straight through while others skip around the sections. We suggest that until you become familiar with an approach that works best for you, consider the following strategy.

First, read the title and abstract carefully. Try to identify the general questions raised. Second, skim the entire article rapidly to get an overview of what the researcher did and what the findings are. Third, read the introduction and discussion sections to understand the starting and ending points of the author's reasoning as well as the conclusions. Underline the hypotheses presented in the introduction and locate them again in the discussion section. Fourth, read the method and results sections to determine how well the procedure allows for testing of the hypotheses and whether the hypotheses were confirmed or not. Underline or make marginal notes that highlight the major points made in the article. Fifth, reread the discussion, keeping in mind the original hypotheses and the reported results. Sixth, put the article aside for a few minutes and take a break. This will allow you to clear your mind of details and focus on the issues raised by this research. Seventh, return to carefully read the article from start to finish, paying attention to your underlining and marginal notes.

Finally, when you are finished reading an article, jot down a few notes about it. Try to summarize the article briefly and assess the logic of the author's thinking from introduction to discussion. You may even write your own abstract, adding your personal questions and comments. Now that you have the complete story, does it all make sense? You still may not be totally convinced by the data and arguments of the study. You have that right, especially now that you have been an intelligent consumer of the research and collected and considered all the facts. Being skeptical and entertaining alternative explanations for behavior is very much a part of being a good social psychologist.

Hopefully, this strategy will help you read research reports. Each author has presented us with challenging and exciting ideas about the ways we operate as social beings. We trust you will find these studies a catalyst for your own thinking about and understanding of human social behavior.

A NOTE ABOUT SEXIST LANGUAGE

In 1977, the American Psychological Association added guidelines encouraging the use of nonsexist language in the journals it publishes. In 1982, those guidelines became a requirement. Compliance with these guidelines requires authors to designate people in less ambiguous, less stereotypical, and less evaluative ways. For instance, the word *man* may be generic and refer to all humans, or it may refer only to males and not to females. A statement such as "Man threatens his own environment" is better posed as "Humans threaten their own environment" or "People threaten their own environment." This is not a trivial issue. Not only are words powerful messengers about who or what they describe, they also may contain evaluative meaning. Consider the phrase "man and wife." Not only is the phrase semantically unbalanced, but it also makes a value judgment. A more precise and nonsexist phrase is either "man and woman" or "husband and wife." You will find few, if any, examples of sexist language in the more recent articles, although many of the older articles reflect the ideology of their times. And, we hope, *you* will not fall into the trap of using sexist language in the psychology papers you write.

A BRIEF STATISTICAL PRIMER

Analysis of variance (ANOVA) is a statistical technique that allows comparison of two or more group means (see **Mean**) to determine if there are significant differences between or among the groups (see Readings 2, 6, 19, 21). The outcome of an analysis of variance is the "F ratio" (usually shortened to "F"), which is a ratio of explained to unexplained variance. Explained variance is attributable to the investigator's intended manipulations (independent variables), and unexplained variance results from all other reasons for subjects' behavior, including chance. F may be tested for statistical significance (see **Statistical significance**). With an analysis of variance, one can examine both main effects and interaction effects (see **Main effects** and **Interaction effects**).

Chi square (χ^2) is a statistical technique that assesses the degree to which two categorical or nominal variables are related (see Reading 21). Although you could measure a person's attractiveness on a scale of 1 to 10, a person's eye color can only fall into one category. Most people are brown-eyed, blue-eyed, or black-eyed. For example, a chi-square analysis might determine whether males or females systematically differ in their political party affiliation. Gender and party affiliation are categories; they do not lend themselves to an analysis dependent on continuous interval scales.

Correlation (r) is a statistical technique that measures the degree of the relationship between two or more variables (see Reading 7). The magnitude of the correlation ranges from 0 (no relationship) to 1 (perfect relationship), and the sign of the correlation ($+$ or $-$) indicates the direction (positive or negative) of the relationship. A positive correlation indicates that the variables change in the same direction. As one variable increases, the other variable also increases. Or, as one variable decreases, the other variable also decreases. For example, the number of years of formal education is positively correlated with income. A negative correlation implies that as one variable increases, the other decreases. For example, students' credit hours earned and their remaining time to graduation are negatively correlated. An important point to remember is that correlation does not necessarily imply causation but rather measures "relatedness."

Dependent variables refer to the particular behaviors of the subjects that will be measured in the study (see especially Reading 28). The investigator is predicting that the subjects' behavior will depend on the independent variable. For example, suppose an investigator wants to test whether the frequency of novel answers to a creativity task is influenced by the presence of an audience. The frequency of novel answers in question is the dependent variable, whereas the presence or absence of an audience is the independent variable.

df is an abbreviation for "degrees of freedom." Degrees of freedom reflect the number of observations that are free to vary and are important in determining statistical significance (see **Statistical significance**). For most statistical techniques, the larger the sample, the smaller the magnitude a difference needs to be for statistical significance to be obtained.

F (see **Analysis of variance**)

Independent variables refer to the differences that are hypothesized to distinguish between or to alter the behavior of subjects (see especially Reading 28). They may be "subject variables," that is, dissimilarities that the subjects bring to the study (for example, age or degree of self-awareness) or they may be the result of manipulations introduced by the investigator (for example, type of persuasive appeal made or whether one observes someone acting aggressively).

Interaction effects are possible when two or more variables are studied at the same time. They occur when one variable has a different effect based on the level of another variable. For example, suppose a hypothetical study examines the influence of two factors, subject sex and the personality variable "need for approval," on how much time is spent playing with a baby (the dependent variable). If females play with the baby more than males do, regardless of their need for approval, then there is a main effect for sex (see **Main effects**). And if those high in need for approval play with the baby more than those low in need for approval, regardless of sex, then there is a main effect for the personality trait of need for approval. However, if males who are low in need for approval and females who are high in need for approval play frequently with the baby, but males high in need for approval and females low in need for approval *do not* play much with the baby, then an interaction exists. Thus, in this example, subject behavior would be "dependent on" both sex (male or female) and need for approval (high or low). Neither variable alone is sufficient to predict behavior; each depends on the other.

Main effects occur when the mean for one level of an independent variable is significantly different from the mean for another level. For example, suppose we have an independent variable labeled "type of classroom." If children in the "cooperative learning" classroom display less racial prejudice than do children in the conventional classroom, there is a main effect for classroom type.

Mean (abbreviated *M*) is the average of a group of scores, i.e., all scores are added and then divided by the total number of scores. An example of a mean is a student's grade-point average.

N or *n* is an abbreviation for the "number of subjects."

Not significant (abbreviated *ns*) indicates that a statistical technique has determined that we cannot rule out chance as the reason for the effects obtained. This can occur when the means of two groups are not sufficiently dissimilar from one another or when two or more variables appear to be unrelated to one another.

Null hypothesis is the assumption that no difference exists between two or more groups in a study. It is usually the negation of the experimental hypothesis. If the investigator hypothesizes that variable X will have a significant effect on the dependent variable (subject behavior), then the null hypothesis is that variable X will have no effect on the dependent variable.

p is the abbreviation for **Probability.** It refers to the odds that a particular finding is due to chance (also known as "significance level"). The conventional standard for an acceptable level of significance is $p < .05$. Thus, if the study were conducted 100 times, the results obtained would be attributable to chance no more than 5 times. The smaller the level (e.g., $p < .01$ or $p < .001$), the less likely that the effect occurred by chance, and the more confidence we have that the finding is actually a true difference.

SD is the abbreviation for **Standard deviation.**

Standard deviation (see **Variance**)

Statistical significance refers to the degree to which a finding is likely to have occurred by chance. By convention, most researchers will not consider a result statistically significant unless a statistical procedure determines that the result has a probability of chance occurrence that is less than 5 percent ($p < .05$). A statistically significant difference is not guaranteed to be a true difference but has a greater likelihood of being a true one compared to a nonsignificant finding (see **Probability**).

t-test and *t* refer to a statistical technique that results from testing the statistical significance of the difference between the means of two groups (see Readings 7, 21, 28). It takes into account how much diversity or variability there is within each group as well as how far the two means are from each other. For example, suppose we want to test the hypothesis that females smile more frequently than males do. We will find that there are some males who smile often and others who smile seldom, and that the same is true for females. A t-test will take into account the variability within the separate groups of males and females while it determines whether, overall, males and females differ in smiling frequency.

Validity is the degree to which a measurement evaluates what it is intended to evaluate. An honest bathroom scale furnishes a valid measurement of weight but has low validity as a measure of height.

Variance is a measure of how spread out or variable the scores are, that is, the degree to which a group of scores deviate from their mean. For example, consider the point total for two basketball teams: Team A's total points in the last five games are 73, 74, 75, 76, and 77; Team B's total points in the last five games are 55, 65, 75, 85, 95. Although both teams have the same mean points scored per game (75), Team B has a greater variability (scores are more spread out from the mean). The square root of the variance is the standard deviation, which represents the average deviation (i.e., distance) from the mean in a particular group of scores.

2

HINDSIGHT DISTORTION AND THE 1980 PRESIDENTIAL ELECTION

Mark R. Leary (1982)

Leary's article is a fine example of a highly readable, empirical study on the hindsight bias, also known as the "I knew-it-all-along" effect. By reading this selection, you can discover how easily the hindsight bias can be demonstrated and measured firsthand. You can look at Table 2-1 to compare the predictions that people actually made one day before the election with the predictions that people made the day after the election about what they would have made before the election. By reading the "Results" section you can determine that the hindsight bias was statistically significant for predictions about both Reagan's and Anderson's votes. Do you understand why the effect did not materialize for the before and after comparison for Carter's votes? Think back to 1992 and the presidential election between George Bush and Bill Clinton. Do you see any parallels between that election and the 1980 election?

Leary is not content to simply demonstrate the "I knew-it-all-along" effect, thus, in his study he considers some of the possibilities as to why the hindsight bias occurs. He contrasts an informational explanation with a motivational explanation, and then sets out to test two kinds of motivational explanations. He manipulates the situational condition of public versus private predictions to test whether the hindsight bias is more likely to occur when people are responding publicly and thus, may want to "save face" with regard to their erroneous predictions. And he assesses the degree to which subjects are knowledgeable and consider political knowledge to be important as a measure of ego involvement. (Leary occasionally uses *self-esteem* and *ego involvement* as synonyms; do you agree?) Because no differences in hindsight bias emerge due to differences in self-presentation or ego involvement, Leary's study supports the informational

Source: Abridged from the *Personality and Social Psychology Bulletin,* 1982, *8,* 257–263. Copyright © 1982 by Sage Publishing Co. Reprinted by permission of the publisher and the author.

hypothesis by default. Now the task remains to identify the informational aspects of the hindsight bias and then to determine how to develop greater accuracy regarding our beliefs about events.

One last question—and be honest in your answer. After reading this article and reviewing the findings, did you feel that you "knew it all along"?

The tendency for people retrospectively to overestimate the degree to which they expected certain events to occur was examined within the context of the 1980 presidential election. Previous research has concluded that distorted hindsight occurs due to people's inability to reconstruct prior probabilities for an event after it has occurred, but the possible mediation of motivational factors, specifically self-esteem and self-presentation, has not been adequately examined. Subjects were asked either before or after the 1980 presidential election, and under public or private response conditions, to predict the outcome of the election (preelection) or to indicate what they would have predicted the outcome to be had they been asked before the election (postelection). In addition, subjects were classified as being either high or low in ego involvement regarding knowledge of politics. Results showed clear evidence of hindsight distortion: Subjects asked after the election said they would have predicted an outcome closer to the results of the election than those asked before, but there was no evidence of mediation by self-esteem or self-presentation concerns.

Although the magnitude of Ronald Reagan's victory over Jimmy Carter in the 1980 presidential election took all but professional political observers by surprise, a great deal of postelection commentary focused retrospectively on preelection signs that a Republican victory was in the works (see "Carter Post-Mortem," 1980). The tone of many of these analyses suggested that the writers were not, after all, particularly surprised by Carter's defeat and that the election outcome was easily understandable in terms of several critical events during the Carter administration, particularly during the campaign itself. Many of these commentaries make one forget that the election was, in reality, "too close to call" until the last few days of the campaign, and appear to reflect the general tendency for people retrospectively to overestimate the degree to which they could have predicted the outcomes of certain events.

Research has repeatedly demonstrated that people overestimate the prior probability of events they believe have occurred. For example, Fischhoff (1975b) asked subjects to read about a historical incident and estimate how likely various outcomes had been at the time the incident occurred. Subjects who thought they knew the outcome of the event considered that outcome to have been more probable than subjects who did not know the outcome. Even when subjects were instructed to respond as if they did not know the actual outcome, they were unable to ignore this information and continued to overestimate the prior probabilities of events they believed had occurred. In another study (Fischhoff & Beyth, 1975), subjects were asked to estimate the probability that certain events would occur during Nixon's 1972 trip to China. After the trip, subjects were asked to recall their own predictions and to state whether or not they thought each event had actually taken place. Results showed that subjects remembered having predicted events they thought had occurred during the trip, whether or not the event had actually taken place. More recently, Fischhoff (1977) and Wood (1978) have shown that people also overestimate the degree to which they had known answers to questions of fact, even when warned of potential bias in their responses and admonished to be as accurate as possible in recalling what they had known before being told the correct answer.

In attempting to explain the occurrence of distorted hindsight, also known as the "knew-it-all-along" effect or "creeping determinism," Fischhoff (1975a, 1975b) suggests that once the outcome of an event is known it is difficult for people to reconstruct what they actually knew prior to the event. By reasoning backward from the event to its possible antecedents, the individual may see relationships among factors that were not easily discernible before the event took place. Factors that are clearly associated with the event in some way are recalled more easily due to the representativeness heuristic employed in estimating probabilities (Tversky & Kahneman, 1974), while factors unrelated to the observed outcome are rendered less salient. Conflicting information that does not fit into the reconstruction of the factors leading up to the event is either ignored or reinterpreted in light of what has subsequently happened.

It is possible, however, that distorted hindsight may arise due to motivational, rather than informational, processes. First, people may retrospectively claim they "knew it would happen" in order to enhance their self-esteem. The conclusion that one was adequately intelligent, perceptive, and/or farsighted to correctly anticipate the outcome of an event may rightfully result in a positive self-evaluation. Such an effect would be more likely with individuals who take pride in their knowledge of such events, since the failure to predict accurately would be more threatening to their self-image (see Walster, 1967).

Second, people might be expected to distort their public statements regarding the event as a self-presentation strategy (Goffman, 1959; Schlenker, 1980), expecting to gain social rewards by demonstrating their perceptiveness to others. Both Fischhoff (1977) and Wood (1978) dismiss a self-presentation explanation of the phenomenon since distorted hindsight has been obtained despite nonevaluative instructions that deemphasized subjects' performance, admonitions to work hard to accurately recall predictions, and warnings to beware of potential hindsight distortion in one's responses. However, previous studies have not completely eliminated factors that may motivate subjects to claim post facto that they knew more than they actually did for self-presentational purposes. If distorted hindsight were obtained even when subjects' responses were entirely anonymous, thus affording them no opportunity to impress others with their perceptiveness, we would have a stronger case for dismissing self-presentation as a mediating factor.

METHOD

Subjects

Subjects were 134 male and 141 female university students between the ages of 18 and 22. They were randomly assigned to experimental conditions before the start of the study.

Procedure

gave up confidentiality

Subjects were contacted in their living quarters (dormitory rooms, fraternity houses, apartments) on either the Monday before or the Wednesday after the 1980 presidential election and asked to participate in an "election survey." In the *public response condition,* subjects were asked to sign their names on the questionnaires, complete them as the experimenter watched, then return them directly to him or her. In the *private response condition,* subjects were asked not to sign their names, were assured that their responses would be completely anonymous, completed the questionnaires out of sight of the experimenter, and returned them to him or her in a sealed envelope.

The first 2 questions were designed to ascertain the degree to which subjects' knowledge of politics was important to their self-esteem. It was reasoned that ego involvement in knowledge of a topic is a joint function of how knowledgeable an individual believes himself or herself to be regarding the topic and how important the individual considers such knowledge to be. Thus, subjects answered questions to assess these 2 factors on 12-point Likert scales. Their responses on these items were later multiplied and the product taken as an index of ego involvement in knowledge of politics.

Subjects were then asked to indicate the percentage of the popular vote that they believed each of the 3 major candidates (Anderson, Carter, and Reagan) would receive in the election (*preelection condition*) or the percentage they would have predicted the candidates would receive had they been asked before the election (*postelection condition*). Subjects were told that their estimates for the 3 candidates should add to 100%.

RESULTS

Subjects' responses to the items assessing self-reported knowledge about the election and the importance they placed on such knowledge were multiplied, and subjects classified as either low or high in ego involvement regarding knowledge of politics (median = 71). The 2 individual items correlated + .32, $p < .01$, indicating a slight correlation between the components of ego involvement. The ego-involvement factor was then entered with timing (before or after election) and response publicness (public or private) into a 2 × 2 × 2 ANOVA for each candidate.

Only a main effect of timing, $F(1, 267) = 4.89$, $p < .03$, was obtained on subjects' estimates of the percentage of votes Ronald Reagan would obtain in the election. Examination of means (see Table 2-1) reveals that, consistent with past research, subjects who knew the outcome of the election said they would have predicted an outcome significantly closer to the actual outcome than subjects who made predictions before the election. Like the media, subjects asked before the election underestimated how well Reagan would perform, then revised their "predictions" upward after the election. No effects of response publicness or ego involvement were obtained, either singly or in interaction.

Both a main effect of timing, $F(1, 267) = 11.86$, $p < .001$, and a main effect of ego involvement in knowledge of politics, $F(1, 267) = 7.71$, $p < .01$, were obtained on estimates of the percentage of the vote John Anderson would receive. First, subjects asked before the election (see Table 2-1) greatly overestimated how well Anderson

TABLE 2-1 PRE- AND POSTELECTION ESTIMATES OF THE PERCENT-
AGE OF THE VOTE OBTAINED BY EACH CANDIDATE

Candidate	Preelection	Postelection	Actual percentage
Reagan	44.3	46.6	51.0
Anderson	14.1	10.5	7.0
Carter	41.7	42.9	41.0

Note: The differences between the pre- and postelection means are significant for
Reagan and Anderson, but not for Carter.

would do, while those asked afterward, although still too high, were significantly
closer to the actual outcome, again demonstrating hindsight distortion.

Second, the main effect of ego involvement shows that subjects classified as high
in ego involvement in knowledgeability of politics ($M = 10.8$) were significantly
more accurate in assessing Anderson's vote-getting power than those low in ego-
involvement ($M = 13.6$). Separate ANOVAs that examined the knowledge and importance components of the ego-involvement measure individually showed that this effect
was associated primarily with subjects' self-reported knowledge of politics. Subjects
who considered themselves knowledgeable about the election were more accurate in
their estimates of how well Anderson would fare than those who were less knowledgeable, $F(1, 267) = 10.35$, p $< .001$. There was no relationship between the importance
subjects placed on knowledge of politics and their estimates of Anderson's vote-
getting power, $p > .50$.

No effects of the independent or subject variables were obtained on subjects' estimates of how well Carter would perform in the election. Examination of means (see
Table 2-1) for the pre- and postelection conditions reveals why. Subjects' preelection
estimates of the percentage of votes Carter would obtain were quite close to the percentage Carter actually received. There is no way in which hindsight distortion can occur when one's preevent predictions are accurate.

DISCUSSION

Consistent with previous research, subjects' postelection recall of how well they had
expected the candidates to fare in the election was more closely in line with the actual
results of the election than subjects' preelection estimates. Yet, despite clear evidence
of hindsight distortion, there was no evidence of mediation by either self-esteem or
self-presentation factors. Thus the present results are consistent with those obtained
previously that supported an information-processing explanation of distorted hindsight
(Fischhoff, 1975b, 1977; Fischhoff & Beyth, 1975; Leary, 1981; Wood, 1978).
Subjects' knowledge of the election outcome appears to have hindered their cognitive
reconstruction of the information that was actually available prior to the election.
Subjects asked after the election seemed to believe, if not that they had foreseen the
outcome, that their preelection expectancies were less discrepant from the election results than they really were.

It may be observed that, although postelection recall was distorted toward the actual election results, those postelection estimates were still somewhat discrepant from the final vote. This suggests that certain factors operated to constrain the degree of hindsight distortion that occurred. It seems likely that preevent predictions serve as an anchor that prevents people from claiming post facto that they had made a perfectly accurate prediction. Although one's initial expectancies cannot be perfectly reconstructed once an outcome is known, enough information is available to hold postevent recall in check. The present subjects appeared unable to accurately recall preelection predictions, but they knew, for example, that few people had expected Reagan to do as well as 51% of the vote and thus could not, in retrospect, claim that they had known he would do that well.

Given the ubiquitousness of distorted hindsight, additional research is needed that examines the conditions under which it does and does not occur, and the behavioral consequences of overestimating one's accuracy in judging events. For example, attributions of blame are often predicated on the belief that the consequences of certain decisions and actions were potentially foreseeable (Shaw & Sulzer, 1964), so that distorted hindsight may lead individuals to unjustifiably blame others for failing to see what was "foreseeable" only in retrospect (Fischhoff, 1975a). Similarly, since disconfirmed expectancies and observed incongruences often serve to facilitate learning and adjustment, the failure to be surprised by certain occurrences may interfere with experience-based learning and lead people to underestimate what may be learned from the past (Fischhoff 1975a, 1977). In short, the "Monday morning quarterback" in us all warrants future research attention.

TWO

SOCIAL THINKING

3

THEY SAW A GAME:
A CASE STUDY

Albert H. Hastorf and Hadley Cantril (1954)

This section on social thinking examines processes by which we make sense of
our own behavior and the behavior of others. In this first reading, Hastorf and
Cantril address more than just the social events in a football game; this study
examines not only how others are perceived but also how that perception may be
faulty, biased, and not entirely reliable. At stake in this study is our understanding
of reality. Hastorf and Cantril suggest that our experiences of the same thing are
not shared, and that, in fact, "the 'thing' simply is *not* the same for different
people." The world we see may at times be more a reflection of what lies behind
our eyes rather than what lies in front of them. Almost 30 years later, Loy and
Andrews (1981) successfully replicated this study using the very same film with
Dartmouth and Princeton students and alumni.

    Although the transactionist viewpoint advocated by Hastorf and Cantril has
not been integrated into mainstream social psychology, the point is extremely
important, especially in regard to our evaluation of scientific "facts." Our
perceptions of others and our perception of data are influenced by what we
already believe that we know about the individuals or about scientific theories.
How much does loyalty to people, colleges, causes, and nations influence our
perceptions of events that indicate possible wrongdoings or shortcomings? To
what degree are our perceptions influenced by what we already "know" to be
true? Bem and Bem (1970, see Reading 1) coined the phrase "nonconscious
ideologies" to describe beliefs that are so basic to our world views that we may
not even be aware that we have them. We are not often aware of how much our

Source: Abridged from the *Journal of Abnormal and Social Psychology,* 1954, *49,* 129–134. Copyright
© 1954 by the American Psychological Association.

allegiances or world views (Unger, Draper, & Pendergrass, 1986) influence our social knowledge.

When obviously compelling evidence is disregarded, it makes one wonder what is needed to change a belief. Are humans always so set in their convictions that no data or circumstances are sufficient to disconfirm these beliefs? And to what degree can you and I count on our "intuition," especially in light of the ways we may be honestly in error when it comes to explaining our behavior, or reconstructing our memories or behavior? The readings that follow in this section will expand on these ideas. We hope that you, as budding social psychologists, will consider what it takes to establish an "objective" stance and, in fact, whether such a stance is possible.

On a brisk Saturday afternoon, November 23, 1951, the Dartmouth football team played Princeton in Princeton's Palmer Stadium. It was the last game of the season for both teams and of rather special significance because the Princeton team had won all its games so far and one of its players, Kazmaier, was receiving All-American mention and had just appeared as the cover man on *Time* magazine, and was playing his last game.

A few minutes after the opening kick-off, it became apparent that the game was going to be a rough one. The referees were kept busy blowing their whistles and penalizing both sides. In the second quarter, Princeton's star left the game with a broken nose. In the third quarter, a Dartmouth player was taken off the field with a broken leg. Tempers flared both during and after the game. The official statistics of the game, which Princeton won, showed that Dartmouth was penalized 70 yards, Princeton 25, not counting more than a few plays in which both sides were penalized.

Needless to say, accusations soon began to fly. The game immediately became a matter of concern to players, students, coaches, and the administrative officials of the two institutions, as well as to alumni and the general public who had not seen the game but had become sensitive to the problem of big-time football through the recent exposures of subsidized players, commercialism, etc. Discussion of the game continued for several weeks.

One of the contributing factors to the extended discussion of the game was the extensive space given to it by both campus and metropolitan newspapers. For example, on November 27 (four days after the game), the *Daily Princetonian* (Princeton's student newspaper) said:

This observer has never seen quite such a disgusting exhibition of so-called "sport." Both teams were guilty but the blame must be laid primarily on Dartmouth's doorstep. Princeton, obviously the better team, had no reason to rough up Dartmouth. Looking at the situation rationally, we don't see why the Indians should make a deliberate attempt to cripple Dick Kazmaier or any other Princeton player. The Dartmouth psychology, however, is not rational itself.

Dartmouth students were "seeing" an entirely different version of the game through the editorial eyes of the *Dartmouth* (Dartmouth's undergraduate newspaper). For example, on November 27 the *Dartmouth* said:

However, the Dartmouth-Princeton game set the stage for the other type of dirty football. A type which may be termed as an unjustifiable accusation.

Dick Kazmaier was injured early in the game. Kazmaier was the star, an All-American. Other stars have been injured before, but Kazmaier had been built to represent a Princeton idol. When an idol is hurt there is only one recourse—the tag of dirty football. So what did the Tiger Coach Charley Caldwell do? He announced to the world that the Big Green had been out to extinguish the Princeton star. His purpose was achieved.

After this incident, Caldwell instilled the old see-what-they-did-go-get-them attitude into his players. His talk got results. Gene Howard and Jim Miller were both injured. Both had dropped back to pass, had passed, and were standing unprotected in the backfield. Result: one bad leg and one leg broken.

The game was rough and did get a bit out of hand in the third quarter. Yet most of the roughing penalties were called against Princeton while Dartmouth received more of the illegal-use-of-the-hands variety.

Basically, then, there was disagreement as to what had happened during the "game." Hence we took the opportunity presented by the occasion to make a "real life" study of a perceptual problem.[1]

PROCEDURE

Two steps were involved in gathering data. The first consisted of answers to a questionnaire designed to get reactions to the game and to learn something of the climate of opinion in each institution. This questionnaire was administered a week after the game to both Dartmouth and Princeton undergraduates who were taking introductory and intermediate psychology courses.

The second step consisted of showing the same motion picture of the game to a sample of undergraduates in each school and having them check on another questionnaire, as they watched the film, any infraction of the rules they saw and whether these infractions were "mild" or "flagrant."[2] At Dartmouth, members of two fraternities were asked to view the film on December 7; at Princeton, members of two undergraduate clubs saw the film early in January.

The answers to both questionnaires were carefully coded and transferred to punch cards.

---

[1]We are not concerned here with the problem of guilt or responsibility for infractions, and nothing here implies any judgment as to who was to blame.

[2]The film shown was kindly loaned for the purpose of the experiment by the Dartmouth College Athletic Council. It should be pointed out that a movie of a football game follows the ball, is thus selective, and omits a good deal of the total action on the field. Also, of course, in viewing only a film of a game, the possibilities of participation as spectator are greatly limited.

RESULTS

Table 3-1 shows the questions which received different replies from the two student populations on the first questionnaire.

Questions asking if the students had friends on the team, if they had ever played football themselves, if they felt they knew the rules of the game well, etc. showed no differences in either school and no relation to answers given to other questions. This is not surprising since the students in both schools come from essentially the same type of educational, economic, and ethnic background.

Summarizing the data of Tables 3-1 and 3-2, we find a marked contrast between the two student groups.

Nearly all *Princeton* students judged the game as "rough and dirty"—not one of them thought it "clean and fair." And almost nine-tenths of them thought the other side started the rough play. By and large they felt that the charges they understood were being made were true; most of them felt the charges were made in order to avoid similar situations in the future.

When Princeton students looked at the movie of the game, they saw the Dartmouth team make over twice as many infractions as their own team made. And they saw the Dartmouth team make over twice as many infractions as were seen by Dartmouth students. When Princeton students judged these infractions as "flagrant" or "mild," the ratio was about two "flagrant" to one "mild" on the Dartmouth team, and about one "flagrant" to three "mild" on the Princeton team.

As for the *Dartmouth* students, while the plurality of answers fell in the "rough and dirty" category, over one-tenth thought the game was "clean and fair" and over a third introduced their own category of "rough and fair" to describe the action. Although a third of the Dartmouth students felt that Dartmouth was to blame for starting the rough play, the majority of Dartmouth students thought both sides were to blame. By and large, Dartmouth men felt that the charges they understood were being made were not true, and most of them thought the reason for the charges was Princeton's concern for its football star.

When Dartmouth students looked at the movie of the game they saw both teams make about the same number of infractions. And they saw their own team make only half the number of infractions the Princeton students saw them make. The ratio of "flagrant" to "mild" infractions was about one to one when Dartmouth students judged the Dartmouth team, and about one "flagrant" to two "mild" when Dartmouth students judged infractions made by the Princeton team.

It should be noted that Dartmouth and Princeton students were thinking of different charges in judging their validity and in assigning reasons as to why the charges were made. It should also be noted that whether or not students were spectators of the game in the stadium made little difference in their responses.

INTERPRETATION: THE NATURE OF A SOCIAL EVENT

It seems clear that the "game" actually was many different games and that each version of the events that transpired was just as "real" to a particular person as other versions were to other people. A consideration of the experiential phenomena that con-

TABLE 3-1   DATA FROM FIRST QUESTIONNAIRE

Question	Dartmouth students (N = 163) %	Princeton students (N = 161) %
1. Did you happen to see the actual game between Dartmouth and Princeton in Palmer Stadium this year?		
Yes	33	71
No	67	29
2. Have you seen a movie of the game or seen it on television?		
Yes, movie	33	2
Yes, television	0	1
No, neither	67	97
3. (Asked of those who answered "yes" to either or both of above questions.) From your observations of what went on at the game, do you believe the game was clean and fairly played, or that it unnecessarily rough and dirty?		w
Clean and fair	6	0
Rough and dirty	24	69
Rough and fair*	25	2
No answer	45	29
4. (Asked of those who answered "no" on both of the first questions.) From what you have heard and read about the game, do you feel it was clean and fairly played, or that it was unnecessarlly rough and dirty?		
Clean and fair	7	0
Rough and dirty	18	24
Rough and fair*	14	1
Don't know	6	4
No answer	55	71
(Combined answers to questions 3 and 4 above)		
Clean and fair	13	0
Rough and dirty	42	93
Rough and fair*	39	3
Don't know	6	4
5. From what you saw in the game or the movies, or from what you have read, which team do you feel started the rough play?		
Dartmouth started it	36	86
Princeton started it	2	0
Both started it	53	11
Neither	6	1
No answer	3	2
6. What is your understanding of the charges being made?**		
Dartmouth tried to get Kazmaier	71	47
Dartmouth intentionally dirty	52	44
Dartmouth unnecessarily rough	8	35
7. Do you feel there is any truth to these charges?		
Yes	10	55
No	57	4
Partly	29	35
Don't know	4	6
8. Why do you think the charges were made?		
Injury to Princeton star	70	23
To prevent repetition	2	46
No answer	28	31

*This answer was not included on the checklist but was written in by the percentage of students indicated.
**Replies do not add to 100% since more than one charge could be given.

TABLE 3-2 DATA FROM SECOND QUESTIONNAIRE CHECKED WHILE SEEING FILM

| | | Total number of infractions checked against | | | |
| | | Dartmouth team | | Princeton team | |
Group	N	Mean	SD	Mean	SD
Dartmouth students	48	4.3*	2.7	4.4	2.8
Princeton students	49	9.8*	5.7	4.2	3.5

*Significant at the .01 level.

stitute a "football game" for the spectator may help us both to account for the results obtained and illustrate something of the nature of any social event.

Like any other complex social occurrence, a "football game" consists of a whole host of happenings. Many different events are occurring simultaneously. Furthermore, each happening is a link in a chain of happenings, so that one follows another in sequence. The "football game," as well as other complex social situations, consists of a whole matrix of events. In the game situation, this matrix of events consists of the actions of all the players, together with the behavior of the referees and linesmen, the action on the sidelines, in the grandstands, over the loud-speaker, etc.

Of crucial importance is the fact that an "occurrence" on the football field or in any other social situation does not become an experiential "event" unless and until some significance is given to it: an "occurrence" becomes an *"event"* only when the happening has significance. And a happening generally has significance only if it reactivates learned significances already registered in what we have called a person's assumptive form-world.

Hence the particular occurrences that different people experienced in the football game were a limited series of events from the total matrix of events *potentially* available to them. People experienced those occurrences that reactivated significances they brought to the occasion; they failed to experience those occurrences which did not reactivate past significances. We do not need to introduce "attention" as an "intervening third" (to paraphrase James on memory) to account for the selectivity of the experiential process.

In this particular study, one of the most interesting examples of this phenomenon was a telegram sent to an officer of Dartmouth College by a member of a Dartmouth alumni group in the Midwest. He had viewed the film which had been shipped to his alumni group from Princeton after its use with Princeton students, who saw, as we noted, an average of over nine infractions by Dartmouth players during the game. The alumnus, who couldn't see the infractions he had heard publicized, wired:

Preview of Princeton movie indicates considerable cutting of important part please wire explanation and possibly air mail missing part before showing scheduled for January 25 we have splicing equipment.

In brief, the data here indicate that there is no such "thing" as a "game" existing "out there" in its own right which people merely "observe." The "game" "exists" for a

person and is experienced by him only in so far as certain happenings have significances in terms of his purpose. Out of all the occurrences going on in the environment,
a person selects those that have some significance for him from his own egocentric position in the total matrix.

Obviously in the case of a football game, the value of the experience of watching
the game is enhanced if the purpose of "your" team is accomplished, that is, if the happening of the desired consequence is experienced—i.e., if your team wins. But the
value attribute of the experience can, of course, be spoiled if the desire to win crowds
out behavior we value and have come to call sportsmanlike.

The sharing of significances provides the links except for which a "social" event
would not be experienced and would not exist for anyone.

A "football game" would be impossible except for the rules of the game which we
bring to the situation and which enable us to share with others the significances of various happenings. These rules make possible a certain repeatability of events such as
first downs, touchdowns, etc. If a person is unfamiliar with the rules of the game, the
behavior he sees lacks repeatability and consistent significance and hence "doesn't
make sense."

And only because there is the possibility of repetition is there the possibility that a
happening has a significance. For example, the balls used in games are designed to
give a high degree of repeatability. While a football is about the only ball used in
games which is not a sphere, the shape of the modern football has apparently evolved
in order to achieve a higher degree of accuracy and speed in forward passing than
would be obtained with a spherical ball, thus increasing the repeatability of an important phase of the game.

The rules of a football game, like laws, rituals, customs, and mores, are registered
and preserved forms of sequential significances enabling people to share the significances of occurrences. The sharing of sequential significances which have value for us
provides the links that operationally make social events possible. They are analogous
to the forces of attraction that hold parts of an atom together, keeping each part from
following its individual, independent course.

From this point of view it is inaccurate and misleading to say that different people
have different "attitudes" concerning the same "thing." For the "thing" simply is *not*
the same for different people whether the "thing" is a football game, a presidential
candidate, Communism, or spinach. We do not simply "react to" a happening or to
some impingement from the environment in a determined way (except in behavior that
has become reflexive or habitual). We behave according to what we bring to the occasion, and what each of us brings to the occasion is more or less unique. And except for
these significances which we bring to the occasion, the happenings around us would
be meaningless occurrences, would be "inconsequential."

From the transactional view, an attitude is not a predisposition to react in a certain
way to an occurrence or stimulus "out there" that exists in its own right with certain
fixed characteristics which we "color" according to our predisposition. That is, a subject does not simply "react to" an "object." An attitude would rather seem to be a complex of registered significances reactivated by some stimulus which assumes its own
particular significance for us in terms of our purposes. That is, the object as experienced would not exist for us except for the reactivated aspects of the form-world
which provide particular significance to the hieroglyphics of sensory impingements.

4

SELF-FULFILLING STEREOTYPES

Mark L. Snyder (1982)

Snyder presents a number of interesting ideas in this short reading about the ways beliefs can generate their own confirmation. The subtle influence now known as "self-fulfilling prophecy" or "behavioral confirmation" was identified many decades ago and is best described by W. I. Thomas: "If men define situations as real, they are real in their consequences (Merton, 1948). Actual research on this phenomenon was first conducted by Rosenthal in the 1960s. The most famous study (Rosenthal and Jacobson, 1968) investigated the influence of teachers' beliefs of children's ability. Teachers received their students' scores on a test predicting "intellectual blossoming." These scores were fictitious, however, and were randomly assigned to the children. Although many of the teachers just glanced at the test scores and did not keep them on file, by the end of the year the classroom "intellectual blossomers" actually did experience greater intellectual spurts than did the other children in the same classrooms. This study and many others since 1968 suggest that teachers may subtly and nonconsciously create behavior in their students that fulfills their expectations.

Snyder expands on this concept by addressing the effect of self-fulfilling stereotypes in both intergender and interracial contexts. In doing so, he challenges the notion of contact theory, which argues that simply spending time with those who are different from you should expose your stereotypes to the harsh light of reality and move you to be less prejudgmental. Thus, Snyder is not entirely optimistic about alleviating those stereotypes and the subsequent prejudices that accompany them. After reading the article, think about these claims. Can we rise above making judgments (often unfairly) that come to

Source: Reprinted from *Psychology Today,* July, 1982, 60–68. Reprinted with permission from *Psychology Today* magazine. Copyright © 1982 (Sussex Publishers, Inc.).

influence the behavior of people around us? Can we avoid becoming the target of such stereotypes that others may make about us?

You may want to think about your own behavior, from sex roles to work-related skills—how much is your behavior a function of others' expectations of you? And the behavior of others around you—how much is their behavior the consequence of your own subtle and nonconscious beliefs about those others? Furthermore, now that we know many of the different ways in which we can create behavior in others, how can we use these phenomena ethically to better all people's lives?

Gordon Allport, the Harvard psychologist who wrote a classic work on the nature of prejudice, told a story about a child who had come to believe that people who lived in Minneapolis were called monopolists. From his father, moreover, he had learned that monopolists were evil folk. It wasn't until many years later, when he discovered his confusion, that his dislike of residents of Minneapolis vanished.

Allport knew, of course, that it was not so easy to wipe out prejudice and erroneous stereotypes. Real prejudice, psychologists like Allport argued, was buried deep in human character, and only a restructuring of education could begin to root it out. Yet many people whom I meet while lecturing seem to believe that stereotypes are simply beliefs or attitudes that change easily with experience. Why do some people express the view that Italians are passionate, blacks are lazy, Jews materialistic, or lesbians mannish in their demeanor? In the popular view, it is because they have not learned enough about the diversity among these groups and have not had enough contact with members of the groups for their stereotypes to be challenged by reality. With more experience, it is presumed, most people of good will are likely to revise their stereotypes.

My research over the past decade convinces me that there is little justification for such optimism—and not only for the reasons given by Allport. While it is true that deep prejudice is often based on the needs of pathological character structure, stereotypes are obviously quite common even among fairly normal individuals. When people first meet others, they cannot help noticing certain highly visible and distinctive characteristics: sex, race, physical appearance, and the like. Despite people's best intentions, their initial impressions of others are shaped by their assumptions about such characteristics.

What is critical, however, is that these assumptions are not merely beliefs or attitudes that exist in a vacuum; they are reinforced by the behavior of both prejudiced people and the targets of their prejudice. In recent years, psychologists have collected considerable laboratory evidence about the processes that strengthen stereotypes and put them beyond the reach of reason and good will.

My own studies initially focused on first encounters between strangers. It did not take long to discover, for example, that people have very different ways of treating those whom they regard as physically attractive and those whom they consider physically unattractive, and that these differences tend to bring out precisely those kinds of behavior that fit with stereotypes about attractiveness.

In an experiment that I conducted with my colleagues Elizabeth Decker Tanke and Ellen Berscheid, pairs of college-age men and women met and became acquainted in telephone conversations. Before the conversations began, each man received a Polaroid snapshot, presumably taken just moments before, of the woman he would soon meet. The photograph, which had actually been prepared before the experiment began, showed either a physically attractive woman or a physically unattractive one. By randomly choosing which picture to use for each conversation, we insured that there was no consistent relationship between the attractiveness of the woman in the picture and the attractiveness of the woman in the conversation.

By questioning the men, we learned that even before the conversations began, stereotypes about physical attractiveness came into play. Men who looked forward to talking with physically attractive women said that they expected to meet decidedly sociable, poised, humorous, and socially adept people, while men who thought that they were about to get acquainted with unattractive women fashioned images of rather unsociable, awkward, serious, and socially inept creatures. Moreover, the men proved to have very different styles of getting acquainted with women whom they thought to be attractive and those whom they believed to be unattractive. Shown a photograph of an attractive woman, they behaved with warmth, friendliness, humor, and animation. However, when the woman in the picture was unattractive, the men were cold, uninteresting, and reserved.

These differences in the men's behavior elicited behavior in the women that was consistent with the men's stereotyped assumptions. Women who were believed (unbeknown to them) to be physically attractive behaved in a friendly, likeable, and sociable manner. In sharp contrast, women who were perceived as physically unattractive adopted a cool, aloof, and distant manner. So striking were the differences in the women's behavior that they could be discerned simply by listening to tape recordings of the women's side of the conversations. Clearly, by acting upon their stereotyped beliefs about the women whom they would be meeting, the men had initiated a chain of events that produced *behavioral confirmation* for their beliefs.

Similarly, Susan Anderson and Sandra Bem have shown in an experiment at Stanford University that when the tables are turned—when it is women who have pictures of men they are to meet on the telephone—many women treat the men according to their presumed physical attractiveness, and by so doing encourage the men to confirm their stereotypes. Little wonder, then, that so many people remain convinced that good looks and appealing personalities go hand in hand.

SEX AND RACE

It is experiments such as these that point to a frequently unnoticed power of stereotypes: the power to influence social relationships in ways that create the illusion of reality. In one study, Berna Skrypnek and I arranged for pairs of previously unacquainted students to interact in a situation that permitted us to control the information that each one received about the apparent sex of the other. The two people were seated in separate rooms so that they could neither see nor hear each other. Using a system of signal lights that they operated with switches, they negotiated a division of labor, deciding which member of the pair would perform each of several tasks that differed in sex-role connotations. The tasks varied along the dimensions of masculinity and femininity: sharpen a hunting knife (masculine), polish a pair of shoes (neutral), iron a shirt (feminine).

One member of the team was led to believe that the other was, in one condition of the experiment, male; in the other, female. As we had predicted, the first member's belief about the sex of the partner influenced the outcome of the pair's negotiations. Women whose partners believed them to be men generally chose stereotypically masculine tasks; in contrast, women whose partners believed that they were women usually chose stereotypically feminine tasks. The experiment thus suggests that much sex-role behavior may be the product of other people's stereotyped and often erroneous beliefs.

In a related study at the University of Waterloo, Carl von Baeyer, Debbie Sherk, and Mark Zanna have shown how stereotypes about sex roles operate in job interviews. The researchers arranged to have men conduct simulated job interviews with women supposedly seeking positions as research assistants. The investigators informed half of the women that the men who would interview them held traditional views about the ideal woman, believing her to be very emotional, deferential to her husband, home-oriented, and passive. The rest of the women were told that their interviewer saw the ideal woman as independent, competitive, ambitious, and dominant. When the women arrived for their interviews, the researchers noticed that most of them had dressed to meet the stereotyped expectations of their prospective interviewers. Women who expected to see a traditional interviewer had chosen very feminine-looking makeup, clothes, and accessories. During the interviews (videotaped through a one-way mirror) these women behaved in traditionally feminine ways and gave traditionally feminine answers to questions such as "Do you have plans to include children and marriage with your career plans?"

Once more, then, we see the self-fulfilling nature of stereotypes. Many sex differences, it appears, may result from the images that people create in their attempts to act out accepted sex roles. The implication is that if stereotyped expectations about sex roles shift, behavior may change, too. In fact, statements by people who have undergone sex-change operations have highlighted the power of such expectations in easing adjustment to a new life. As the writer Jan Morris said in recounting the story of her transition from James to Jan: "The more I was treated as a woman, the more woman I became."

The power of stereotypes to cause people to confirm stereotyped expectations can also be seen in interracial relationships. In the first of two investigations done at Princeton University by Carl Word, Mark Zanna, and Joel Cooper, white undergraduates interviewed both white and black job applicants. The applicants were actually confederates of the experimenters, trained to behave consistently from interview to interview, no matter how the interviewers acted toward them.

To find out whether or not the white interviewers would behave differently toward white and black job applicants, the researchers secretly videotaped each interview and then studied the tapes. From these, it was apparent that there were substantial differences in the treatment accorded blacks and whites. For one thing, the interviewers' speech deteriorated when they talked to blacks, displaying more errors in grammar and pronunciation. For another, the interviewers spent less time with blacks than with whites and showed less "immediacy," as the researchers called it, in their manner. That is, they were less friendly, less outgoing, and more reserved with blacks.

In the second investigation, white confederates were trained to approximate either the immediate or the nonimmediate interview styles that had been observed in the first investigation as they interviewed white job applicants. A panel of judges who evaluated the tapes agreed that applicants subjected to the nonimmediate styles performed less adequately and were more nervous than job applicants treated in the immediate style. Apparently, then, the blacks in the first study did not have a chance to display their qualifications to the best advantage. Considered together, the two investigations suggest that in interracial encounters, racial stereotypes may constrain behavior in ways that cause both blacks and whites to behave in accordance with those stereotypes.

REWRITING BIOGRAPHY

Having adopted stereotyped ways of thinking about another person, people tend to notice and remember the ways in which that person seems to fit the stereotype, while resisting evidence that contradicts the stereotype. In one investigation that I conducted with Seymour Uranowitz, student subjects read a biography of a fictitious woman named Betty K. We constructed the story of her life so that it would fit the stereotyped images of both lesbians and heterosexuals. Betty, we wrote, never had a steady boyfriend in high school, but did go out on dates. And although we gave her a steady boyfriend in college, we specified that he was more of a close friend than anything else. A week after we had distributed this biography, we gave our subjects some new information about Betty. We told some students that she was now living with another woman in a lesbian relationship; we told others that she was living with her husband.

To see what impact stereotypes about sexuality would have on how people remembered the facts of Betty's life, we asked each student to answer a series of questions about her life history. When we examined their answers, we found that the students had reconstructed the events of Betty's past in ways that supported their own stereotyped beliefs about her sexual orientation. Those who believed that Betty was a lesbian remembered that Betty had never had a steady boyfriend in high school, but tended to neglect the fact that she had gone out on many dates in college. Those who believed that Betty was now a heterosexual tended to remember that she had formed a steady relationship with a man in college, but tended to ignore the fact that this relationship was more of a friendship than a romance.

The students showed not only selective memories but also a striking facility for interpreting what they remembered in ways that added fresh support for their stereotypes. One student who accurately remembered that a supposedly lesbian Betty never had a steady boyfriend in high school confidently pointed to that fact as an early sign of her lack of romantic or sexual interest in men. A student who correctly remembered that a purportedly lesbian Betty often went out on dates in college was sure that these dates were signs of Betty's early attempts to mask her lesbian interests.

Clearly, the students had allowed their preconceptions about lesbians and heterosexuals to dictate the way in which they interpreted and reinterpreted the facts of

Betty's life. As long as stereotypes make it easy to bring to mind evidence that supports them and difficult to bring to mind evidence that undermines them, people will cling to erroneous beliefs.

STEREOTYPES IN THE CLASSROOM AND WORK PLACE

The power of one person's beliefs to make other people conform to them has been well demonstrated in real life. Back in the 1960s, as most people well remember, Harvard psychologist Robert Rosenthal and his colleague Lenore Jacobson entered elementary-school classrooms and identified one out of every five pupils in each room as a child who could be expected to show dramatic improvement in intellectual achievement during the school year. What the teachers did not know was that the children had been chosen on a random basis. Nevertheless, something happened in the relationships between teachers and their supposedly gifted pupils that led the children to make clear gains in test performance.

It can also do so on the job. Albert King, now a professor of management at Northern Illinois University, told a welding instructor in a vocational training center that five men in his training program had unusually high aptitude. Although these five had been chosen at random and knew nothing of their designation as high-aptitude workers, they showed substantial changes in performance. They were absent less often than were other workers, learned the basics of the welder's trade in about half the usual time, and scored a full 10 points higher than other trainees on a welding test. Their gains were noticed not only by the researcher and by the welding instructor, but also by other trainees, who singled out the five as their preferred co-workers.

Might not other expectations influence the relationships between supervisors and workers? For example, supervisors who believe that men are better suited to some jobs and women to others may treat their workers (wittingly or unwittingly) in ways that encourage them to perform their jobs in accordance with stereotypes about differences between men and women. These same stereotypes may determine who gets which job in the first place. Perhaps some personnel managers allow stereotypes to influence, subtly or not so subtly, the way in which they interview job candidates, making it likely that candidates who fit the stereotypes show up better than job-seekers who do not fit them.

Unfortunately, problems of this kind are compounded by the fact that members of stigmatized groups often subscribe to stereotypes about themselves. That is what Amerigo Farina and his colleagues at the University of Connecticut found when they measured the impact upon mental patients of believing that others knew their psychiatric history. In Farina's study, each mental patient cooperated with another person in a game requiring teamwork. Half of the patients believed that their partners knew they were patients; the other half believed that their partners thought they were nonpatients. In reality, the nonpatients never knew a thing about anyone's psychiatric history. Nevertheless, simply believing that others were aware of their history led the patients to feel less appreciated, to find the task more difficult, and to perform poorly. In addition, objective observers saw them as more tense, more anxious, and more poorly adjusted than patients who believed that their status was not known. Seemingly, the belief that others perceived them as stigmatized caused them to play the role of stigmatized patients.

CONSEQUENCES FOR SOCIETY

Apparently, good will and education are not sufficient to subvert the power of stereotypes. If people treat others in such a way as to bring out behavior that supports stereotypes, they may never have an opportunity to discover which of their stereotypes are wrong.

I suspect that even if people were to develop doubts about the accuracy of their stereotypes, chances are they would proceed to test them by gathering precisely the evidence that would appear to confirm them.

The experiments I have described help to explain the persistence of stereotypes. But, as is so often the case, solving one puzzle only creates another. If by acting as if false stereotypes were true, people lead others, too, to act as if they were true, why do the stereotypes not come to *be* true? Why, for example, have researchers found so little evidence that attractive people are generally friendly, sociable, and outgoing and that unattractive people are generally shy and aloof?

I think that the explanation goes something like this: Very few among us have the kind of looks that virtually everyone considers either very attractive or very unattractive. Our looks make us rather attractive to some people but somewhat less attractive to other people. When we spend time with those who find us attractive, they will tend to bring out our more sociable sides, but when we are with those who find us less attractive, they will bring out our less sociable sides. Although our actual physical appearance does not change, we present ourselves quite differently to our admirers and to our detractors. For our admirers we become attractive people, and for our detractors we become unattractive. This mixed pattern of behavior will prevent the development of any consistent relationship between physical attractiveness and personality.

Now that I understand some of the powerful forces that work to perpetuate social stereotypes, I can see a new mission for my research. I hope, on the one hand, to find out how to help people see the flaws in their stereotypes. On the other hand, I would like to help the victims of false stereotypes find ways of liberating themselves from the constraints imposed on them by other members of society.

5

ON BEING SANE IN INSANE PLACES

D. L. Rosenhan (1973)

We hypothesize every day about a variety of topics: "She loves me, she loves me not." "He's a hard teacher; I won't be able to get an *A* in that course." "I've learned to trust my first impressions; they've been right in the past." And we use a variety of measures to test others' behaviors. But, as Rosenhan (1973) shows, even the scientifically educated among us fail to use appropriate means of testing hypotheses much of the time. His report of psychiatric hospitals includes multiple examples of clinical workers doing what we all do, looking for data that will confirm our beliefs. Yet this practice leads to erroneous conclusions, and it is only by looking for disconfirmatory as well as confirmatory information that we can really test our hypotheses. A major goal of ours, as teachers, is to help students develop disconfirmatory thinking. This critical thinking skill, the ability to disconfirm hypotheses, has enormous value for one's interpersonal relationships, financial expenditures, careers, and health maintenance.

Critical thinking is not an easy skill to develop. Throughout our childhood we are told what to do, what to think, and what to believe. Questioning is not always encouraged. "Because I'm your parent—that's why" or "As long as you're living under my roof, you'll abide by my rules" discourages us from looking elsewhere for answers. In social psychological terms, our ability to develop or express disconfirmatory hypotheses is inhibited.

One final point about the Rosenhan study is the identification of the powerlessness and the depersonalization that patients experience in psychiatric hospitals. Although much has changed in the last two decades, these issues are still very grave concerns in psychiatric settings (note the consequences of the label in Farina's work described by Snyder in Reading 4). Believing that you are "out of control" has negative consequences throughout our life cycle (see Rodin and Langer, Reading 8).

If sanity and insanity exist, how shall we know them?

The question is neither capricious nor itself insane. However much we may be personally convinced that we can tell the normal from the abnormal, the evidence is simply not compelling. It is commonplace, for example, to read about murder trials wherein eminent psychiatrists for the defense are contradicted by equally eminent psychiatrists for the prosecution on the matter of the defendant's sanity. More generally, there are a great deal of conflicting data on the reliability, utility, and meaning of such terms as "sanity," "insanity," "mental illness," and "schizophrenia." Finally, as early as 1934, Benedict suggested that normality and abnormality are not universal. What is viewed as normal in one culture may be seen as quite aberrant in another. Thus, notions of normality and abnormality may not be quite as accurate as people believe they are.

To raise questions regarding normality and abnormality is in no way to question the fact that some behaviors are deviant or odd. Murder is deviant. So, too, are hallucinations. Nor does raising such questions deny the existence of the personal anguish that is often associated with "mental illness." Anxiety and depression exist. Psychological suffering exists. But normality and abnormality, sanity and insanity, and the diagnoses that flow from them may be less substantive than many believe them to be.

At its heart, the question of whether the sane can be distinguished from the insane (and whether degrees of insanity can be distinguished from each other) is a simple matter: do the salient characteristics that lead to diagnoses reside in the patients themselves or in the environments and contexts in which observers find them? From Bleuler, through Kretchmer, through the formulators of the recently revised *Diagnostic and Statistical Manual* of the American Psychiatric Association, the belief has been strong that patients present symptoms, that those symptoms can be categorized, and, implicitly, that the sane are distinguishable from the insane. More recently, however, this belief has been questioned. Based in part on theoretical and anthropological considerations, but also on philosophical, legal, and therapeutic ones, the view has grown that psychological categorization of mental illness is useless at best and downright harmful, misleading, and pejorative at worst. Psychiatric diagnoses, in this view, are in the minds of the observers and are not valid summaries of characteristics displayed by the observed.

Gains can be made in deciding which of these is more nearly accurate by getting normal people (that is, people who do not have, and have never suffered, symptoms of serious psychiatric disorders) admitted to psychiatric hospitals and then determining whether they were discovered to be sane and, if so, how. If the sanity of such pseudopatients were always detected, there would be prima facie evidence that a sane individual can be distinguished from the insane context in which he is found. Normality (and presumably abnormality) is distinct enough that it can be recognized wherever it occurs, for it is carried within the person. If, on the other hand, the sanity of the pseudopatients were never discovered, serious difficulties would arise for those who support traditional modes of psychiatric diagnosis. Given that the hospital staff was not incompetent, that the pseudopatient had been behaving as sanely as he had been outside of the hospital, and that it had never been previously suggested that he belonged in a psychiatric hospital, such an unlikely outcome would support the view that psychiatric diagnosis betrays little about the patient but much about the environment in which an observer finds him.

This article describes such an experiment. Eight sane people gained secret admission to 12 different hospitals. Their diagnostic experiences constitute the data of the first part of this article; the remainder is devoted to a description of their experiences in psychiatric institutions. Too few psychiatrists and psychologists, even those who have worked in such hospitals, know what the experience is like. They rarely talk about it with former patients, perhaps because they distrust information coming from the previously insane. Those who have worked in psychiatric hospitals are likely to have adapted so thoroughly to the settings that they are insensitive to the impact of that experience. And while there have been occasional reports of researchers who submitted themselves to psychiatric hospitalization, these researchers have commonly remained in the hospitals for short periods of time, often with the knowledge of the hospital staff. It is difficult to know the extent to which they were treated like patients or like research colleagues. Nevertheless, their reports about the inside of the psychiatric hospital have been valuable. This article extends those efforts.

PSEUDOPATIENTS AND THEIR SETTINGS

The eight pseudopatients were a varied group. One was a psychology graduate student in his 20's. The remaining seven were older and "established." Among them were three psychologists, a pediatrician, a psychiatrist, a painter, and a housewife. Three pseudopatients were women, five were men. All of them employed pseudonyms, lest their alleged diagnoses embarrass them later. Those who were in mental health professions alleged another occupation in order to avoid the special attentions that might be accorded by staff, as a matter of courtesy or caution, to ailing colleagues. With the exception of myself (I was the first pseudopatient and my presence was known to the hospital administrator and chief psychologist and, so far as I can tell, to them alone), the presence of pseudopatients and the nature of the research program was not known to the hospital staffs.

The settings were similarly varied. In order to generalize the findings, admission into a variety of hospitals was sought. The 12 hospitals in the sample were located in five different states on the East and West coasts. Some were old and shabby, some were quite new. Some were research-oriented, others not. Some had good staff-patient ratios, others were quite understaffed. Only one was a strictly private hospital. All of the others were supported by state or federal funds or, in one instance, by university funds.

After calling the hospital for an appointment, the pseudopatient arrived at the admissions office complaining that he had been hearing voices. Asked what the voices said, he replied that they were often unclear, but as far as he could tell they said "empty," "hollow," and "thud." The voices were unfamiliar and were of the same sex as the pseudo-patient. The choice of these symptoms was occasioned by their apparent similarity to existential symptoms. Such symptoms are alleged to arise from painful concerns about the perceived meaninglessness of one's life. It is as if the hallucinating person were saying, "My life is empty and hollow." The choice of these symptoms was also determined by the *absence* of a single report of existential psychoses in the literature.

Beyond alleging the symptoms and falsifying name, vocation, and employment, no further alterations of person, history, or circumstances were made. The significant events of the pseudopatient's life history were presented as they had actually occurred. Relationships with parents and siblings, with spouse and children, with people at work and in school, consistent with the aforementioned exceptions, were described as they were or had been. Frustrations and upsets were described along with joys and satisfactions. These facts are important to remember. If anything, they strongly biased the subsequent results in favor of detecting sanity, since none of their histories or current behaviors were seriously pathological in any way.

Immediately upon admission to the psychiatric ward, the pseudopatient ceased simulating *any* symptoms of abnormality. In some cases, there was a brief period of mild nervousness and anxiety, since none of the pseudopatients really believed that they would be admitted so easily. Indeed, their shared fear was that they would be immediately exposed as frauds and greatly embarrassed. Moreover, many of them had never visited a psychiatric ward; even those who had, nevertheless had some genuine fears about what might happen to them. Their nervousness, then, was quite appropriate to the novelty of the hospital setting, and it abated rapidly.

Apart from that short-lived nervousness, the pseudopatient behaved on the ward as he "normally" behaved. The pseudopatient spoke to patients and staff as he might ordinarily. Because there is uncommonly little to do on a psychiatric ward, he attempted to engage others in conversation. When asked by staff how he was feeling, he indicated that he was fine, that he no longer experienced symptoms. He responded to instructions from attendants, to calls for medication (which was not swallowed), and to dining-hall instructions. Beyond such activities as were available to him on the admissions ward, he spent his time writing down his observations about the ward, its patients, and the staff. Initially these notes were written "secretly," but as it soon became clear that no one much cared, they were subsequently written on standard tablets of paper in such public places as the dayroom. No secret was made of these activities.

The pseudopatient, very much as a true psychiatric patient, entered a hospital with no foreknowledge of when he would be discharged. Each was told that he would have to get out by his own devices, essentially by convincing the staff that he was sane. The psychological stresses associated with hospitalization were considerable, and all but one of the pseudopatients desired to be discharged almost immediately after being admitted. They were, therefore, motivated not only to behave sanely, but to be paragons of cooperation. That their behavior was in no way disruptive is confirmed by nursing reports, which have been obtained on most of the patients. These reports uniformly indicate that the patients were "friendly," "cooperative," and "exhibited no abnormal indications."

THE NORMAL ARE NOT DETECTABLY SANE

Despite their public "show" of sanity, the pseudopatients were never detected. Admitted, except in one case, with a diagnosis of schizophrenia, each was discharged with a diagnosis of schizophrenia "in remission." The label "in remission" should in no way be dismissed as a formality, for at no time during any hospitalization had any question been raised about any pseudopatient's simulation. Nor are there any indications in the hospital records that the pseudopatient's status was suspect. Rather, the evidence is strong that, once labeled schizophrenic, the pseudopatient was stuck with that label. If the pseudopatient was to be discharged, he must naturally be "in remission"; but he was not sane, nor, in the institution's view, had he ever been sane.

The uniform failure to recognize sanity cannot be attributed to the quality of the hospitals, for, although there were considerable variations among them, several are considered excellent. Nor can it be alleged that there was simply not enough time to observe the pseudopatients. Length of hospitalization ranged from 7 to 52 days, with an average of 19 days. The pseudopatients were not, in fact, carefully observed, but this failure clearly speaks more to traditions within psychiatric hospitals than to lack of opportunity.

Finally, it cannot be said that the failure to recognize the pseudopatients' sanity was due to the fact that they were not behaving sanely. While there was clearly some tension present in all of them, their daily visitors could detect no serious behavioral consequences—nor, indeed, could other patients. It was quite common for the patients to "detect" the pseudopatients' sanity. During the first three hospitalizations, when accurate counts were kept, 35 of a total of 118 patients on the admissions ward voiced their suspicions, some vigorously. "You're not crazy. You're a journalist, or a professor [referring to the continual note-taking]. You're checking up on the hospital." While most of the patients were reassured by the pseudopatient's insistence that he had been sick before he came in but was fine now, some continued to believe that the pseudopatient was sane throughout his hospitalization.[1] The fact that the patients often recognized normality when staff did not raises important questions.

Failure to detect sanity during the course of hospitalization may be due to the fact that physicians operate with a strong bias toward what statisticians call the type 2 error. This is to say that physicians are more inclined to call a healthy person sick (a false positive, type 2) than a sick person healthy (a false negative, type 1). The reasons for this are not hard to find: it is clearly more dangerous to misdiagnose illness than health. Better to err on the side of caution, to suspect illness even among the healthy.

But what holds for medicine does not hold equally well for psychiatry. Medical illnesses, while unfortunate, are not commonly pejorative. Psychiatric diagnoses, on the contrary, carry with them personal, legal, and social stigmas. It was therefore important to see whether the tendency toward diagnosing the sane insane could be reversed.

---

[1] It is possible, of course, that patients have quite broad latitudes in diagnosis and therefore are inclined to call many people sane, even those whose behavior is patently aberrant. However, although we have no hard data on this matter, it was our distinct impression that this was not the case. In many instances, patients not only singled us out for attention, but came to imitate our behaviors and styles.

The following experiment was arranged at a research and teaching hospital whose staff had heard these findings but doubted that such an error could occur in their hospital. The staff was informed that at some time during the following 3 months, one or more pseudopatients would attempt to be admitted into the psychiatric hospital. Each staff member was asked to rate each patient who presented himself at admissions or on the ward according to the likelihood that the patient was a pseudopatient. A 10-point scale was used, with a 1 and 2 reflecting high confidence that the patient was a pseudopatient.

Judgments were obtained on 193 patients who were admitted for psychiatric treatment. All staff who had had sustained contact with or primary responsibility for the patient—attendants, nurses, psychiatrists, physicians, and psychologists—were asked to make judgments. Forty-one patients were alleged, with high confidence, to be pseudopatients by at least one member of the staff. Twenty-three were considered suspect by at least one psychiatrist. Nineteen were suspected by one psychiatrist *and* one other staff member. Actually, no genuine pseudopatient (at least from my group) presented himself during this period.

The experiment is instructive. It indicates that the tendency to designate sane people as insane can be reversed when the stakes (in this case, prestige and diagnostic acumen) are high. But what can be said of the 19 people who were suspected of being "sane" by one psychiatrist and another staff member? Were these people truly "sane," or was it rather the case that in the course of avoiding the type 2 error the staff tended to make more errors of the first sort—calling the crazy "sane"? There is no way of knowing. But one thing is certain: any diagnostic process that lends itself so readily to massive errors of this sort cannot be a very reliable one.

THE STICKINESS OF PSYCHODIAGNOSTIC LABELS

Beyond the tendency to call the healthy sick—a tendency that accounts better for diagnostic behavior on admission than it does for such behavior after a lengthy period of exposure—the data speak to the massive role of labeling in psychiatric assessment. Having once been labeled schizophrenic, there is nothing the pseudopatient can do to overcome the tag. The tag profoundly colors others' perceptions of him and his behavior.

From one viewpoint, these data are hardly surprising, for it has long been known that elements are given meaning by the context in which they occur. Gestalt psychology made this point vigorously, and Asch demonstrated that there are "central" personality traits (such as "warm" versus "cold") which are so powerful that they markedly color the meaning of other information in forming an impression of a given personality. "Insane," "schizophrenic," "manic-depressive," and "crazy" are probably among the most powerful of such central traits. Once a person is designated abnormal, all of his other behaviors and characteristics are colored by that label. Indeed, that label is so powerful that many of the pseudopatients' normal behaviors were overlooked entirely or profoundly misinterpreted. Some examples may clarify this issue.

As far as I can determine, diagnoses were in no way affected by the relative health or the circumstances of a pseudopatient's life. Rather, the reverse occurred: the perception of his circumstances was shaped entirely by the diagnosis. A clear example of such translation is found in the case of a pseudopatient who had had a close relationship with his mother but was rather remote from his father during his early childhood. During adolescence and beyond, however, his father became a close friend, while his relationship with his mother cooled. His present relationship with his wife was characteristically close and warm. Apart from occasional angry exchanges, friction was minimal. The children had rarely been spanked. Surely there is nothing especially pathological about such a history. Indeed, many readers may see a similar pattern in their own experiences, with no markedly deleterious consequences. Observe, however, how such a history was translated in the psychopathological context, this from the case summary prepared after the patient was discharged.

> This white 39-year-old male . . . manifests a long history of considerable ambivalence in close relationships, which begins in early childhood. A warm relationship with his mother cools during his adolescence. A distant relationship to his father is described as becoming very intense. Affective stability is absent. His attempts to control emotionality with his wife and children are punctuated by angry outbursts and, in the case of the children, spankings. And while he says that he has several good friends, one senses considerable ambivalence embedded in those relationships also. . . .

The facts of the case were unintentionally distorted by the staff to achieve consistency with a popular theory of the dynamics of a schizophrenic reaction. Nothing of an ambivalent nature had been described in relations with parents, spouse, or friends. To the extent that ambivalence could be inferred, it was probably not greater than is found in all human relationships. It is true the pseudopatient's relationships with his parents changed over time, but in the ordinary context that would hardly be remarkable—indeed, it might very well be expected. Clearly, the meaning ascribed to his verbalizations (that is, ambivalence, affective instability) was determined by the diagnosis: schizophrenia. An entirely different meaning would have been ascribed if it were known that the man was "normal."

All pseudopatients took extensive notes publicly. Under ordinary circumstances, such behavior would have raised questions in the minds of observers, as, in fact, it did among patients.

But no questions were asked of the pseudopatients. How was their writing interpreted? Nursing records for three patients indicate that the writing was seen as an aspect of their pathological behavior. "Patient engages in writing behavior" was the daily nursing comment on one of the pseudopatients who was never questioned about his writing. Given that the patient is in the hospital, he must be psychologically disturbed. And given that he is disturbed, continuous writing must be a behavioral manifestation of that disturbance, perhaps a subset of the compulsive behaviors that are sometimes correlated with schizophrenia.

One tacit characteristic of psychiatric diagnosis is that it locates the sources of aberration within the individual and only rarely within the complex of stimuli that surrounds him. Consequently, behaviors that are stimulated by the environment are commonly misattributed to the patient's disorder. For example, one kindly nurse found a pseudopatient pacing the long hospital corridors. "Nervous, Mr. X?" she asked. "No, bored," he said.

One psychiatrist pointed to a group of patients who were sitting outside the cafeteria entrance half an hour before lunchtime. To a group of young residents he indicated that such behavior was characteristic of the oral-acquisitive nature of the syndrome. It seemed not to occur to him that there were very few things to anticipate in a psychiatric hospital besides eating.

A psychiatric label has a life and an influence of its own. Once the impression has been formed that the patient is schizophrenic, the expectation is that he will continue to be schizophrenic. When a sufficient amount of time has passed, during which the patient has done nothing bizarre, he is considered to be in remission and available for discharge. But the label endures beyond discharge, with the unconfirmed expectation that he will behave as a schizophrenic again. Such labels, conferred by mental health professionals, are as influential on the patient as they are on his relatives and friends, and it should not surprise anyone that the diagnosis acts on all of them as a self-fulfilling prophecy. Eventually, the patient himself accepts the diagnosis, with all of its surplus meanings and expectations, and behaves accordingly.

THE EXPERIENCE OF PSYCHIATRIC HOSPITALIZATION

The term "mental illness" is of recent origin. It was coined by people who were humane in their inclinations and who wanted very much to raise the station of (and the public's sympathies toward) the psychologically disturbed from that of witches and "crazies" to one that was akin to the physically ill. And they were at least partially successful, for the treatment of the mentally ill *has* improved considerably over the years. But while treatment has improved, it is doubtful that people really regard the mentally ill in the same way that they view the physically ill. A broken leg is something one recovers from, but mental illness allegedly endures forever. A broken leg does not threaten the observer, but a crazy schizophrenic? There is by now a host of evidence that attitudes toward the mentally ill are characterized by fear, hostility, aloofness, suspicion, and dread. The mentally ill are society's lepers.

That such attitudes infect the general population is perhaps not surprising, only upsetting. But that they affect the professionals—attendants, nurses, physicians, psychologists, and social workers—who treat and deal with the mentally ill is more disconcerting, both because such attitudes are self-evidently pernicious and because they are unwitting. Most mental health professionals would insist that they are sympathetic toward the mentally ill, that they are neither avoidant nor hostile. But it is more likely that an exquisite ambivalence characterizes their relations with psychiatric patients, such that their avowed impulses are only part of their entire attitude. Negative attitudes are there too and can easily be detected. Such attitudes should not surprise us. They are the natural offspring of the labels patients wear and the places in which they are found.

POWERLESSNESS AND DEPERSONALIZATION

Powerlessness was evident everywhere. The patient is deprived of many of his legal rights by dint of his psychiatric commitment. He is shorn of credibility by virtue of his psychiatric label. His freedom of movement is restricted. He cannot initiate contact with the staff, but may only respond to such overtures as they make. Personal privacy is minimal. Patient quarters and possessions can be entered and examined by any staff member, for whatever reason. His personal history and anguish is available to any staff member (often including the "grey lady" and "candy striper" volunteer) who chooses to read his folder, regardless of their therapeutic relationship to him. His personal hygiene and waste evacuation are often monitored. The water closets may have no doors.

At times, depersonalization reached such proportions that pseudopatients had the sense that they were invisible, or at least unworthy of account. Upon being admitted, I and other pseudopatients took the initial physical examinations in a semipublic room, where staff members went about their own business as if we were not there.

On the ward, attendants delivered verbal and occasionally serious physical abuse to patients in the presence of other observing patients, some of whom (the pseudopatients) were writing it all down. Abusive behavior, on the other hand, terminated quite abruptly when other staff members were known to be coming. Staff are credible witnesses. Patients are not.

A nurse unbuttoned her uniform to adjust her brassiere in the presence of an entire ward of viewing men. One did not have the sense that she was being seductive. Rather, she didn't notice us. A group of staff persons might point to a patient in the dayroom and discuss him animatedly, as if he were not there.

THE SOURCES OF DEPERSONALIZATION

What are the origins of depersonalization? I have already mentioned two. First are attitudes held by all of us toward the mentally ill—including those who treat them—attitudes characterized by fear, distrust, and horrible expectations on the one hand, and benevolent intentions on the other. Our ambivalence leads, in this instance as in others, to avoidance.

Second, and not entirely separate, the hierarchical structure of the psychiatric hospital facilitates depersonalization. Those who are at the top have least to do with patients, and their behavior inspires the rest of the staff. Average daily contact with psychiatrists, psychologists, residents, and physicians combined ranged from 3.9 to 25.1 minutes, with an overall mean of 6.8 (six pseudopatients over a total of 129 days of hospitalization). Included in this average are time spent in the admissions interview, ward meetings in the presence of a senior staff member, group and individual psychotherapy contacts, case presentation conferences, and discharge meetings. Clearly, patients do not spend much time in interpersonal contact with doctoral staff. And doctoral staff serve as models for nurses and attendants.

SUMMARY AND CONCLUSIONS

It is clear that we cannot distinguish the sane from the insane in psychiatric hospitals. The hospital itself imposes a special environment in which the meanings of behavior can easily be misunderstood. The consequences to patients hospitalized in such an environment—the powerlessness, depersonalization, segregation, mortification, and self-labeling—seem undoubtedly countertherapeutic.

I do not, even now, understand this problem well enough to perceive solutions. But two matters seem to have some promise. The first concerns the proliferation of community mental health facilities, of crisis intervention centers, of the human potential movement, and of behavior therapies that, for all of their own problems, tend to avoid psychiatric labels, to focus on specific problems and behaviors, and to retain the individual in a relatively nonpejorative environment. Clearly, to the extent that we refrain from sending the distressed to insane places, our impressions of them are less likely to be distorted. (The risk of distorted perceptions, it seems to me, is always present, since we are much more sensitive to an individual's behaviors and verbalizations than we are to the subtle contextual stimuli that often promote them. At issue here is a matter of magnitude. And, as I have shown, the magnitude of distortion is exceedingly high in the extreme context that is a psychiatric hospital.)

The second matter that might prove promising speaks to the need to increase the sensitivity of mental health workers and researchers to the *Catch 22* position of psychiatric patients. Simply reading materials in this area will be of help to some such workers and researchers. For others, directly experiencing the impact of psychiatric hospitalization will be of enormous use. Clearly, further research into the social psychology of such total institutions will both facilitate treatment and deepen understanding.

I and the other pseudopatients in the psychiatric setting had distinctly negative reactions. We do not pretend to describe the subjective experiences of true patients. Theirs may be different from ours, particularly with the passage of time and the necessary process of adaptation to one's environment. But we can and do speak to the relatively more objective indices of treatment within the hospital. It could be a mistake, and a very unfortunate one, to consider that what happened to us derived from malice or stupidity on the part of the staff. Quite the contrary, our overwhelming impression of them was of people who really cared, who were committed and who were uncommonly intelligent. Where they failed, as they sometimes did painfully, it would be more accurate to attribute those failures to the environment in which they, too, found themselves than to personal callousness. Their perceptions and behavior were controlled by the situation, rather than being motivated by a malicious disposition. In a more benign environment, one that was less attached to global diagnosis, their behaviors and judgments might have been more benign and effective.

6

SEX DIFFERENCES IN ATTRIBUTIONS FOR FRIENDLY BEHAVIOR: DO MALES MISPERCEIVE FEMALES' FRIENDLINESS?

Antonia Abbey (1982)

Abbey's study identifies another way in which attributions can affect our interactions with others. Her work identifies sex differences in simple perceptions about others' friendliness and seductiveness. In Abbey's study, college-age men perceived their interactions with college-age women in more sexual terms than did the women. It seems that friendly actions of women may be misinterpreted by men as sexual interest on the part of women, and this can result in cross-sex misunderstandings that confuse both men and women. Women may have reason to be wary of touching a man. This type of attribution error may also be a contributing factor in date rape and sexual violence (see Reading 25). As an aside, in our society females are much more likely to touch other females compared to males touching other males. Why do you think there is this difference in same-sex touching?

Abbey's study indicates the value of attribution theory in understanding a wide range of human behavior. If Abbey is right that men apply more of a sexually oriented perspective than women in their attempts to understand and organize social behavior, then what other belief differences might exist between males and females? This question highlights for us the notion of nonconscious ideologies (Bem and Bem, 1970, see Reading 1) and the effects that our hidden assumptions may have on our behavior.*

Source: Abridged from the *Journal of Personality and Social Psychology,* 1982, *42,* 830–838. Copyright © 1982 by the American Psychological Association. Reprinted by permission of the publisher and the author.

*Editors' note: At this point, we want to report on another attribution study that may be relevant to your own academic experiences. Poor academic performance or dropping out of school are often accompanied by personal beliefs that one is not smart enough or hard-working enough to succeed academically. Either way, the attribution being made is about one's self and one's ability to do good academic work. Wilson and

ABSTRACT

This investigation tested the hypothesis that friendliness from a member of the opposite sex might be misperceived as a sign of sexual interest. Previous research in the area of acquaintance and date rape suggests that males frequently misunderstand females' intentions. A laboratory experiment was conducted in which a male and female participated in a 5-minute conversation while a hidden male and female observed this interaction. The results indicate that there were sex differences in subjects' rating of the actors. Male actors and observers rated the female actor as being more promiscuous and seductive than female actors and observers rated her. Males were also more sexually attracted to the opposite-sex actor than females were. Furthermore, males also rated the male actor in a more sexualized fashion than females did. These results were interpreted as indicating that men are more likely to perceive the world in sexual terms and to make sexual judgments than women are. Males do seem to perceive friendliness from females as seduction, but this appears to be merely one manifestation of a broader male sexual orientation.

The research described in this article grew out of the observation that females' friendly behavior is frequently misperceived by males as flirtation. Males tend to impute sexual interest to females when it is not intended. For example, one evening the author and a few of her female friends shared a table at a crowded campus bar with two male strangers. During one of the band's breaks, they struck up a friendly conversation with their male table companions. It was soon apparent that their friendliness had been misperceived by these men as a sexual invitation, and they finally had to excuse themselves from the table to avoid an awkward scene. What had been intended as platonic friendliness had been perceived as sexual interest.

After discussions with several other women verified that this experience was not unique, the author began to consider several related, researchable issues. Do women similarly misjudge men's intentions or is this bias limited to men only? How frequently do these opposite-sex misunderstandings occur? What causes them and what circumstances elicit them?

Research on other subcultural groups indicates that intergroup misperceptions may be common. For example, La France and Mayo (1976, 1978a, 1978b) have examined racial differences in the interpretations of various nonverbal cues. They have found that black and white Americans frequently interpret the same nonverbal cues, such as a direct gaze, quite differently. For example, white listeners gaze at the speaker more than black listeners do. Consequently, interracial encounters may be cumbersome be-

---

Linville (1985) developed an attributional intervention—in their study, they suggested to some first-year students that they view their academic problems as temporary and within their control. The first-year students who learned that college students generally improve academically from the first to upperclass years had significantly lower dropout rates, significantly higher grade-point averages, and significantly better performance on sample items on the GRE compared to first-year students not receiving information about academic improvement over time. Thus, attributions about causes for poor grades can mediate future academic performance! Wilson and Linville retested their hypotheses in two additional studies (1985) and found similar results. Thus, one's own academic performance can sometimes be positively influenced by attributions of unstable and temporary causes. As budding social psychologists, you may want to generate hypotheses as to why this attribution might be successful. You may also want to examine Myers's Module 10 for another type of attribution therapy.

cause the participants' signals for yielding the floor or ending the conversation may differ. Because neither individual realizes that their nonverbal vocabularies conflict, they are likely to mistakenly attribute the awkwardness of the conversation to the other's dislike of them.

Although similar research has not been conducted concerning opposite-sex misunderstandings, a great deal has been written about date and acquaintance rape that may be applicable. Although a simple verbal misunderstanding is in no way comparable to rape in either magnitude or consequences, the underlying process that produces these two events may be related. Several authors have described how our cultural beliefs about the dating situation might lead to sexual misunderstandings and, in the extreme case, rape (Bernard, 1969; Brodyaga, Gates, Singer, Tucker, & White, 1975; Medea & Thompson, 1974; Russell, 1975; Weis & Borges, 1973; Hendrick, 1976; Goodchilds, 1977). These authors argue that women are socialized to flirt and play "hard to get." Even when sexually attracted to a man, a woman is expected to say "no" to his sexual advances, at least at first. And, in a complementary fashion, men are taught to initiate all sexual encounters and to believe that women prefer lovers who are aggressive, forceful, and dominant.

According to this argument these social mores may cause men to unwittingly force sexual relations on their dates, mistaking their true lack of sexual interest for mere coyness. Date and acquaintance rape are prevalent. Researchers estimate that 48–58% of all reported rapes are committed by someone the victim knows (Amir, 1971; Kanin, 1957, 1967; Katz & Mazur, 1979; Kirkpatrick and Kanin, 1957). Kanin and Parcell (1977) found that 50.7% of the 292 female undergraduates they polled had experienced some level of sexual aggression on a date during the previous year. Of these, 23.8% involved forced intercourse (see also Kirkpatrick and Kanin, 1957, and Kanin, 1967). After interviewing college males who had engaged in sexual aggression toward their dates, Kanin (1969) argues that

> The typical male enters into heterosexual interaction as an eager recipient of any subtle signs of sexual receptivity broadcasted by his female companion. In some instances, however, these signs are innocently emitted by a female naive in erotic communication. He perceives erotic encouragement, eagerly solicits further erotic concessions, encounters rebuff, and experiences bewilderment (pp. 18–19).

In order to test empirically the hypothesis that men misperceive women's intentions, an experiment was designed in which a male and female would interact with each other while another male and female would observe this interaction. Hence, unlike Hendrick's (1976) experiment in which subjects reacted to the behavior of confederates on a videotape, in this case half of the subjects were participants in the interaction. This paradigm also permits examination of both actors' reactions to their partners. If the results do indicate that males misperceive females' intentions, such result would be difficult to interpret without knowing if females similarly misperceive males' intentions.

The observers were included in the design to provide greater insight into this phenomenon. Although it was hypothesized that males are unable to distinguish females' friendly behavior from their seductive behavior because of the differential meaning that the relevant cues have for the two sexes, other explanations of this effect are tenable. For instance, it could be argued that males mistakenly perceive sexual interest in females for ego-enhancing motives; it makes them feel good to think that a woman is sexually attracted to them. However, if male observers as well as male actors perceive the female as being sexually attracted to the male actor, then this lends support to the notion of a general male bias. By comparing the male actors' ratings of the female actor to the male observers' ratings of her, one can assess the extent to which these ratings are due to ego-enhancing motives as opposed to a more general masculine orientation toward female behavior.

The inclusion of female observers provides additional information about the boundaries of this effect. Again, because it was proposed that the hypothesized effect is due to differences in sex role socialization, one would expect the female observers' ratings to be similar to the female actors' ratings and unlike the males' ratings. However, alternatively, one could argue that this phenomenon is due to some kind of actor-observer difference. It may be that all outsiders, regardless of sex, misperceive the female actors' intentions. By comparing the female observers' ratings to the male observers' ratings, we can test these competing explanations.

Although it was predicted that male subjects would misperceive the female actor, it was less clear as to how female subjects would rate the male actor. The evidence in the nonverbal-cues literature, which indicates that women are better at interpreting nonverbal cues than men are (Buck, Miller, & Caul, 1974; Hall, 1978; Rosenthal, Hall, DiMatteo, Rogers, & Archer, 1979), suggests that women may be capable of correctly distinguishing men's friendly behavior from their seductive behavior. However, the pervasiveness of the cultural myth that men are primarily interested in women for sexual reasons may lead one to predict that women may also mistake a man's friendly behavior as a sign of sexual interest. Therefore, no predictions were made as to how the male actor would be judged by the female subjects.

METHOD

Subjects

Subjects were 144 white Northwestern University undergraduates who received credit toward a course requirement of research participation. Subjects were scheduled in groups of four such that none of the students scheduled for the same session knew each other. In all, 36 complete sessions were run (72 males, 72 females).

Procedure

Subjects reported to a large anteroom with five connecting cubicles. Subjects were reminded by the experimenter that the study concerned the acquaintance process and were told that the purpose of the experiment was to determine the ways in which the topic of conversation affects the smoothness of initial interactions. Pairs of subjects would each be assigned a different topic, which they would discuss for 5 minutes. Then they would fill out a questionnaire that would assess their opinion of the conversation. Finally, they would engage in a second conversation about a different topic either with the same or a different partner and fill out a second questionnaire. Subjects were told that the experimenter wanted a male and a female in each pair, and they drew pieces of paper to determine who would interact with whom. (Unbeknown to the subjects, this random draw was also used to determine their role assignment.) Although subjects were told by the experimenter that each pair would have a slightly different task, they were led to believe that both pairs would be engaging in conversations. This was done to keep the actors from correctly guessing that they were being observed.

After the draw the experimenter asked the subjects to fill out a brief questionnaire "before the actual study begins." Subjects were placed in individual cubicles to complete this questionnaire. They were given this questionnaire solely to provide the experimenter with the opportunity to give the observers their instructions. After waiting 3 minutes, the experimenter placed both observers in the same room and explained their task to them. Then they were asked to wait quietly and avoid talking while the actors were prepared.

The experimenter then escorted the actors into the "conversation" room in which the one-way mirror through which the observers were watching was hidden by sheer pastel curtains. The actors were seated in chairs facing each other about 4 ft. (1.2 m) apart. They were instructed to talk for 5 minutes about their experiences of that year at Northwestern.

The experimenter immediately joined the observers and turned on a microphone that allowed them to hear the conversation. The observers had a clear view of the actors' profiles. After 5 minutes the experimenter turned off the microphone, reminded the observers to remain silent, and returned to the actors' room to stop the conversation. The experimenter gave the actors questionnaires containing the dependent measures and asked them to fill them out in their individual cubicles. Then the experimenter gave the observers their questionnaires and asked them to return to their original rooms to complete them. When all four subjects were finished, they were brought together in the center room and thoroughly debriefed.

Dependent Measures

After the conversation, subjects completed a questionnaire that asked them to evaluate the quality of the conversation (this was included in order to make the cover story more convincing) and their reactions to the male and female actors. First, subjects were asked to describe one actor's personality in an open-ended question. Then they rated that actor on a variety of trait terms using a 7-point Likert-type scale. Then they answered the same questions about the other actor.[1] The subjects were asked to base their ratings on how they thought the actor was "trying to behave" because according to the experimental hypothesis it is the target person's intentions that are misjudged.

---

[1]The order in which observers completed these questions was counterbalanced so half of them rated the female actor first, whereas the other half rated the male actor first.

The key trait terms were the adjectives *flirtatious, seductive,* and *promiscuous;* these words were selected because they were thought to measure the construct "sexuality." Additional trait terms such as *considerate, interesting, likeable,* and *intelligent* were included to avoid alerting subjects to the true focus of the study. Other important dependent variables were subjects' responses to questions asking them if they would like to get to know the actors, if they were sexually attracted to the opposite-sex actor, if they would like to date him or her, and why or why not. The observers were also asked if they thought each of the actors was sexually attracted to and would like to date his or her partner and why or why not. Finally, the actors were asked to respond "yes" or "no" to a question asking them if they would like to interact with the same partner in the second half of the experiment.

RESULTS

Sex of Experimenter

Two male and two female experimenters conducted the study. The results of a $2 \times 2 \times 2$ (Sex of Subject $\times$ Role of Subject $\times$ Sex of Experimenter) analysis of variance indicated that the sex of experimenter did not have an effect on subjects' responses. Therefore, all further analyses were conducted by summing across this variable.

Sex Differences

As expected, there were no sex differences in subjects' ratings of the female actor's friendliness and these ratings were quite high (female $M = 6.0$; male $M = 5.7$). A multivariate analysis of variance combining subjects' ratings of the female actor on the three sexual adjectives—*flirtatious, seductive,* and *promiscuous*—into a Sexuality Index (interitem correlations ranged from .39 to .62, $p < .001$) indicated that there was a significant sex-of-subject effect for this variable, $F(3, 138) = 3.09, p < .03$. An examination of the univariate findings indicated that, as predicted, male subjects rated the female actor as being significantly more promiscuous than female subjects did, $F(1, 140) = 7.67, p < .01$ (see Table 6-1). Similarly, there was a marginal effect, $F(1, 140) = 2.98, p < .09$, for males to rate the female actor as being more seductive than did females. However, there were no sex differences in subjects' ratings of the female actor's flirtatiousness.

TABLE 6-1 MEAN SCORES FOR RATINGS OF THE FEMALE ACTOR ON THE SEXUALITY ITEMS AS A FUNCTION OF SEX OF SUBJECT

	Sex of subject		
Ratings of female actor	Male	Female	$p <$
Promiscuous	2.2	1.7	.01
Seductive	2.3	1.9	.09
Flirtatious	2.9	2.8	ns

A multivariate analysis of variance combining actors' responses to the questions "Would you like to get to know your partner better?"; "Would you be interested in becoming friends with your partner?"; "Are you sexually attracted to your partner?"; and "Would you be interested in dating your partner?" into a Future Interaction Index for actors (interitem correlations ranged from .56 to .88, $p < .001$) yielded a significant sex-of-subject effect, $F(4, 67) = 2.83$, $p < .03$. Responses to the question asking the actors if they were sexually attracted to their partner indicated that the male actors were more sexually attracted to their partners than the female actors were, $F(1, 70) = 7.17$, $p < .01$ (male $M = 3.5$, female $M = 2.4$). None of the other univariate results were significant.

Also, a multivariate analysis of variance combining observers' responses to questions asking them how sexually attracted they were to the opposite-sex actor and how interested they were in dating her or him into a Sexual Attraction Index for observers ($r = .85, p < .001$) showed a significant effect for sex of subject, $F(2, 69) = 4.83$, $p < .01$, again indicating greater male interest than female interest. Univariate analyses indicated that the male observers were more sexually attracted to, $F(1, 70) = 9.10$, $p < .004$, and eager to date, $F(1, 70) = 8.87$, $p < .004$, the opposite-sex actor than were the female observers (sexually attracted: male $M = 3.3$, female $M = 2.1$; date: male $M = 3.3$, female $M = 2.2$). Similarly, the male observer thought that the female actor wanted to be friends with the male actor, $F(1, 70) = 3.25$, $p < .08$, was sexually attracted to the male actor, $F(1, 70) = 6.58$, $p < .01$, and wanted to date the male actor, $F(1, 70) = 6.80$, $p < .01$, more than the female observer did (friends: male $M = 4.1$, female $M = 3.5$; sexually attracted: male $M = 3.2$, female $M = 2.4$; date: male $M = 3.1$, female $M = 2.3$).

Analyses of subjects' ratings of the male actor exhibited some surprising sex-of-subject effects. A multivariate analysis of variance combining subjects' ratings of the male actor on the Sexuality Index (interitem correlations ranged from .40 to .72, $p < .001$)—flirtatious, seductive, and promiscuous—indicated that there was a significant sex-of-subject effect, $F(3, 138) = 2.99$, $p < .03$. The univariate analyses indicated that the male actors and observers rated the male actor as being significantly more flirtatious, $F(1, 140) = 4.21$, $p < .04$, and seductive, $F(1, 140) = 9.07$, $p < .003$, than the

TABLE 6-2 MEAN SCORES FOR RATINGS OF THE MALE ACTOR ON THE SEXUALITY ITEMS AS A FUNCTION OF SEX OF SUBJECT AND ROLE OF SUBJECT

	Rating of the male actor								
	Flirtatious[a]			Seductive[b]			Promiscuous[c]		
Sex of Subject	Actor	Observer	M	Actor	Observer	M	Actor	Observer	M
Female	2.1	2.4	2.3	1.5	1.9	1.7	1.8	1.8	1.8
Male	3.1	2.4	2.8	2.5	2.1	2.3	2.1	2.1	2.1

[a]Sex of Subject × Role interaction, $p < .04$. Sex-of-subject effect, $p < .04$.
[b]Sex of Subject × Role interaction, $p < .04$. Sex-of-subject effect, $p < .003$.
[c]Sex of Subject × Role interaction, ns. Sex-of-subject effect, $p < .07$.

female subjects did. There was also a significant sex by role interaction for each of these variables, $F(1, 140) = 4.21$, $p < .04$, $F(1, 140) = 4.12$, $p < .04$, respectively. Tukey *(b)* tests indicated that the female actors' and the male actors' ratings were significantly different ($p < .05$) with the male actor rating himself as significantly more flirtatious and seductive than the female actor rated him (see Table 6-2). There was a marginal trend for males to rate the male actor as being more promiscuous than females did, $F(1, 140) = 3.34$, $p < .07$. Male actors and observers also rated the male actor as being more attractive than females did, $F(1, 140) = 7.94$, $p < .01$ (male $M = 4.4$; female $M = 3.8$).

DISCUSSION

Sex Differences

The results of the experiment were generally consistent with our predictions. Males rated the female actor as being more promiscuous and seductive than females did. Male actors were more sexually attracted to their partners than their partners were to them. Similarly, the male observers were more sexually attracted to and eager to date the opposite-sex actor than the female observers were. Finally, the male observers rated the female actors as being more sexually attracted to and willing to date their partners than the female observers did.

It is noteworthy that most of the significant differences were found with the traits and behaviors most obviously sexual in nature. There were no sex differences in subjects' ratings of the female actor's flirtatiousness, the mildest trait term. In fact, the finding that both sexes rated the female actor as being more flirtatious than the male actor substantiates the interpretation that this term has a connotation that implies female gender. There were also no sex differences in actors' desire to get to know their partner better, to become friends, or to date their partner. This sex difference in perception of the opposite sex is only apparent when unmistakably sexual terms are used.

As mentioned earlier, if this effect was due to a self-serving bias on the male actors' part, then the male actors' ratings should have been significantly higher than the male observers' ratings. Similarly, if it was due to actor-observer differences, then the female actors' (the target persons') ratings should have been different from the other three participants' (her observers) ratings. Therefore, the absence of any significant sex by role interactions for these key dependent variables is consistent with the hypothesis that this effect is due to a general masculine style of viewing female behavior.

In sum, the above results provide support for the hypothesis that men mistakenly interpret women's friendliness as an indication of sexual interest. According to the female actors' self-ratings, they intended to be friendly yet they were perceived as being seductive and promiscuous by the male subjects. Clearly, one has no way of judging if the women's behavior truly was seductive or not. What is important, however, is her own perception of her behavior. If she felt she was not being sexually provocative, then she would be offended if a man interpreted her behavior this way, regardless of how an unbiased observer would rate her behavior. In future research similar interactions can be videotaped and later rated by judges, thereby providing a clearer interpretation of these findings.

Although most of the predictions were substantiated by the results, an examination of the subjects' ratings of the male actor necessitated rethinking the initial hypothesis. Not only were males inclined to rate the female actor in sexual terms but they also rated the male actor in a similar manner. Male actors perceived themselves as being more flirtatious and seductive than the female actors rated them. Furthermore, male actors perceived themselves and male observers perceived the male actor as being more attractive and promiscuous than females did.

The results of this experiment indicate that men are more likely to perceive the world in sexual terms and to make sexual judgments than women are. The predicted effect that men misperceive friendliness from women as seduction, appears to be merely one manifestation of this broader male sexual orientation.

Alternatively, one could explain these findings by arguing that males and females in our experiment were equally likely to make sexual judgments but that males were simply more willing than females to admit them. Although this explanation is feasible, we consider it to be unlikely. Respondents' explanations as to why they were or were not interested in dating the opposite-sex actor were coded. Males and females were equally likely to mention sexual factors such as "I'm not physically attracted to her" or "The magnetism was not there" as influencing their decision (females = 22%, males = 25%; interrater reliability = .91). If females and males were equally willing to admit their sexual judgments in open-ended responses, then it is likely that they were both being equally honest about these feelings throughout the questionnaire. Also, an approximately equal number of males and females volunteered the information that they were currently dating (females = 19%; males = 17%). Therefore, differential levels of sexual availability do not explain the findings.

A thorough explanation as to why males and females differ in their propensity to make sexual judgments is beyond the scope of this paper. An explanation based on differential socialization could probably be proposed. Certainly the stereotypes of our culture, as evidenced by the mass media's depiction of men and women, portray men as having a greater interest in sexual matters than do women. Once men develop this sexual orientation, it may act as a generalized expectancy, causing them to interpret ambiguous information, such as that presented in our study, as evidence in support of their beliefs. As Markus (1977) suggests, events that fit one's self-schemas have a greater impact than those that do not. Consequently, if the issue of sexuality is more central to men's concerns than those of women, then males may be aware of the potential sexual meaning of others' behavior. Future research that delineates the extent of this phenomenon and the conditions under which it does and does not occur may help elucidate its origin.

SUMMARY AND CONCLUSIONS

In conclusion, the results of this laboratory investigation corroborate the author's personal experience: Men do tend to read sexual intent into friendly behavior. However, this appears to occur because of a general male bias rather than an attitude about fe-males only. Evidently, women are not subject to this bias (at least not under these cir-cumstances) and are, therefore, unlikely to misjudge male intentions in the way that men misjudge those of women. It is for future researchers to determine the underlying causal factors that contribute to this male bias and the specific circumstances that elicit it.

7

THE ILLUSION OF UNIQUE INVULNERABILITY AND THE USE OF EFFECTIVE CONTRACEPTION

Jerry M. Burger and Linda Burns (1988)

If Burger and Burns are correct, many people engage in unsafe behaviors because of the illusion of unique invulnerability. Unsafe behaviors such as smoking, drunk driving, and drug abuse may be seen as behaviors that are dangerous for other people but not for us. A student was once overheard by one of your editors telling his friend that he had totaled his car over the weekend: "I was really wasted. Had way too much to drink. But I don't understand it. I'm usually an even better driver when I'm drunk because I know I'm drunk, so I drive safer to make up for it." Every spring brings not only flowers and baseball but, unfortunately, a rash of seemingly obligatory postprom car crashes with a car full of very finely dressed and very highly intoxicated teenagers leaving the road at a high rate of speed.

Similarly, engaging in sex without contraception does not just expose one to the the possibility of an unplanned pregnancy, but in today's world we also must deal with the harsh realities of potential transmission of the HIV virus and AIDS between two people. When used correctly, many contraceptives are highly effective in minimizing the chances of a pregnancy; however these contraceptives provide little or no protection against sexually transmitted diseases. The feeling that "it can't happen to me," while understandable as a self-serving bias, is not an adequate defense. This is a serious issue; life and death decisions hang in the balance. Special as we'd like to be, the odds play no favorites.

It was proposed that one reason people often fail to use effective contraception methods is that they engage in a systematic distortion of their likelihood of being involved in an unwanted pregnancy relative to others. A survey of undergraduate

Source: Abridged from the *Personality and Social Psychology Bulletin*, 1986, *14*, 264–70. Copyright © 1988 by Sage Publishing Co. Reprinted by permission of the publisher and the authors.

females found that sexually active women tended to see themselves as less likely than other students, other women their age, and women of childbearing age to become pregnant. The tendency to utilize this illusion of unique invulnerability was related to the use of effective contraception. The more subjects discounted their chances of becoming pregnant relative to others, the less likely they were to use effective methods of birth control.

Despite the availability of relatively effective methods of birth control, unwanted pregnancy continues to be a major problem in this country. American women are seeking out abortions to deal with many of these unwanted pregnancies at a rate of one and a half million per year. Naturally, many psychologists have been interested in understanding this seemingly irrational failure to utilize contraception when having intercourse (see Byrne & Fisher, 1983). Among the many variables that have been identified in the search to predict contraceptive behavior are sex guilt (Gerrard, 1982), contraceptive knowledge (Allgeier, 1983), communication between partners (Burger & Inderbitzen, 1985), and self-image (McKinney, Sprecher, & DeLamater, 1984).

Another approach to understanding the failure to utilize effective birth control that will be presented here concerns the use of information-processing errors by those not using contraception. More specifically, we were interested in the manner in which women perceive their chances of becoming pregnant. It has been noted (Cvetkovich & Grote, 1983) that victims of unwanted pregnancies often report that they did not believe that they or their partner would become pregnant, even though they clearly understood the biological reasons for the pregnancy. These people seem to be saying that they knew what they were doing might cause a pregnancy, but they didn't believe it would happen to them.

Researchers investigating other behaviors have discovered a similar style of thinking (Perloff, 1983; Perloff & Fetzer, 1986; Weinstein 1980). For example, people have been found to rate themselves as significantly less likely than others to fall victim to health problems, such as cancer or heart attacks; assaults, such as muggings or car theft; or unpleasant life events, such as divorce or losing one's job (Perloff & Fetzer, 1986; Weinstein, 1980). This systematic biasing of one's likelihood of victimization has been termed an "illusion of unique invulnerability" by Perloff and Fetzer (1986) and has been used to suggest why people may fail to take adequate precautions to avoid such unfortunate, but partially preventable, events as lung cancer and car theft. It is recognized that these things happen, but people typically see themselves as unlikely victims.

When the illusion-of-unique invulnerability phenomenon is applied to the question of unwanted pregnancies, it seems possible that this systematic distortion may account in part for the failure by many people to use effective contraception. It may be that many sexually active people are underestimating their chances of becoming involved in an unwanted pregnancy. They recognize that other people get pregnant from sexual activity, but perceive their own chances as so slim as to not require the trouble to obtain and use birth control.

Several explanations have been advanced to account for the illusion-of-unique-invulnerability effect (see Perloff, 1983). Some emphasize motivational mechanisms, such as reducing the anxiety associated with perceived vulnerability or satisfying a need to feel in control of events rather than at the mercy of diseases and criminals. Sexually active people who do not want the woman to become pregnant may be able to reduce the anxiety of possible pregnancy by convincing themselves that it won't happen. Other interpretations point to cognitive mechanisms. Weinstein (1980), for example, has proposed that people often compare themselves with inappropriate prototypes of victims that cause them to conclude that they are not a likely candidate for victimization. In asking themselves if they will become an unmarried pregnant woman, some women may generate a stereotyped image of a pregnant female. Because this image resembles them very little, they may conclude that they are not the type of person unwanted pregnancies happen to.

The purpose of the present investigation was twofold. First, the study was designed to determine if sexually active female adults fall victim to the illusion of unique invulnerability when making decisions about their chances of becoming pregnant. If this proved to be the case, then it was expected that these individuals would estimate their chances of becoming pregnant as significantly less than those of others. Second, if this systematic distortion of one's chances of becoming pregnant is related to the failure to take precautions—that is, to use contraception—then it was predicted that the more people engage in the illusion of unique invulnerablilty, the less likely they will be to use contraception.

METHOD

Subjects

A survey was distributed to 76 female undergraduates enrolled in several different upper division (juniors and seniors) psychology classes at a liberal arts university. Fiftynine (77.6%) of these returned the questionnaire, and thus composed the final sample. No incentive beyond helping the experimenter and the opportunity to see the results was offered for participation.

Procedure

Female students attending one of the class meetings selected for the study were given a survey package. Only those who had been or were married (very few) and those who had already received a survey were excluded. The package contained a cover letter, the survey questionnaire, and a stamped, self-addressed envelope. It was explained to the subjects at that time and in the cover letter that the researcher was interested in the sexual attitudes and behaviors of university students. Subjects were asked to take the survey home with them and to return it via the mail after completion. All subjects were assured that their responses would remain anonymous and confidential, and the voluntary nature of participation was emphasized.

Following a short personality measure not relevant to the present investigation (the Desirability of Control Scale, Burger & Cooper, 1979), the survey questionnaire asked subjects to indicate on a 101-point scale, with 0 = *no chance* and 100 = *certainty,* the likelihood that they would become pregnant in the next 12 months. Using the same scale, subjects then indicated the likelihood that the average female student at the university would have an unwanted pregnancy, the likelihood that the average American female her age would have an unwanted pregnancy, and the likelihood that the average American female of childbearing age would have an unwanted pregnancy during the next 12 months.

Next, subjects were asked to indicate, if applicable, the percentage of the times they had engaged in sexual intercourse during the past 6 months in which they had used contraception. The questionnaire asked subjects to indicate this percentage for each of the following methods: birth control pill, condom, condom with spermicide, diaphragm, douching, intrauterine device, rhythm (as plotted by knowledgeable source), intuitive feelings about good and bad times of the month, spermicide, contraceptive sponge, withdrawal, none, and other. (No subject indicated any use of an "other" method.) For example, a subject who had used birth control pills 80% of the time and a condom 20% of the time would indicate 80 and 20 by these two methods on the survey. Subjects were reminded that their responses should total 100%.

Subjects then were asked about their sexual behavior. Of relevance to the present study, subjects were asked to indicate if they had engaged in sexual intercourse at all during the past 6 months. Finally, subjects were asked if they had ever been pregnant.

RESULTS

Thirty-four of the 59 subjects (57.6%) indicated that they had engaged in sexual intercourse at least once during the past 6 months. Because the study was interested only in understanding the contraceptive behavior of those who are at risk for becoming pregnant, the nonactive subjects were not included in the analyses.

The first question was whether the students perceived themselves as being less vulnerable to pregnancy than others. To calculate this, the likelihood-of-pregnancy rating the subjects gave themselves was compared with each of the other three likelihood-of-pregnancy ratings through dependent t-tests. As shown in Table 7-1, the subjects indicated that they were less likely to have an unwanted pregnancy during the upcoming year than the average female at the school, $t(33) = 5.11$, $p < .001$, than the average woman their age, $t(33) = 8.93$, $p < .001$, and than the average woman of childbearing

TABLE 7-1   MEAN LIKELIHOOD OF PREGNANCY RATINGS

You (the subject)	9.24
Average female at the university	26.97
Average American female your age	42.59
Average American female of childbearing age	46.03

Note: Based on scale with 0 = no chance and 100 = certainty.

age, $t(33) = 8.66$, $p < .001$. Thus these women appeared to show the illusion-of-unique-invulnerability effect. This effect is especially pronounced given that all of the subjects were sexually active, whereas many of the women in the comparison groups (e.g., the average female at the school) were not.

The second question was whether this illusion of unique invulnerability was related to the use of contraception. To test this, the likelihood-of-pregnancy ratings the subjects gave themselves were subtracted from each of the other three likelihood-of-pregnancy ratings. These three values were then summed to form an overall illusion-of-unique-invulnerability score. That is, the higher the score, the more the student believed that others would more likely become pregnant than she. This score then was correlated with the value the subjects reported for the percentage of time they had used contraception when engaging in intercourse during the last 6 months. The contraception percentage score was calculated by summing the percentages subjects reported for using legitimate contraceptive methods. That is, the percentage of time subjects reported using a method other than withdrawal, douching, or intuitively guessing at a safe time of the month were summed (e.g., if a subject reported using condoms 50% of the time, a diaphragm 40% of the time, and withdrawal 10% of the time, a contraception score of 90 was calculated).

The average percentage of legitimate contraceptive use by the sexually active females was 67.9%. The correlation between the contraception percentage measure and the illusion-of-unique-invulnerability measure was $-.34$, $p < .05$. Thus the higher the illusion-of-unique-invulnerability score, the less likely the subject was to use effective contraception when having intercourse.

DISCUSSION

The results provide support for the notion that undergraduate females engage in a systematic distortion of their perceptions of becoming pregnant relative to others. Sexually active subjects rated other women attending the university as almost three times as likely to become pregnant as they were, even though the average college female is not necessarily even sexually active. It seems safe to say that these students understand that engaging in sexual intercourse can lead to pregnancy, but they tend to see this as happening to someone else, rather than to themselves.

In addition, it was found that the more the women engaged in this illusion of unique invulnerability, the less likely they were to use effective methods of contraception. One interpretation of this finding is that the illusion of unique invulnerability is one of the reasons for this poor use of contraception. Women who believe they have little chance of becoming pregnant are less likely to take the precautions that rational judgment dictates. On the other hand, because the data are correlational, we cannot rule out the possibility that the poor use of contraception comes first and that this causes the cognitions. That is, women who risk pregnancy may rationalize their behavior by convincing themselves that they are not likely to become pregnant. This interpretation is consistent with a cognitive dissonance (Festinger, 1957) or self-perception (Bem, 1972) view, both of which propose that people often bring their attitudes in line with their behaviors. Future investigations that assess both contraceptive behavior and cognitions about vulnerability to pregnancy at more than one time might help to disentangle the causal link in this phenomenon.

Yet another possibility is that these women are simply overestimating other people's chances of becoming pregnant and accurately appraising their own. However, the high rate of unwanted pregnancies (in this sample, 8 of the 34 sexually active females, 23.5%, indicated that they had been pregnant) suggests this is not the case.

One direction for future work in this area is in obtaining a better understanding of the mechanisms underlying the illusion-of-unique-invulnerability effect. One possibility suggested by the work of Weinstein (1980) is that the women in the present sample used an inappropriate comparison of themselves to other potential victims. According to Weinstein, people often generate, for example, a prototypic alcoholic when assessing their likelihood of developing an alcohol problem. Because these people typically see themselves as being very dissimilar to the prototype, they conclude that they are unlikely to be like this alcoholic. Consistent with this reasoning, Perloff and Fetzer (1986) found that people tended to see someone very similar to themselves (their closest friend or a sibling) as also being relatively invulnerable. In the present investigation it seems likely that the college students' prototypic images of an unwed, pregnant woman were very dissimilar to their self-images. Thus they may have concluded that they were not the type who got pregnant. Another possibility is that some of the motivational processes described earlier may have been operating. Subjects may have been protecting themselves from the anxiety-provoking thought of pregnancy by downplaying their chances of becoming pregnant.

Finally, if one of the factors contributing to the failure to use contraception is the illusion of unique invulnerability, then some implications may be drawn for those working to reduce the problem of unwanted pregnancy. As suggested by the above reasoning, it may be important for men and women to realize that they are as vulnerable as anyone else to becoming involved in an unwanted pregnancy. Undergraduates may believe that this kind of thing does not happen to nice college students because they do not see or hear about all of the many unwanted pregnancies encountered by college students each year. Making people aware that pregnancy does happen to someone like them may help in part to encourage those choosing to engage in sexual intercourse to also engage in the use of effective contraception.

8

AGING LABELS: THE DECLINE OF CONTROL AND THE FALL OF SELF-ESTEEM

Judith Rodin and Ellen J. Langer (1980)

What are your images of the aging process and the elderly? Have you ever thought about what it would be like to be old, really old? If we are lucky, we will all become old someday. American stereotypes of aging are grim. Usually, we assume a slowing or loss of function with aging; we expect that speed in walking, thinking, and responding will gradually slow down. Then hearing and/or sight will diminish as well, and memory will begin to slip. Will our bodies and minds betray us? The ads for bladder control undergarments aimed at the elderly increase our negative expectations. We all started out in diapers—will we be wearing them again down the line?

Not being in control of one's destiny is scary—be it control of one's living arrangements, control of one's daily activities, even being in control of one's bodily functions. Control can even extend to the issue of how and when and who is in control of the end of our lives. Increasing public concern and debate focus on such issues as quality of life, assisted suicides, and who should make the decision as to whether extreme measures should be taken in the case of medical crises. Durable powers of attorney for health care allow individuals to designate someone who knows their wishes to make medical decisions for them if they are incapacitated. The issues addressed in this reading (self-efficacy and stereotyping of the elderly) are even more timely today than they were when Rodin and Langer wrote them in 1980.

Many elderly report, however, that the physical aspects of aging are not as frustrating as the negative assumptions and treatment they receive from a society that has so little respect or time for the elderly. Myers' Module 8 discusses the importance of optimism, self-determination, and self-efficacy; the present reading reveals the many ways in which the situation and our cultural beliefs systematically chip away at these personality characteristics in aging individuals. Rodin and Langer show how our stereotypes of aging and our responses to the aged (as a consequence of our stereotypes) are an important aspect of what makes aging difficult in U. S. society. But being optimistic, the authors also utilize some of social psychology's ideas for reducing prejudice, for example, motivational and attribution therapy, developing new self-fulfilling prophecies, an improved media image, perceived similarity, and greater and more equal contact (see also Readings 4, 6, 23).

By the year 2000, it is estimated that over 15 percent of the population, 30 million people, will be 65 or over. Although aging affords status to people in some countries, in the United States and other industrialized nations the elderly often suffer a loss of status, reduction in personal contacts and income, and a social climate that views aging with fearfulness and distaste. Since in the United States less than 5 percent of all people over 65 actually require custodial care (Berezin, 1972; Brotman, 1974), it may be asserted that at least 95 percent of the aged do not conform to the stereotype of the helpless and sick old person. Nevertheless, such stereotypes exist (cf. Butler, 1970). Indeed, a number of studies examining such diverse cultural influences as children's and adolescents' literature (Blue, 1978; Peterson & Karnes, 1976), contemporary fiction and poetry (Sohngen, 1977; Sohngen & Smith, 1978), and popular jokes (Davis, 1977; Richman, 1977), all found at least some negative stereotypes of the elderly.

In this paper, we describe several studies that investigated the social psychological correlates of aging. Our goal was to understand how negative labeling and stigmatization of the elderly might contribute to behavior that actually confirmed prevalent stereotypes of old age and led to lowered self-esteem and diminished feelings of control. Given that stereotypes and social labels are in a sense simply summaries of cultural expectations, such expectations might be assumed to affect all members of the culture, including those about whom the labels are held. If one's self-image and behavior come to portray these negative stereotypes (cf. Kelley, 1967; Rosenthal, 1971; Snyder & Swann, 1978), self-esteem should decline. As self-esteem decreases, belief in one's ability to exercise control over the environment also declines (Rodin, 1980).

Aging individuals may therefore overestimate decrements in their capacities that may be experienced as discrepant with their evaluative standards for competent behavior (Bandura, 1971), and the effects of this awareness may be more debilitating than the change itself (Langer, 1979b). When, in addition, there actually is a reduction of the number and kinds of potential options for control of the environment, as is the case for the elderly, this self-view is reconfirmed.

If these deleterious causal relationships can in fact be demonstrated, the underlying mechanisms determined, and the effects reversed, we expect that there would follow a restoration of both a more positive self-concept and a greater sense of control for the aged, as well as less age-stereotyped behavior. A simplified diagrammatic illustration of this process appears below.

The next section examines some of the research bearing on these questions.

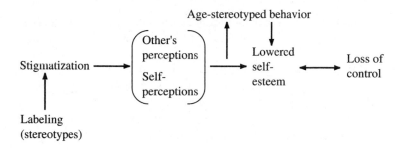

Negative Stereotypes Toward Old Age

If our society has developed labels that create certain sets of negative expectations with regard to aging, it is likely that people will act in a manner that is consistent with these labels. To the extent that a particular stereotype is actually believed, elderly persons may also begin to act in a manner that is consistent with that stereotype. Expectations based on the label senility, for example, may have a great impact on the way old people and those approaching old age view themselves.

Every time a mistake is made or a thought is forgotten, older people may question whether their mental capacities are diminishing. If people are worrying about their failing memory while in a situation where new learning could take place (e.g., learning the name of a new acquaintance), they might indeed "forget" what they had just learned. However, the problem would have been in the conditions surrounding the learning (distraction) and not a problem of memory at all. But how could the elderly come to this more benign conclusion in the face of the salient stereotypes that exist with respect to their cognitive capacities? Any such fears the elderly have about themselves are exacerbated by the dearth of appropriate role models who could serve as counter examples of what life after seventy might be like. Thus, it is critical to determine what negative stereotypes exist about the elderly, what behaviors they produce, and the extent to which older people also accept these views.

Consequently, we designed a study to determine the extent to which different subject populations spontaneously apply the label "senility" and to assess the consequences of those labels for other attitudes.

Forty female high school students, 40 middle-age women, and 40 older women were recruited for a study on person perception. To reduce differences among the age groups due to socioeconomic status and religion, the adults were the mothers and grandmothers of the students, who were randomly selected from a local high school. Each of the three groups of subjects was randomly assigned to one of two experimental conditions described below.

The three members of each family, tested individually, were shown three videotaped scenes involving dyadic interactions that they were asked to rate. The experimental question was tested in the third scene, which for half the subjects in each age group depicted an interview where the target person, the interviewee, appeared forgetful by asking the interviewer to repeat something he said earlier on three separate occasions. The third scene for the remaining subjects also depicted an interview, but here the target person responded to the interviewer's questions without engaging in forgetful behavior.

Each group was further subdivided so that for half of the subjects in each group above, the person engaging in the senility-related or non-related behavior appeared to be about 35 years old, and for the other half, about 75 years old. These manipulations also provided an opportunity to assess the generality of the negative labeling process. Specifically, we were interested in learning whether even non-age related behaviors of the elderly were likely to be labeled as evidence of senility and whether any of these behaviors, regardless of the label, were seen as more negative in older than younger persons.

To summarize, the study was a 3 × 2 × 2 design where age of subject (approximately 18 years old, 40 years old, and 65 years old), behavior of target (senility-related or non-related), and age of target (young or old) were the independent variables. The relevant measures were responses to a questionnaire that followed each scene. The items were designed to determine whether the behavior of elderly persons was spontaneously labeled as senile and/or whether their behavior was generally evaluated more negatively. Subjects were asked to rate, for example, how much they liked the target person, how alert they thought she was, and how stable she appeared to be, on a series of 10-point scales. Open-ended questions asked for description of the people and interactions in the videotaped sequences.

We found a main effect for age of the target person for both measures. Regardless of the subjects' age, they were more likely to label the older target as "senile" than the young target person, which is hardly surprising. However, subjects also evaluated the same behaviors more negatively in the older target person than in the younger. We also found that the older, not the younger, respondents tended to evaluate the forgetful elderly target most negatively, suggesting that the older one gets, the more frightened one is of being or becoming senile or showing other presumably age-related negative traits. This fear is likely to motivate older people to distance themselves, psychologically, from old people with difficulties such as forgetfulness, by evaluating them as negatively as possible, and thereby making them seem different from themselves. Taking this finding, together with the data from the Langer and Mulvey study, it appears that older people are more positive towards the elderly overall than are younger people, but are also more negative than young people about the negative features of old age.

In general, this study also suggests that old age per se carries with it enough negative expectations so that a behavior that is seen as normal in a young person may be seized upon when engaged in by an elderly person as confirmation of the stereotype, and cloud the perception of the rest of the (target) individual's behavior.

Attribution about Aging

We have observed that chronological age per se is not sufficient to provide a person with the self-definition of "old," although obviously there is some relationship between chronological age and self-perception. Rather, a series of events or experiences forces acceptance, although reluctantly, of the fact that one is old, and often these events have avoidance and/or the loss of control at their core. Once this occurs, it may be that older people then evaluate themselves on the basis of feelings and behaviors that they attribute to aging rather than to the environment and circumstance.

Negative attributional processes deriving from feeling avoided and from reduced feelings of control can create at least two different types of problems for older people that may lower their number of coping attempts and thus detrimentally affect their health (see Rodin, 1978, for a longer discussion of the effects of attributions on health in general). First, there is a tendency to overattribute most of their negative physical symptoms to aging per se, especially to the presumed physical decline with which aging is associated. Biological attributions may incorrectly focus the person away from situational and social factors such as the loss of a loved one or feeling unsafe; these are stress-inducing in part because they are associated with a loss of control. Recent work has shown that even among healthy college students, loss of control is related to increased experience of symptoms (Pennebaker & Skelton, 1978). Second, when events are attributed to the aging process, they are seen as inevitable; and remedial steps that could be extremely beneficial may not be undertaken.

The negative self-concept of elderly persons would further increase the likelihood that they will make damaging self, rather than situational, attributions when they perceive, whether veridically or not, that they are being avoided, or when they experience reduced feelings of control. Interventions might then be developed to redirect these attributions. We have already conducted some work on this question, looking more generally at the consequences of attributional processes and the possibility of changing them.

We interviewed people in the week that followed their entering a nursing home, and selected the 80 percent who made explicit negative attributions to physical decline associated with aging as either causing or contributing greatly to some of their problems. We took a variety of premeasures including interviews, health measures, and observations of level of participation. There were three randomly assigned groups: one group was untreated; one group was simply given information trying to argue against physical decline in aging as being the real source of their problems (using material taken from doctors' reports and journal articles); and the third group was given environmental explanations (or at least age-environment interactional attributions) as being the source of their problems.

As an example of some environmental attributions that were used, subjects in the latter group were told that the floors in the nursing home are very slippery because they are tiled in order to keep them clean. Even young people slip on them. By this means, we tried to reduce the attribution that slipping was due to weak knees or poor movement that resulted from their age. As another example, they were reminded that they were awakened at 5:30 in the morning, which would make most people tired by evening. Again, we tried to minimize the likelihood that they would attribute their weariness to aging per se. Thus, we simply attempted to refocus their explanations for their own feelings and behavior onto plausible factors in the environment that could have been producing some of the physical symptoms they were likely to be experiencing.

As a result of the reattribution intervention, patients showed greatly improved behavior, including an increase in active participation and sociability relative to groups
simply given information or to untreated controls. There were also benefits in the area
of general health and indices of stress. Thus, debilitating and often excessive attribution to physical states associated with aging and decline can be refocused, with beneficial effects, onto more easily changed aspects of the environment.

In another study (Langer, Rodin, Beck, Weinman, & Spitzer, 1979) we demonstrated that attributions about whether the same task was a memory test, or was a new
activity being introduced into the nursing home, dramatically influenced subjects' subsequent performance. Those expecting to be tested performed significantly less well
than those expecting to try out a new "activity."

Reversing Memory "Loss"

Over-attribution to aging rather than to environmental sources, coupled with the negative labeling process described above, work together to decrease self-esteem and diminish performance. Often this results in a lack of motivation to engage in a variety of
behaviors, rather than an inability to do so. Over time, and with disuse, the abilities
themselves may also decline.

Taking loss of memory as an example, we speculated that some component of
memory loss may be due to the operation of these social psychological factors, which
produce symptoms of forgetfulness and confusion that have nothing to do with aging
per se. We reasoned that, in some older individuals, apparently diminished memory
could be reversed by increasing motivation for thinking and remembering.

In two studies, we attempted to motivate elderly nursing home residents to adhere to
a recommended course of action over time that asked them to think about and remember a variety of events (Langer et al., 1979). In the first study, we tried to increase motivation to remember by providing the opportunity for reciprocal self-disclosure between the subject and an interviewer who recommended the particular course of
cognitive activity. Janis and Rodin (1979) have hypothesized that establishing referent
power (French & Raven, 1959) is an important way to increase motivation and promote commitment. Persons have referent power for those who perceive them as
benevolent and accepting. Eliciting and sometimes reciprocating self-disclosure is one
factor that is critical in helping a person to establish referent power (Rodin & Janis,
1979). In the second study we tried to increase motivation to use one's memory by setting up a contingency in which greater cognitive effort resulted in greater tangible reward (chips that could be traded for gifts). In both studies, the recommended course of
action involved remembering a series of questions and probing the environment and
one's long-term memory for information relevant to their answers. Both studies had
"no treatment" controls as well as a control group treated in all ways identical to experimental subjects except that, in the first study, *low* reciprocal self-disclosure was
elicited and, in the second study, the rewards were *not contingent* upon performance.

In both studies, experimental subjects showed a significant improvement on standard short-term memory tests including probe and pattern recall, as well as improvements on nurses' ratings of alertness, mental activity and social adjustment, relative to

controls. Thus, we found that restructuring the environment to make it more demanding, and then motivating elderly people to increase their cognitive activity, leads to improvements in memory that are generalizable. It is critical to note that the experimental treatments provided no explicit training for the memory tests that constituted the dependent variables of greatest interest. While we did not measure self-esteem directly, we found that experimental subjects were rated as happier and more involved following the intervention, and we may infer that they were feeling better about themselves.

Thus, it appears that the consequences of major changes associated with aging, over-attribution to physical decline associated with aging, and the effects of negative stereotypes regarding aging, can be reversed by appropriate environmental manipulations. We predict that this will be true for many factors other than apparent memory loss, which have been adduced to be inevitable consequences of aging for most persons (see Langer, 1979a, for a discussion of the environmental determinants of aging). Our earliest work in this area showed that when even relatively debilitated nursing home residents were given the opportunity to make decisions and to feel increased responsibility, thus potentially reducing their negative self-labeling, they became more involved, active and self-initiating, as well as considerably happier, and they showed dramatic health-related benefits (Langer & Rodin, 1976; Rodin & Langer, 1977). Thus, reversals are even possible in nursing home environments, which foster a sense of dependency and loss of control (see Wack & Rodin, 1978, for a full discussion of the reasons for creation and effects of nursing homes).

CONCLUSIONS

In this paper, we described our studies examining the relationship between aging and cognitive social psychological factors with specific references to labeling, control and self-concept. In this research, we investigated if and how the aged are negatively stereotyped, and the consequences of negative labels associated with aging. We demonstrated how such labels and attributions may, in turn, affect the self-concept and behavior of the elderly, and lead to decrements in perceived control. We then investigated how changing labels, and giving control experiences, can serve to reinstate motivation in some elderly individuals, thereby promoting more self-benefiting behavior. However, we also believe that making these changes at the individual level is only a short-term solution.

Social change is a complex process that does not lend itself to easy analysis. Nevertheless, it seems that every successful movement has at least included the following elements: (1) There is a public protest when media or important professional groups are intentionally or unintentionally (usually the latter) insulting. (2) The social stereotype of the affected group becomes so well-known that it becomes a public joke and an emblem of bigotry. Comic villians like Archie Bunker bring home the message. (3) There is exposure of the person for whom acceptance in sought. The first black was seen on a television commercial in New York City in the late sixties. Now it is routine. The exposure seems to shift first from merely including the person in situations from which they were previously omitted, for example, an office setting, to gradually presenting them in a positive light, and then making them the focal heroes or heroines (Wooley & Wooley, 1977). The elderly have not yet been this fortunate.

We end with two important caveats. First, the solicitousness and increased care that this type of consciousness-raising may bring could result in even greater debilitation for the elderly (Langer & Benevento, 1978; Langer & Rodin, 1976; Rodin, 1980; Rodin & Langer, 1977). What is needed is not simply attention or pampering, which foster dependency, but rather increased opportunities for esteem-building and self-control. Second, this line of reasoning argues strongly for social change that provides opportunities for real control, not simply strategies that increase perceived control while options for actual control remain unavailable. If older persons are led to expect more control over their destinies, which they then find themselves unable to exercise, they are most likely to blame themselves. Once again, this could produce great debilitation and even death, given the strong association between chronic stress, induced by a lack of control, and ill health among the elderly (Rodin, 1980).

9

ATTITUDES VERSUS ACTIONS

Richard T. LaPiere (1934)

The following article by LaPiere is a classic study in social psychology and a turning point for the field. It brought the issue of the link between attitudes and behavior to the front and center in social psychology. Along with feelings and beliefs, part of the classic definition of an attitude includes a behavioral component (a predisposition or readiness to act, usually in positive or negative ways). It was assumed that attitudes and behavior had to be linked in some way or else the study of attitudes would be an exercise in futility. LaPiere's finding that attitudes did not predict behavior began an important debate that continues today.

In defense of attitudes, many studies have shown the ability of attitudes to predict at least some behavior some of the time. After examining 109 studies, Ajzen and Fishbein (1977) concluded that attitudes predict behavior when the measures of both the attitude and behavior have similar degrees of specificity (how exact and precise they are). Also, both measures should assess both the behavior and the target (person or thing) at which the behavior is directed. Thus, if the attitude survey is general, the measurements of behavior must tap a similarly general domain in order for the attitude survey to be predictive of behavior. And, measuring specific attitudes corresponding to specific behaviors is much more likely to predict those behaviors than very general measures of attitudes. Lastly, Ajzen and Fishbein also suggest that multiple measures of an attitude are more likely to correlate with the attitude than will only a single measure of that attitude.

In light of these considerations, the LaPiere findings are not so surprising. In addition, there were a number of methodological problems in the original

Source: Reprinted from *Social Forces,* 1934, *13,* 290–297. Copyright © 1934 by Waverly Press, Inc., Baltimore, MD.

research design. Were the people who answered LaPiere's letter the same people who dealt with his traveling party during the summer before? Was there a difference between the well-dressed Chinese tourists and the prevalent (and quite negative) stereotype of Chinese in the 1930s? And speaking of the times, the Great Depression was very much in effect in the early 1930s, and here was money at the door when LaPiere and his traveling companions presented themselves. Would the Chinese couple have been treated differently if a university professor were not their guide? These and other questions (about which you are encouraged to speculate) do not detract from the importance of LaPiere's work in influencing and spurring forward the study of attitudes. And it makes for interesting reading as well!

By definition, a social attitude is a behavior pattern, anticipatory set or tendency, predisposition to specific adjustment to designated social situations, or, more simply, a conditioned response to social stimuli. Terminological usage differs, but students who have concerned themselves with attitudes apparently agree that they are acquired out of social experience and provide the individual organism with some degree of preparation to adjust, in a well-defined way, to certain types of social situations if and when these situations arise. It would seem, therefore, that the totality of the social attitudes of a single individual would include all his socially acquired personality which is involved in the making of adjustments to other human beings.

But by derivation social attitudes are seldom more than a verbal response to a symbolic situation. For the conventional method of measuring social attitudes is to ask questions (usually in writing) which demand a verbal adjustment to an entirely symbolic situation. Because it is easy, cheap, and mechanical, the attitudinal questionnaire is rapidly becoming a major method of sociological and socio-psychological investigation. The technique is simple. Thus from a hundred or a thousand responses to the question "Would you get up to give an Armenian woman your seat in a street car?" the investigator derives the "attitude" of non-Armenian males towards Armenian females. Now the question may be constructed with elaborate skill and hidden with consummate cunning in a maze of supplementary or even irrelevant questions, yet all that has been obtained is a symbolic response to a symbolic situation. The words "Armenian woman" do not constitute an Armenian woman of flesh and blood, who might be tall or squat, fat or thin, old or young, well or poorly dressed—who might, in fact, be a goddess or just another old and dirty hag. And the questionnaire response, whether it be "yes" or "no," is but a verbal reaction and this does not involve rising from the seat or stolidly avoiding the hurt eyes of the hypothetical woman and the derogatory stares of other street-car occupants. Yet, ignoring these limitations, the diligent investigator will jump briskly from his factual evidence to the unwarranted conclusion that he has measured the "anticipatory behavior patterns" of non-Armenian males towards Armenian females encountered on street cars. Usually he does not stop here, but proceeds to deduce certain general conclusions regarding the social relationships between Armenians and non-Armenians. Most of us have applied the questionnaire technique with greater caution, but not I fear with any greater certainty of success. Nothing could be used as a more accurate index of color prejudice than the admission or non-admission of colored people to hotels. For the proprietor must reflect the group attitude in his policy regardless of his own feelings in the matter. Since he determines what the group attitude is towards Negroes through the expression of that attitude in overt behavior and over a long period of actual experience, the results will be exceptionally free from those disturbing factors which inevitably affect the effort to study attitudes by direct questioning.

Beginning in 1930 and continuing for two years thereafter, I had the good fortune to travel rather extensively with a young Chinese student and his wife. Both were personable, charming, and quick to win the admiration and respect of those they had the opportunity to become intimate with. But they were foreign-born Chinese, a fact that could not be disguised. Knowing the general "attitude" of Americans towards the Chinese as indicated by the "social distance" studies which have been made, it was with considerable trepidation that I first approached a hotel clerk in their company. Perhaps that clerk's eyebrows lifted slightly, but he accommodated us without a show of hesitation. And this in the "best" hotel in a small town noted for its narrow and bigoted "attitude" towards Orientals. Two months later I passed that way again, phoned the hotel and asked if they would accommodate "an important Chinese gentleman." The reply was an unequivocal "No." That aroused my curiosity and led to this study.

In something like ten thousand miles of motor travel, twice across the United States, up and down the Pacific Coast, we met definite rejection from those asked to serve us just once. We were received at 66 hotels, auto camps, and "Tourist Homes," refused at one. We were served in 184 restaurants and cafes scattered throughout the country and treated with what I judged to be more than ordinary consideration in 72 of them. Accurate and detailed records were kept of all these instances. An effort, necessarily subjective, was made to evaluate the overt response of hotel clerks, bell boys, elevator operators, and waitresses to the presence of my Chinese friends. The factors entering into the situations were varied as far and as often as possible. Control was not, of course, as exacting as that required by laboratory experimentation. But it was as rigid as is humanly possible in human situations. For example, I did not take the "test" subjects into my confidence fearing that their behavior might become self-conscious and thus abnormally affect the response of others towards them. Whenever possible I let my Chinese friend negotiate for accommodations (while I concerned myself with the car or luggage) or sent them into a restaurant ahead of me. In this way I attempted to "factor" myself out. We sometimes patronized high-class establishments after a hard and dusty day on the road and stopped at inferior auto camps when in our most presentable condition.

In the end I was forced to conclude that those factors which most influenced the behavior of others towards the Chinese had nothing at all to do with race. Quality and condition of clothing, appearance of baggage (by which, it seems, hotel clerks are prone to base their quick evaluations), cleanliness and neatness were far more significant for person to person reaction in the situations I was studying than skin pigmentation, straight black hair, slanting eyes, and flat noses. And yet an air of self-confidence might entirely offset the "unfavorable" impression made by dusty clothes and the usual disorder to appearance consequent upon some hundred miles of motor travel. A supercilious desk clerk in a hotel of noble aspirations could not refuse his master's hospitality to people who appeared to take their request as a perfectly normal and conventional thing, though they might look like tin-can tourists and two of them belong to the racial category "Oriental." On the other hand, I became rather adept at approaching hotel clerks with that peculiar crab-wise manner which is so effective in provoking a somewhat scornful disregard. And then a bland smile would serve to reverse the entire situation. Indeed, it appeared that a genial smile was the most effective password to acceptance. My Chinese friends were skillful smilers, which may account, in part, for the fact that we received but one rebuff in all our experience. Finally, I was impressed with the fact that even where some tension developed due to the strangeness of the Chinese it would evaporate immediately when they spoke in unaccented English.

In only one out of 251 instances in which we purchased goods or services necessitating intimate human relationships did the fact that my companions were Chinese adversely affect us. Factors entirely unassociated with race were, in the main, the determinant of significant variations in our reception. It would appear reasonable to conclude that the "attitude" of the American people, as reflected in the behavior of those who are for pecuniary reasons presumably most sensitive to the antipathies of their white clientele, is anything but negative towards the Chinese. In terms of "social distance" we might conclude that native Caucasians are not averse to residing in the same hotels, auto-camps, and "Tourist Homes" as Chinese and will with complacency accept the presence of Chinese at an adjoining table in restaurant or cafe. It does not follow that there is revealed a distinctly "positive" attitude towards the Chinese, that whites prefer the Chinese to other whites. But the facts as gathered certainly preclude the conclusion that there is an intense prejudice towards the Chinese.

Yet the existence of this prejudice, very intense, is proven by a conventional "attitude" study. To provide a comparison of symbolic reaction to symbolic social situations with actual reaction to real social situations, I "questionnaired" the establishments which we patronized during the two year period. Six months were permitted to lapse between the time I obtained the overt reaction and the symbolic. It was hoped that the effects of the actual experience with Chinese guests, adverse or otherwise, would have faded during the intervening time. To the hotel or restaurant a questionnaire was mailed with an accompanying letter purporting to be a special and personal plea for response. The questionnaires all asked the same question, "Will you accept members of the Chinese race as guests in your establishment?" Two types of questionnaire were used. In one this question was inserted among similar queries concerning Germans, French, Japanese, Russians, Armenians, Jews, Negroes, Italians, and Indians. In the other the pertinent question was unencumbered. With persistence, completed replies were obtained from 128 of the establishments we had visited; 81 restaurants and cafes and 47 hotels, auto-camps, and "Tourist Homes." In response to the relevant question 92 per cent of the former and 91 per cent of the latter replied "No." The remainder replied "Uncertain; depend upon circumstances." From the woman proprietor of a small auto-camp I received the only "Yes," accompanied by a chatty letter describing the nice visit she had had with a Chinese gentleman and his sweet wife during the previous summer.

A rather unflattering interpretation might be put upon the fact that those establishments who had provided for our needs so graciously were, some months later, verbally antagonistic towards hypothetical Chinese. To factor this experience out, responses were secured from 32 hotels and 96 restaurants located in approximately the same regions, but uninfluenced by this particular experience with Oriental clients. In this, as in the former case, both types of questionnaires were used. The results indicate that neither the type of questionnaire nor the fact of previous experience had important bearing upon the symbolic response to symbolic social situations.

It is impossible to make direct comparison between the reactions secured through questionnaires and from actual experience. On the basis of the above data it would appear foolhardy for a Chinese to attempt to travel in the United States. And yet, as I have shown, actual experience indicates that the American people, as represented by the personnel of hotels, restuarants, etc., are not at all averse to fraternizing with Chinese within the limitations which apply to social relationships between Americans themselves. The evaluations which follow are undoubtedly subject to the criticism which any human judgment must withstand. But the fact is that, although they began their travels in this country with considerable trepidation, my Chinese friends soon lost all fear that they might receive a rebuff. At first somewhat timid and considerably dependent upon me for guidance and support, they came in time to feel fully self-reliant and would approach new social situations without the slightest hesitation.

No doubt a considerable part of the data which the social scientist deals with can be obtained by the questionnaire method. The census reports are based upon verbal questionnaires and I do not doubt their basic integrity. If we wish to know how many children a man has, his income, the size of his home, his age, and the condition of his parents, we can reasonably ask him. These things he has frequently and conventionally converted into verbal responses. He is competent to report upon them, and will do so accurately, unless indeed he wishes to do otherwise. A careful investigator could no doubt even find out by verbal means whether the man fights with his wife (frequently, infrequently, or not at all), though the neighbors would be a more reliable source. But we should not expect to obtain by the questionnaire method his "anticipatory set or tendency" to action should his wife pack up and go home to Mother, should Elder Son get into trouble with the neighbor's daughter, the President assume the status of a dictator, the Japanese take over the rest of China, or a Chinese gentleman come to pay a social call.

Only a verbal reaction to an entirely symbolic situation can be secured by the questionnaire. It may indicate what the responder would actually do when confronted with the situation symbolized in the question, but there is no assurance that it will. And so to call the response a reflection of a "social attitude" is to entirely disregard the definition commonly given for the phrase "attitude." If social attitudes are to be conceptualized as partially integrated habit sets which will become operative under specific circumstances and lead to a particular pattern of adjustment they must, in the main, be derived from a study of humans behaving in actual social situations. They must not be imputed on the basis of questionnaire data.

The questionnaire is cheap, easy, and mechanical. The study of human behavior is time consuming, intellectually fatiguing, and depends for its success upon the ability of the investigator. The former method gives quantitative results, the latter mainly qualitative. Quantitative measurements are quantitatively accurate; qualitative evaluations are always subject to the errors of human judgment. Yet it would seem far more worth while to make a shrewd guess regarding that which is essential than to accurately measure that which is likely to prove quite irrelevant.

10

THE MINDSET OF HEALTH

Ellen J. Langer (1989)

In Module 10, Myers discusses people's miseries: depression, loneliness, and social anxiety, and suggests some social-psychological approaches to treating these problems. These are problems with which you are probably familiar if you are a typical North American. All of us have had circumstances that trigger these very real human emotions. Life is at times depressing, and there's no way around it. Rare is the person who avoids feelings of loneliness and anxiety. The key to working through such problems (with or without the aid of helping professionals) may revolve around what Langer refers to as our "mindset."

Having read these modules on social thinking, we are now in a position to link basic theory with application, that is, to use our science to help people with specific problems. We now know that the way we think very much influences how depressed or cheerful we feel; in this reading, Langer shows that the way we think very much influences our physical health as well. She builds on our understanding of social thinking to suggest specific ways in which our thoughts influence how we feel physically as well as mentally, e.g., in fighting disease, pain, and addictions. We agree with Langer that successful medicine of the future will include the patient in the cure.

Consider this scenario: During a routine physical, your doctor notices a small lump in your breast and orders a biopsy as a cancer-screening measure. Your immediate reaction is fear, probably intense fear. Yet in some cases, a tiny breast lump or mole requires only a tiny incision, comparable to removing a large splinter. Fear in such a situation is based not on the procedure but on your interpretation of what the doctor is doing. You're not thinking splinters or minor cuts; you're thinking biopsy, cancer, death.

Our thoughts create the context that determines our feelings. In thinking about health, and especially in trying to change the consequences of an illness or the behavior that leads to it, an awareness of context—or what I have come to call a "mindfulness"—is crucial.

UNDERSTANDING THE POWER OF CONTEXT

"Is there a split between mind and body?" the comedian Woody Allen once asked. "And if so, which is better to have?" With these questions he penetrates to one of our most potent mindsets. From earliest childhood we learn to see mind and body as separate—and to regard the body as without question the more essential of the two. We are taught that "sticks and stones can break my bones, but names can never hurt me." And later, we take our physical problems to one sort of doctor, our mental problems to another. But the mind/body split is not only one of our strongest beliefs, it is a dangerous and premature psychological commitment.

When we think of various influences on our health, we tend to think of many of them as coming from the outside environment. But each outside influence is mediated by context. Our perceptions and interpretations influence the ways in which our bodies respond to information in the world. If we automatically—"mindlessly"—accept preconceived notions of the context of a particular situation, we can jeopardize the body's ability to handle that situation. Sometimes, for the sake of our health, we need to place our perceptions intentionally, that is, mindfully in a different context.

Context can be so powerful that it influences our basic needs. In an experiment on hunger, subjects who chose to fast for a prolonged time for personal reasons tended to be less hungry than those who fasted for external reasons—for money, for example. Freely choosing to perform a task means that one has adopted a certain attitude toward it. In this experiment, those who had made a personal psychological commitment not only were less hungry on a subjective measure, but they also showed a smaller increase in free fatty acid levels, a physiological indicator of hunger. The obvious conclusion: State of mind shapes state of body.

BUILDING IMMUNITY THROUGH EMOTION

A wide body of recent research has been devoted to investigating the influence of attitudes on the immune system, which is thought to be the intermediary between psychological states and physical illness. The emotional context, our interpretation of the events around us, could thus be the first link in a chain leading to serious illness. And since context is something we can control, the clarification of these links between psychology and illness is good news. Diseases that were once thought to be purely physiological and probably incurable may be more amenable to personal control than we once believed.

Even when a disease may appear to progress inexorably, our reactions to it can be mindful or mindless and thus influence its effects. A very common mindset, as mentioned before, is the conviction that cancer means death. Even if a tumor has not yet had any effect on any body function, or how you feel physically, rarely will you think of yourself as healthy after having a malignancy diagnosed. At the same time, there are almost certainly people walking around with undiagnosed cancer who consider themselves healthy, and may remain so. Yet many doctors have noticed that, following a diagnosis of cancer, some patients seem to go into a decline that has little to do with the actual course of the disease. They appear, in a sense, to "turn their faces to the wall" and begin to die. But they needn't. By reinterpreting the context, they might avoid the unnecessary failure attributable to fear alone.

HARNESSING THE POWER OF THE MIND

In recent years there has been much new research that now supports the value of a mindful approach in handling a variety of health situations such as:

Pain: Patients have been successfully taught to tolerate rather severe pain by seeing how pain varies depending on context (thinking of bruises incurred during a football game that are easily tolerated, versus the attention we require to nurse a mere paper cut).

This mindful exercise helped the patients get by with fewer pain relievers and sedatives and to leave the hospital earlier than a comparison group of patients. And the results seem to indicate more than a simple, temporary distraction of the mind, because once the stimulus—the source of pain—has been reinterpreted so that the person has a choice of context, one painful, one not, the mind is unlikely to return to the original interpretation. It has, in effect, changed contexts.

Hospitals: Part of the hospital context is its strangeness, a strangeness that has been found to be life-threatening in some cases. In a dramatic investigation, Klaus Jarvinen, lecturer in internal medicine at the University of Helsinki, studied patients who had suffered severe heart attacks and found that they were five times as likely to die suddenly when unfamiliar staff members made the rounds.

Had these patients been able to meet these staff members and helped to see the way they were much like the people the patients already knew and cared for, making the new staff seem less strange, the consequences might have been different.

OUTSMARTING TEMPTATION

We all know people who have quit smoking "cold turkey." Do they succeed because their commitment to stop puts withdrawal symptoms into a new context? For many years I quit smoking from time to time, found it too difficult, and began again, as many people do. But when I stopped the last time, almost ten years ago, I surprisingly felt no withdrawal symptoms. There was no willpower involved. I simply did not have an urge to continue smoking. Where did it go?

Jonathan Margolis, a graduate student at Harvard, and I explored this question in two stages. First we tried to find out if smokers in a nonsmoking context experienced strong cravings for cigarettes. We questioned smokers in three situations that prohibited smoking: in a movie theater, at work, and on a religious holiday (Orthodox Jews are not permitted to smoke on the Sabbath). The results in each setting were very similar. People did not suffer withdrawal symptoms when they were in any of the nonsmoking contexts. But when they returned to a context where smoking was allowed—a smoke break at work, for instance—their cravings resurfaced.

All of these people escaped the urge to smoke in a mindless manner. Could they have achieved the same thing deliberately? Can people control the experience of temptation?

In designing a second experiment to answer this question, we assumed that a mindful person would look at addiction from more than one perspective. For instance, it is clear that there are actually advantages as well as disadvantages to addictions. But this is not the usual point of view of someone trying to break a habit.

People who want to stop smoking usually remind themselves of the health risks, the bad smell, the cost, others' reactions to their smoking—the drawbacks of smoking. But these effects are not the reasons they smoke, so trying to quit for those reasons alone often leads to failure. The problem is that all of the *positive* aspects of smoking are still there and still have strong appeal—the relaxation, the concentration, the taste, the sociable quality of smoking.

A more mindful approach would be to look carefully at these pleasures and find other, less harmful, ways of obtaining them. If the needs served by an addiction or habit can be satisfied in different ways, it should be easier to shake.

To test whether this dual perspective was at work when people quit smoking, we picked a group of people who had already quit and complimented each one for their success. We then paid careful attention to their responses to our compliments on their will power.

To understand our strategy, imagine being complimented for being able to spell three-letter words. A compliment doesn't mean much when the task is very easy. If you solve a horrendously difficult problem and then receive a compliment, it is probably most welcome.

We then asked these former smokers what factors they considered when they decided to stop smoking. Those who gave single-minded answers, citing only the negative consequences, were more likely to be the ones who accepted the compliment. Those who saw both sides usually shrugged it off, suggesting that quitting was easier for them. And months later, these people who did not experience a hardship when quitting were more likely to remain successful in staying off cigarettes.

PUTTING ADDICTION OUT OF MIND

Similar evidence of the importance of context in dealing with temptation comes from work on alcoholism and drug addiction, both often seen as intractable problems. For instance, even the degree of intoxication experienced can be changed by altering the drinker's expectations.

In one experiment, psychologists G. Alan Marlatt of the University of Washington and Damaris J. Rohsenow of the V.A. Medical Center in Providence, Rhode Island, divided a group of subjects according to whether they expected to receive an alcoholic drink (vodka and tonic) or a nonalcoholic drink (tonic alone). Despite the presumed physiological effects of alcohol on behavior, expectations were the major influence. What the people expected, tonic or vodka and tonic, determined how aggressively they behaved and how socially anxious and sexually aroused they became. In a similar study, researchers found that groups of men who believed they had been given alcohol, whether or not they had, showed a tendency for reduced heart rate, a condition associated with drinking.

These are just two of the many investigations showing that thoughts may be a more important determinant of the physiological reactions believed to be alcohol-related than the actual chemical properties of alcohol. The antics of high school kids at parties, generation after generation, are probably also influenced by context just as much as they are by the quantity of beer guzzled.

Here is another example. Informal reports from people who work with heroin addicts show that those addicts who are sent to prisons with the reputation of being "clean" (that is, the addicts believe there is absolutely no chance they will be able to get drugs there) did not seem to suffer withdrawal symptoms, while addicts sent to prisons whose reputations included easy access to drugs and who believed they would be able to get their hands on drugs—but didn't—experienced the pain of withdrawal.

FOOLING THE MIND

The deliberate nature of mindfulness is what makes its potential so enormous. And that potential has important precursors in methods we've developed to "fool" ourselves into better health. In the 1960s, experiments with biofeedback made it clear that it was possible to gain intentional control of such "involuntary" functions as heart rate, blood flow and brain activity. Through trial and error, people learned to control the workings of their own bodies and, for example, lower their blood pressure or counteract painful headaches.

Another method for harnessing the healing powers of the mind in a passive way is through the use of placebos, inert substances that in appearance resemble active drugs. Although inert, placebos are known to have powerful effects on health. But who is doing the healing? Why can't we just say to our minds, "Repair this ailing body." Why must we fool our minds in order to enlist our own powers of self-healing?

Placebos, hypnosis, autosuggestion, faith healing, visualization, positive thinking, biofeedback—these are among the ways we have learned to invoke our own powers. Each can be seen as a device for changing mindsets, enabling us to move from an unhealthy to a healthy context. The more we can learn about how to do this mindfully and deliberately, rather than having to rely on elaborate, indirect strategies, the more control we will gain over our own health.

THE MIND'S ACTIVE PLACEBO

Ever since we relied on our mothers to make a bruised knee better with a Band-Aid and a kiss, we have held on to the assumption that someone out there, somewhere, can make us better. If we go to a specialist and are given a Latin name for our problem, and a prescription, this old mindset of that magical someone helping is reconfirmed.

But what if we get the Latin name without the prescription? Imagine going to the doctor for some aches and pains and being told you have Zapalitis and that little can be done for this condition. Before you were told it was Zapalitis, you paid attention to each symptom in a mindful way and did what you could to feel better. But now you have been told that nothing can be done. So you do nothing. Your motivation to do something about the aches, to listen to your body, has been thwarted by a label. With the loss of motivation eventually comes the loss of the skill of caring for ourselves, to whatever degree we otherwise would have been able.

In the past decade or so, a new brand of empowered patient/consumer movement has tried to restore our control over our own health. Many of the alternative therapies sought out by these people have as their most active ingredient the concept of mindfulness.

Whenever we try to heal ourselves and do not abdicate this responsibility completely to doctors, each step is mindful. We welcome new information, whether from our bodies or from books. We look at our illness from more than the single perspective of medicine. We work on changing contexts, whether it is a stressful workplace or a depressing view of the hospital. And finally, when we attempt to stay healthy rather than to be made well, we become involved in the process rather than the outcome.

In applying mindfulness theory to health, I have worked a good deal with elderly people. Success in increasing longevity by making more mental demands on nursing-home residents or by teaching meditation or techniques of flexible, novel thinking gives us strong reason to believe that the same techniques could be used to improve health and shorten illness earlier in life. In a recent experiment we gave arthritis sufferers various interesting word problems to increase their mental activity. Compared to a group given a less stimulating task, the mindful patients not only reported increased comfort and enjoyment, but some of the chemistry of the disease changed as well.

There are two ways in which we have learned to influence our health: exchanging unhealthy mindsets for healthy ones and increasing a generally mindful state. The latter method is more lasting and results in more personal control. Understanding the importance of abandoning the mind/body dualism that has shaped both our thinking and the practice of medicine for so long can make a profound difference in both what we do and how we feel. The real value of fostering the idea of "active placebos" will come when people put them to work for themselves.

Consider how you learned to ride a bike. Someone older held on to the seat as you peddled to keep you from falling until you found your balance. Then, without your knowledge, that strong hand let go and you were riding on your own. You controlled the bicycle without even knowing you had learned how.

The same is true for all of us most of our lives. We control our health, and the course of disease, without really knowing that we do. But just as on the bike, at some point we all discover that we are in control. Now may be the time for many of us to learn how to recognize and use the control we possess over illness through mindfulness.

11

EXCERPT FROM
HEALTH AND OPTIMISM

Christopher Peterson and Lisa M. Bossio (1991)

In this last selection on Social Thinking, the importance of how one thinks about events is again stressed. Social thinking is not just control over the events themselves (primary control), it is also control over how we feel about the events and our ability both to accommodate ourselves to those events and to find a silver lining in the storm cloud (secondary control). Reading this selection, I (AGH) realized how much my beliefs and attitudes about the world have changed over time. While I was growing up (until at least age 30), I used to think that if I could just get the world to go my way, then I would be happy! Slowly I came to the realization (it took another decade) that I was not going to get the world to go my way all or even most of the time. I have not given up trying, that is, I have not become passive or helpless in the face of adversity, but I have refocused my perspective in two ways. First, if I make any impact on complex outcomes, I recognize that as success—thus increasing my sense of empowerment (see Myers, 1994, p. 108). Second, I have begun to look at difficult circumstances as positive challenges—there is always something to learn from them. Both of these changes in my thinking reflect aspects of secondary control.

Although optimism seems to have developed a reputation for being the philosophy of the fool and cynicism and pessimism mark the intellectual ("The place where optimism most flourishes is a lunatic asylum"—Havelock Ellis, 1923), Peterson and Bossio make the case that the optimist has much to gain in mental and physical health. After reading this selection, you may want to consider what characteristics of happy people you already have in your psychological makeup and which ones you would like to develop to a greater degree. And furthermore, now that you have a list of characteristics that seem related to happiness, as a budding social psychologist, do you think it is complete? What characteristics might you add?

THE FUTURE

Many contemporary Americans look healthy and happy on the surface. Recent studies of changes in the incidence of depression over the decades, however, suggest that today's young adults are much more likely to be depressed than their parents or grandparents—perhaps ten times more so (Seligman, 1988). Given the strong link between depression and pessimism, we infer that pessimism itself is also becoming more prevalent.

The opposite of collective optimism is collective pessimism, what sociologists for years have been calling alienation. The traditional explanation of alienation is that it occurs in a society in which the relationship between what people do and what then happens to them is obscured: the societal equivalent of a learned helplessness experiment. There are other routes to collective pessimism as well, not the least important of which is via the information about the countless hazards to life and happiness with which the general public is bombarded.

Here popular books on personal problems must shoulder part of the blame for the difficulties they purport to solve. In calling people's problems with work, shopping, sexuality, and chocolate "addictions" rather than bad habits, some writers make these more imposing than they need to be.[1] Addiction is an internal, stable, and global explanation for a problem in life; in our terms, it is a pessimistic construal that leads to helplessness and hopelessness.

WHEN OPTIMISM IS NOT ENOUGH

Rothbaum, Weisz, and Snyder chide contemporary psychologists—including us—for focusing unduly on what they call primary control: whether or not people can change actual events in the world (Rothbaum, Weisz, & Snyder, 1982). Sometimes primary control is impossible; optimism may be at odds with reality. Some people in difficult circumstances become helpless and hopeless, depressed and ill. Other people continue to cope by accommodating themselves to uncontrollable events.

Primary control represents an attempt to change the *world*. In contrast, accommodating oneself to uncontrollable bad events involves changing the *self*. Rothbaum et al. call the strategies at one's disposal for changing the self secondary control. One such strategy is finding meaning or purpose in otherwise traumatic occurrences. "I learned what was really important in life," say some people after a brush with death.

---

[1]Addiction proves a difficult to define concept even when applied narrowly to problems with alcohol and drugs (Peele, 1989). Historically, people were considered to be addicted to a substance if they were physically dependent upon it, showing tolerance following increased use and withdrawal following decreased use. But this definition rested on the ability to distinguish physical dependence from psychological dependence, and we know this is difficult if not downright impossible. Many mental health professionals today speak no longer of addiction to drugs but instead of their abuse. Some popular authors have not been so cautious with the concept of addiction, extending it widely, even including other people as addictions.

To the degree that people can make sense of bad events, they can blunt their harmful effects. Numerous philosophies, secular and religious, are available for the purpose of secondary control. We endorse no one philosophy in particular. A person must find one that fits with her own web of belief. But regardless of its content, Rothbaum et al. conclude that such a philosophy is useful.

Sociologist Aaron Antonovsky introduces a similar idea, sense of coherence, which he defines as the ability to find structure, meaning, and regularity in the events that one experiences. Sense of coherence is related to how one copes with demands posed by the world, but it is a broader notion than simply exerting control over outcomes. The person with a sense of coherence regards demands as challenges worthy of attention. Antonovsky (1987) argues that sense of coherence is linked to good health, and its absence to poor health.

With Jennifer Bryce, Ned Kirsch, and Kim Lachman, we are in the process of testing some of these hypotheses about the benefits of finding significance in life's traumas. Just as we did for optimism (see Table 11-1), we developed a questionnaire that measures the degree to which someone tries to find meaning in bad events (see Table 11-2) as well as a content analysis procedure that can be used to score secondary control (or its absence) from verbal material.

TABLE 11-1. EXAMPLE OF AN ATTRIBUTIONAL STYLE OPTIMISM QUESTIONNAIRE ITEM

Please try to imagine yourself in the situation that follows. If such a situation happened to you, what do you feel would have caused it? While events may have many causes, we want you to pick only one—*the major cause if this event happened to you.*

Please write the cause in the blank provided after each event. Next we want you to answer three questions about the cause you provided. First, is the cause of this event something about you or something about other people or circumstances? Second, is the cause of this event something that will occur in the future or not? Third, is the cause of this event something that affects all situations in your life or something that just affects this type of event?

Event: You cannot get all the work done that your supervisor has assigned.

A. Write down the one major cause: _____

B. Is the cause of this something about you or something about other people or circumstances? (circle one number)

totally due to others	1	2	3	4	5	6	7	totally due to me

C. In the future, will this cause again be present? (circle one number)

never present	1	2	3	4	5	6	7	always present

D. Is this cause something that affects just this type of situation, or does it also influence other areas of your life? (circle one number)

just this situation	1	2	3	4	5	6	7	all situations

TABLE 11-2. ITEMS FROM THE SECONDARY CONTROL QUESTIONNAIRE

Respondents are asked to indicate their relative agreement or disagreement with statements like these.

1. I take a philosophical approach to what happens to me.

2. What's good or bad depends entirely on your point of view.

3. There are lessons to be learned from every experience.

4. I try to understand the meaning of life.

5. God has a specific plan for me.

6. I'm a believer in the idea that disappointments and setbacks can be good experiences if you learn from them.

7. I adapt myself to what happens.

In our first study, we examined the first-person narratives of two groups of people who arguably experienced a great number of uncontrollable life events but nonetheless survived quite well. The first was former American slaves who told their stories to interviewers during the 1930s in conjunction with the Federal Writers Project, a massive undertaking in which survivors of slavery were located and interviewed (Yetman, 1970). At the time they told their stories, the people were elderly. They necessarily had survived the trauma of slavery and its aftermath. By the logic of Rothbaum et al., secondary control strategies should be prominent in their accounts. Here was a group of people for whom primary control was not possible, yet they still coped effectively, as shown by their longevity.

The second was a group of mothers raising their families in the war zone of contemporary Beirut (Bryce, 1986). Again, these people were physically and mentally healthy, despite their lack of control over events happening around them. Again, according to Rothbaum et al., they should be using secondary control strategies.

For comparison purposes, we also looked at first-person narratives from two samples of contemporary Americans: students at an exclusive college and upper middle-class adults. Obviously, these are not ideal comparison groups. They differ from the slaves and the Lebanese mothers in terms of the objective uncontrollability of the events befalling them, but also in other ways.

Regardless, we predicted that the use of secondary control would be more prevalent in the first two samples than in the latter two, by virtue of the greater stress to which these people were exposed and in light of their continued thriving. This pattern is exactly what we found. The former slaves and the mothers in Beirut were much more likely to describe attempts to find meaning in bad events around them than were the American college students and adults. These individuals typically described bad events in terms of their attempts to change them.

We also undertook a more tightly controlled investigation of the mitigating effect of secondary control. Where our first study used a content analysis procedure to search for mention of secondary control, our second investigation used the questionnaire we devised that measures the degree to which a respondent endorses strategies of secondary control.

This questionnaire was administered to a group of students, along with others assessing explanatory style, stressful life events, and depressive symptoms. We expected an overall correlation between bad events and depression, but we further predicted that the use of secondary control strategies would mitigate this relationship. So, we sought to test the same prediction as in the first study: that secondary control is associated with doing well in the face of bad life events. Again, the results were as predicted. Secondary control reduced the depressing effects of stress. We also found that optimistic explanatory style was associated with less depression in the wake of bad events—*independently* of secondary control.

Thus, two different strategies are associated with robustness in the face of stress. Optimism is one of these. But secondary control—the ability to find meaning in misfortune even when the world itself cannot be changed—is also useful.[2] These strategies are not incompatible. The person who has both available is better able to cope than the person who has but one or neither.

---

[2]As the noted philosopher Kenny Rogers once observed, one has to know when to hold cards and know when to fold them.

SOCIAL INFLUENCE

12

EXCERPT FROM
THE MOUNTAIN PEOPLE

Colin M. Turnbull (1972)

People generally consider their values to be very private aspects of their lives and a matter of individual choice. They also recognize that ethics, morals, and beliefs are shaped by family and perhaps by religious upbringing. Few of us, however, have carefully explored the many ways that our particular social groups shape our perceptions regarding what is important to us in our interactions with each other, as well as in our lives overall. Throughout this section on social influence, we explore how some of our values are developed and expressed as a consequence of the presence of others, either in terms of the influence of society as a whole or the presence of specific individual others.

We begin that exploration by considering an extreme case. It is sometimes easier to see our own values when contrasted with values that we do not share. Looking across culture, we find the Ik (pronounced "eek") of Uganda, a people with a culture that was initially very different from ours, and who have since experienced extreme survival stress. Turnbull's important study of the Ik highlights the capacity for human behavior to be diverse and changeable. One might take the view that humans are inherently self-interested, or a situational perspective, which recognizes the impact of extreme long-term stresses on human behavior. Turnbull (personal communication, February, 1989) takes the situational perspective. He believes ". . . that we all have the capability of responding as the Ik did, in that (context) or some other context. Equally, we have a potential for what we consider 'civilized' or 'humane' behavior—and the potential will also be related to a possible plurality of contexts." From our perspective on social values, this case suggests that many values are group derived and can change dramatically when groups meet with massive situational change.

Source: Excerpted from *The mountain people,* by Colin M. Turnbull, 1972, New York: Simon & Schuster. Copyright © 1972 by Colin M. Turnbull. Reprinted by permission of the publisher, Simon & Schuster, Inc., and the author.

Turnbull is an excellent writer and for those of you who would like to read more by him, we strongly recommend *The Forest People,* a description of the BaMbuti pygmies of the Ituri rain forest in the Congo. If the individualistic Ik of Uganda provide "bad news" with reason for pessimism about the future of humanity, then the collectivist BaMbuti give us "good news" and hope for the future of humans on this planet. In a radically different environment, the BaMbuti enjoy a kind, loving, and productive life in harmony with their surroundings.

ABSTRACT

Anthropologist Colin M. Turnbull, author of The Forest People *and* The Lonely Africans, *went to study the Ik of Uganda, who he believed were still primarily hunters, in order to compare them with other hunting-and-gathering societies he had studied in totally different environments. He was surprised to discover that they were no longer hunters but primarily farmers, well on their way to starvation and something worse in a drought-stricken land.*

In what follows, there will be much to shock, and the reader will be tempted to say, "how primitive, how savage, how disgusting," and, above all, "how inhuman." The first judgments are typical of the kind of ethno- and egocentricism from which we can never quite escape. But "how inhuman" is of a different order and supposes that there are certain values inherent in humanity itself, from which the people described here seem to depart in a most drastic manner. In living the experience, however, and perhaps in reading it, one finds that it is oneself one is looking at and questioning; it is a voyage in quest of the basic human and a discovery of his potential for inhumanity, a potential that lies within us all.

Just before World War II the Ik tribe had been encouraged to settle in northern Uganda, in the mountainous northeast corner bordering on Kenya to the east and Sudan to the north. Until then they had roamed in nomadic bands, as hunters and gatherers, through a vast region in all three countries. The Kidepo Valley below Mount Morungole was their major hunting territory. After they were confined to a part of their former area, Kidepo was made a national park and they were forbidden to hunt or gather there.

The concept of family in a nomadic society is a broad one; what really counts most in everyday life is community of residence, and those who live close to each other are likely to see each other as effectively related, whether there is any kinship bond or not. Full brothers, on the other hand, who live in different parts of the camp may have little concern for each other.

It is not possible then, to think of the family as a simple, basic unit. A child is brought up to regard any adult living in the same camp as a parent, and age-mate as a brother or sister. The Ik had this essentially social attitude toward kinship, and it readily lent itself to the rapid and disastrous changes that took place following the restriction of their movement and hunting activities. The family simply ceased to exist.

It is a mistake to think of small-scale societies as "primitive" or "simple." Hunters and gatherers, most of all, appear simple and straightforward in terms of their social organization, yet that is far from true. If we can learn about the nature of society from a study of small-scale societies, we can also learn about human relationships. The smaller the society, the less emphasis there is on the formal system and the more there

is on interpersonal and intergroup relations. Security is seen in terms of these relationships, and so is survival. The result, which appears so deceptively simple, is that
hunters frequently display those characteristics that we find so admirable in man: kind-
ness, generosity, consideration, affection, honesty, hospitality, compassion, charity.
For them, in their tiny, close-knit society, these are necessities for survival. In our society anyone possessing even half these qualities would find it hard to survive, yet we
think these virtues are inherent in man. I took it for granted that the Ik would possess
these same qualities. But they were as unfriendly, uncharitable, inhospitable and generally mean as any people can be. For those positive qualities we value so highly are
no longer functional for them; even more than in our own society they spell ruin and
disaster. It seems that, far from being basic human qualities, they are luxuries we can
afford in times of plenty or are mere mechanisms for survival and security. Given the
situation in which the Ik found themselves, man has no time for such luxuries, and a
much more basic man appears, using more basic survival tactics.

*Turnbull had to wait in Kaabong, a remote administration outpost, for permission
from the Uganda government to continue to Pirre, the Ik water hole and police post.
While there he began to learn the Ik language and became used to their constant demands for food and tobacco. An official in Kaabong gave him, as a "gift," 20 Ik workers to build a house and a road up to it. When they arrived at Pirre, however, wages
for the workers were negotiated by wily Atum, "the senior of all the Ik on
Morungole."*

I was always up before dawn, but by the time I got up to the villages they were always deserted. One morning I followed the little *oror* [gulley] up from *oror a pirre'i*
[Ravine of Pirre] while it was still quite dark, and I met Lomeja on his way down. He
took me on my first illicit hunt in Kidepo. He told me that if he got anything he would
share it with me and with anyone else who managed to join us but that he certainly
would not take anything back to his family. "Each one of them is out seeing what he
can get for himself, and do you think they will bring any back for me?"

Lomeja was one of the very few Ik who seemed glad to volunteer information.
Unlike many of the others, he did not get up and leave as I approached. Apart from
him, I spent most of my time, those days, with Losike, the potter. She told me that
Nangoli, the old lady in the adjoining compound, and her husband, Amuarkuar, were
rather peculiar. They helped each other get food and water, and they brought it back to
their compound to eat together.

I still do not know how much real hunger there was at that time, for most of the
younger people seemed fairly well fed, and the few skinny old people seemed healthy
and active. But my laboriously extracted genealogies showed that there were quite a
number of old people still alive and allegedly in these villages, though they were never
to be seen. Then Atum's wife died.

Atum told me nothing about it but kept up his demands for food and medicine.
After a while the beady-eyed Lomongin told me that Atum was selling the medicine I
was giving him for his wife. I was not unduly surprised and merely remarked that that
was too bad for his wife. "Oh no," said Lomongin, "she has been dead for weeks."

It must have been then that I began to notice other things that I suppose I had chosen to ignore before. Only a very few of the Ik helped me with the language. Others
would understand when it suited them and would pretend they did not understand

when they did not want to listen. I began to be forced into a similar isolationist attitude myself, and although I cannot say I enjoyed it, it did make life much easier. I even began to enjoy, in a peculiar way, the company of the silent Ik. And the more I accepted it, the less often people got up and left as I approached. On one occasion I sat on the *di* [sitting place] by Atum's rain tree for three days with a group of Ik, and for three days not one word was exchanged.

Once I settled down into my new home, I was able to work more effectively. Having recovered at least some of my anthropological detachment, when I heard the telltale rustling of someone at my stockade, I merely threw a stone. If when out walking I stumbled during a difficult descent and the Ik shrieked with laughter, I no longer even noticed it.

Anyone falling down was good for a laugh, but I never saw anyone actually trip anyone else. The adults were content to let things happen and then enjoy them; it was probably conservation of energy. The children, however, sought their pleasures with vigor. The best game of all, at this time, was teasing poor little Adupa. She was not so little—in fact she should have been an adult, for she was nearly 13 years old—but Adupa was a little mad. Or you might say she was the only sane one, depending on your point of view. Adupa did not jump on other people's play houses, and she lavished enormous care on hers and would curl up inside it. That made it all the more jump-on-able. The other children beat her viciously.

Children are not allowed to sleep in the house after they are "put out," which is at about three years old, four at the latest. From then on they sleep in the open courtyard, taking what shelter they can against the stockade. They may ask for permission to sit in the doorway of their parents' house but may not lie down or sleep there. "The same thing applies to old people," said Atum, "if they can't build a house of their own and, of course, *if* their children let them stay in their compounds."

I saw a few old people, most of whom had taken over abandoned huts. For the first time I realized that there really was starvation and saw why I had never known it before: it was confined to the aged. Down in Giriko's village the old ritual priest, Lolim, confidentially told me that he was sheltering an old man who had been refused shelter by his son. But Lolim did not have enough food for himself, let alone his guest; could I . . . I liked old Lolim, so, not believing that Lolim had a visitor at all, I brought him a double ration that evening. There was a rustling in the back of the hut, and Lolim helped ancient Lomeraniang to the entrance. They shook with delight at the sight of the food.

When the two old men had finished eating, I left; I found a hungry-looking and disapproving little crowd clustered outside. They muttered to each other about wasting food. From then on I brought food daily, but in a very short time Lomeraniang was dead, and his son refused to come down from the village above to bury him. Lolim scratched a hole and covered the body with a pile of stones he carried himself, one by one.

Hunger was indeed more severe than I knew, and, after the old people, the children were the next to go. It was all quite impersonal—even to me, in most cases, since I had been immunized by the Ik themselves against sorrow on their behalf. But Adupa was an exception. Her madness was such that she did not know just how vicious humans could be. Even worse, she thought that parents were for loving, for giving as well as receiving. Her parents were not given to fantasies. When she came for shelter, they drove her out, and when she came because she was hungry, they laughed that Icien laugh, as if she had made them happy.

Adupa's reactions became slower and slower. When she managed to find food— fruit peels, skins, bit of bone, half-eaten berries—she held it in her hand and looked at it with wonder and delight. Her playmates caught on quickly; they put tidbits in her way and watched her simple drawn little face wrinkle in a smile. Then as she raised her hand to her mouth, they set on her with cries of excitement, fun and laughter, beating her savagely over the head. But that is not how she died. I took to feeding her, which is probably the cruelest thing I could have done, a gross selfishness on my part to try to salve my own rapidly disappearing conscience. I had to protect her, physically, as I fed her. But the others would beat her anyway, and Adupa cried, not because of the pain in her body but because of the pain she felt at the great, vast, empty wasteland where love should have been.

It was *that* that killed her. She demanded that her parents love her. Finally they took her in, and Adupa was happy and stopped crying. She stopped crying forever because her parents went away and closed the door tight behind them, so tight that weak little Adupa could never have moved it.

The Ik seem to tell us that the family is not such a fundamental unit as we usually suppose, that it is not essential to social life. In the crisis of survival facing the Ik, the family was one of the first institutions to go, and the Ik as a society have survived.

The other quality of life that we hold to be necessary for survival—love—the Ik dismiss as idiotic and highly dangerous. But we need to see more of the Ik before their absolute lovelessness becomes truly apparent.

In this curious society there is one common value to which all Ik hold tenaciously. It is *ngag,* "food." That is the one standard by which they measure right and wrong, goodness and badness. The very word for "good" is defined in terms of food. "Goodness" is "the possession of food," or the "*individual* possession of food." If you try to discover their concept of a "good man," you get the truly Icien answer: one who has a full stomach.

We should not be surprised, then, when the mother throws her child out at three years old. At that age a series of *rites de passage* begins. In this environment a child has no chance of survival on his own until he is about 13, so children form age bands. The junior band consists of children between three and seven, the senior of eight-to-twelve-year-olds. Within the band each child seeks another close to him in age for defense against the older children. These friendships are temporary, however, and inevitably there comes a time when each turns on the one that up to then had been the closest to him: that is the *rite de passage,* the destruction of the fragile bond called friendship. When this has happened three or four times, the child is ready for the world.

The weakest are soon thinned out, and the strongest survive to achieve leadership of the band. Such a leader is eventually driven out, turned against by his fellow band members. Then the process starts all over again; he joins the senior age band as its most junior member.

The final *rite de passage* is into adulthood, at the age of 12 or 13. By then the candidate has learned the wisdom of acting on his own, for his own good, while acknowledging that on occasion it is profitable to associate temporarily with others.

There seemed to be increasingly little among the Ik that could by any stretch of the imagination be called social life, let alone social organization. The family does not hold itself together; economic interest is centered on as many stomachs as there are people; and cooperation is merely a device for furthering an interest that is consciously selfish. We often do the same thing in our so-called "altruistic" practices, but we tell ourselves it is for the good of others. The Ik have dispensed with the myth of altruism. Though they have no centralized leadership or means of physical coercion, they do hold together with remarkable tenacity.

In our world, where the family has also lost much of its value as a social unit and where religious belief no longer binds us into communities, we maintain order only through coercive power that is ready to uphold a rigid law and through an equally rigid penal system. The Ik, however, have learned to do without coercion, either spiritual or physical. It seems that they have come to a recognition of what they accept as man's basic selfishness, of his natural determination to survive as an individual before all else. This they consider to be man's basic right, and they allow others to pursue that right without recrimination.

Lolim, the oldest and greatest of the ritual priests, was also the last. He was not much in demand any longer, but he was still held in awe, which means kept at a distance. Whenever he approached a *di,* people cleared a space for him, as far away from themselves as possible. The Ik rarely called on his services, for they had little to pay him with, and he had equally little to offer them. The main things they did try to get out of him were certain forms of medicine, both herbal and magical.

Lolim said that he had inherited his power from his father. His father had taught him well but could not give him the power to hear the *abang*—that had to come from the *abang* themselves. He had wanted his oldest son to inherit and had taught him everything he could. But his son, Longoli, was bad, and the *abang* refused to talk to him. They talked instead to his oldest daughter, bald Nangoli. But there soon came the time when all the Ik needed was food in their stomachs, and Lolim could not supply that. The time came when Lolim was too weak to go out and collect the medicines he needed. His children all refused to go except Nangoli, and then she was jailed for gathering in Kidepo Park.

Lolim became ill and had to be protected while eating the food I gave him. Then the children began openly ridiculing him and teasing him, dancing in front of him and kneeling down so that he would trip over them. His grandson used to creep up behind him and with a pair of hard sticks drum a lively tattoo on the old man's bald head.

I fed him whenever I could, but often he did not want more than a bite. Once I found him rolled up in his protective ball, crying. He had had nothing to eat for four days and no water for two. He had asked his children, who all told him not to come near them.

The next day I saw him leaving Atum's village, where his son Longoli lived. Longoli swore that he had been giving his father food and was looking after him. Lolim was not shuffling away; it was almost a run, the run of a drunken man, staggering from side to side. I called to him, but he made no reply, just a kind of long, contin-

uous and horrible moan. He had been to Longoli to beg him to let him into his compound because he knew he was going to die in a few hours, Longoli calmly told me afterward. Obviously Longoli could not do a thing like that; a man of Lolim's importance would have called for an enormous funeral feast. So he refused. Lolim begged
Longoli then to open up Nangoli's *asak* for him so that he could die in *her* compound.
But Longoli drove him out, and he died alone.

Insofar as ritual survived at all, it could hardly be said to be religious, for it did little or nothing to bind Icien society together. But the question still remained: Did this
lack of social behavior and communal ritual or religious expression mean that there
was no community of belief?

Belief may manifest itself, at either the individual or the communal level, in what
we call morality, when we behave according to certain principles supported by our belief even when it seems against our personal interest. When we call ourselves moral,
however, we tend to ignore that ultimately our morality benefits us even as individuals, insofar as we are social individuals and live in a society. In the absence of belief,
law takes over and morality has little role. If there was such a thing as an Icien morality, I had not yet perceived it, though traces of a moral past remained. But it still remained a possibility, as did the existence of an unspoken, unmanifest belief that might
yet reveal itself and provide a basis for the reintegration of society. I was somewhat
encouraged in this hope by the unexpected flight of old Nangoli, widow of
Amuarkuar.

When Nangoli returned and found her husband dead, she did an odd thing: she
grieved. She tore down what was left of their home, uprooted the stockade, tore up
whatever was growing in her little field. Then she fled with a few belongings.

Some weeks later I heard that she and her children had gone over to the Sudan and
built a village there. This migration was so unusual that I decided to see whether this
runaway village was different.

Lojieri led the way, and Atum came along. One long day's trek got us there. Lojieri
pulled part of the brush fence aside, and we went in and wandered around. He and
Atum looked inside all the huts, and Lojieri helped himself to tobacco from one and
water from another. Surprises were coming thick and fast. That households should be
left open and untended with such wealth inside . . . That there should have been such
wealth, for as well as tobacco and jars of water there were baskets of food, and meat
was drying on racks. There were half a dozen or so compounds, but they were separated from each other only by a short line of sticks and brush. It was a village, and
these were homes, the first and last I was to see.

The dusk had already fallen, and Nangoli came in with her children and grandchildren. They had heard us and came in with warm welcomes. There was no hunger here,
and in a very short time each kitchen hearth had a pot of food cooking. Then we sat
around the central fire and talked until late, and it was another universe.

There was no talk of "how much better it is here than there"; talk revolved around
what had happened on the hunt that day. Loron was lying on the ground in front of the
fire as his mother made gentle fun of him. His wife, Kinimei, whom I had never seen
even speak to him at Pirre, put a bowl of fresh-cooked berries and fruit in front of him.
It was all like a nightmare rather than a fantasy, for it made the reality of Pirre seem all
the more frightening.

The unpleasantness of returning was somewhat alleviated by Atum's suffering on the way up the stony trail. Several times he slipped, which made Lojieri and me laugh. It was a pleasure to move rapidly ahead and leave Atum gasping behind so that we could be sitting up on the *di* when he finally appeared and could laugh at his discomfort.

The days of drought wore on into weeks and months and, like everyone else, I became rather bored with sickness and death. I survived rather as did the young adults, by diligent attention to my own needs while ignoring those of others.

Early one morning, before dawn, the village moved. In the midst of a hive of activity were the aged and crippled, soon to be abandoned, in danger of being trampled but seemingly unaware of it. Lolim's widow, Lo'ono, whom I had never seen before, also had been abandoned and had tried to make her way down the mountainside. But she was totally blind and had tripped and rolled to the bottom of the *oror a pirre'i;* there she lay on her back, her legs and arms thrashing feebly, while a little crowd laughed.

At this time a colleague was with me. He kept the others away while I ran to get medicine and food and water, for Lo'ono was obviously near dead from hunger and thirst as well as from the fall. We treated her and fed her and asked her to come back with us. But she asked us to point her in the direction of her son's new village. I said I did not think she would get much of a welcome there, and she replied that she knew it but wanted to be near him when she died. So we gave her more food, put her stick in her hand and pointed her the right way. She suddenly cried. She was crying, she said, because we had reminded her that there had been a time when people had helped each other, when poeople had been kind and good. Still crying, she set off.

The Ik up to this point had been tolerant of my activities, but all this was too much. They said that what we were doing was wrong. Food and medicine were for the living, not the dead. I thought of Lo'ono. And I thought of other old people who had joined in the merriment when they had been teased or had a precious morsel of food taken from their mouths. They knew that it was silly of them to expect to go on living, and, having watched others, they knew that the spectacle really was quite funny. So they joined in the laughter. Perhaps if we had left Lo'ono, she would have died laughing. But we prolonged her misery for no more than a few brief days. Even worse, we reminded her of when things had been different, of days when children had cared for parents and parents for children. She was already dead, and we made her unhappy as well. At the time I was sure we were right, doing the only "human" thing. In a way we *were*—we were making life more comfortable for ourselves. But now I wonder if the Ik way was not right, if I too should not have laughed as Lo'ono flapped about, then left her to die.

And now that all the old are dead, what is left? Every Ik who is old today was thrown out at three and has survived, and in consequence has thrown his own children out and knows that they will not help him in his old age any more than he helped his parents. The system has turned one full cycle and is now self-perpetuating; it has eradicated what we know as "humanity" and has turned the world into a chilly void where man does not seem to care even for himself, but survives. Yet into this hideous world Nangoli and her family quietly returned because they could not bear to be alone.

For the moment abandoning the very old and the very young, the Ik as a whole must be searched for one last lingering trace of humanity. They appear to have disposed of virtually all the qualities that we normally think of as differentiating us from other primates, yet they survive without seeming to be greatly different from ourselves in terms of behavior. Their behavior is more extreme, for we do not start throwing our children out until kindergarten. We have shifted responsibility from family to state; the Ik have shifted it to the individual.

Those values we cherish so highly may indeed be basic to human society but not to humanity, and that means that the Ik show that society itself is not indispensable for man's survival and that man is capable of associating for purposes of survival without being social. The Ik have replaced human society with a mere survival system that does not take human emotion into account. As yet the system is imperfect, for although survival is assured, it is at a minimal level and there is still competition between individuals. With our intellectual sophistication and advanced technology we should be able to perfect the system and eliminate competition, guaranteeing survival for a given number of years for all, reducing the demands made upon us by a social system, abolishing desire and consequently that ever-present and vital gap between desire and achievement, treating us, in a word, as individuals with one basic individual right—the right to survive.

Such interaction as there is within this system is one of mutual exploitation. That is how it already is with the Ik. In our own world the mainstays of a society based on a truly social sense of mutuality are breaking down, indicating that perhaps society as we know it has outworn its usefulness and that by clinging to an outworn system we are bringing about our own destruction. Family, economy, government and religion, the basic categories of social activity and behavior, no longer create any sense of social unity involving a shared and mutual responsibility among all members of our society. At best they enable the individual to survive as an individual. It is the world of the individual, as is the world of the Ik.

13

X: A FABULOUS CHILD'S STORY

Lois Gould (1978)

Gould examines an intriguing issue, the importance of bringing up a child in accordance with appropriate gender roles. Although many people give lip service to the idea of raising children in nonsexist ways, in fact, most parents expect or require gender-role-appropriate behavior in their children. This hypothetical case is more a fantasy than a thought experiment, but it highlights, nonetheless, two important considerations. First, it points out some of the difficulties in actually trying to raise children who are not traditional in their gender-role behaviors, and, second, it shows some of the difficulties of defying commonly held beliefs. Living in society has some costs, and these are most notable when applying a distinctive and different set of values. One of us (AGH) now has a three-year-old and a three-month-old and can attest to the incredible complexity of the process. For example, when asked "Boy or girl?" and we reply ever so sweetly, "It's a baby!" people think us hostile. We have yet to find a children's book that doesn't require some changes in it before we can read to our three-year-old. And, despite repeated explanations to family and friends without becoming ranting ideologues, we constantly note their gendered verbalizations to our children. Although we are delighted with how our children are developing, we now think that 85759 pages in the *Instruction Manual* to which Gould alludes might not be enough advice!

We find that our students intellectually admire Baby X's parents, yet very few of them plan to try to follow in their footsteps in the least. Exactly how important is it for *you* to raise either gender-role-oriented or nontraditional (androgynous) children, and how far might you go in providing a different type of upbringing?

Source: Reprinted by permission of Lois Gould and Daughters Publishing Company, copyright © 1978.

Once upon a time, a baby named X was born. This baby was named X so that nobody could tell whether it was a boy or a girl. Its parents could tell, of course, but they couldn't tell anybody else. They couldn't even tell Baby X, at first.

You see, it was all part of a very important Secret Scientific Xperiment, known officially as Project Baby X. The smartest scientists had set up this Xperiment at a cost of Xactly 23 billion dollars and 72 cents, which might seem like a lot for just one baby, even a very important Xperimental baby. But when you remember the prices of things like strained carrots and stuffed bunnies, and popcorn for the movies and booster shots for camp, let alone 28 shiny quarters from the tooth fairy, you begin to see how it adds up.

Also, long before Baby X was born, all those scientists had to be paid to work out the details of the Xperiment, and to write the *Official Instruction Manual* for Baby X's parents and, most important of all, to find the right set of parents to bring up Baby X. These parents had to be selected very carefully. Thousands of volunteers had to take thousands of tests and answer thousands of tricky questions. Almost everybody failed because, it turned out, almost everybody really wanted either a baby boy or a baby girl, and not Baby X at all. Also, almost everybody was afraid that a Baby X would be a lot more trouble than a boy or a girl. (They were probably right, the scientists admitted, but Baby X needed parents who wouldn't *mind* the Xtra trouble.)

There were families with grandparents named Milton and Agatha, who didn't see why the baby couldn't be named Milton or Agatha instead of X, even if it *was* an X. There were families with aunts who insisted on knitting tiny dresses and uncles who insisted on sending tiny baseball mitts. Worst of all, there were families that already had other children who couldn't be trusted to keep the secret. Certainly not if they knew the secret was worth 23 billion dollars and 72 cents—and all you had to do was take one little peek at Baby X in the bathtub to know if it was a boy or a girl.

But, finally, the scientists found the Joneses, who really wanted to raise an X more than any other kind of baby—no matter how much trouble it would be. Ms. and Mr. Jones had to promise they would take equal turns caring for X, and feeding it, and singing it lullabies. And they had to promise never to hire any baby-sitters. The government scientists knew perfectly well that a baby-sitter would probably peek at X in the bathtub, too.

The day the Joneses brought their baby home, lots of friends and relatives came over to see it. None of them knew about the secret Xperiment, though. So the first thing they asked was what kind of a baby X was. When the Joneses smiled and said, "It's an X!" nobody knew what to say. They couldn't say, "Look at her cute little dimples!" And they couldn't say, "Look at his husky little biceps!" And they couldn't even say just plain "kitchycoo." In fact, they all thought the Joneses were playing some kind of rude joke.

But, of course, the Joneses were not joking. "It's an X" was absolutely all they would say. And that made the friends and relatives very angry. The relatives all felt embarrassed about having an X in the family. "People will think there's something wrong with it!" some of them whispered. "There *is* something wrong with it!" others whispered back.

"Nonsense!" the Joneses told them all cheerfully. "What could possibly be wrong with this perfectly adorable X?"

Nobody could answer that, except Baby X, who had just finished its bottle. Baby X's answer was a loud, satisfied burp.

Clearly, nothing at all was wrong. Nevertheless, none of the relatives felt comfortable about buying a present for Baby X. The cousins who sent the baby a tiny football helmet would not come and visit any more. And the neighbors who sent a pink-flowered romper suit pulled their shades down when the Joneses passed their house.

The *Official Instruction Manual* had warned the new parents that this would happen, so they didn't fret about it. Besides, they were too busy with Baby X and the hundreds of different Xercises for treating it properly.

Ms. and Mr. Jones had to be Xtra careful about how they played with little X. They knew that if they kept bouncing it up in the air and saying how *strong* and *active* it was, they'd be treating it more like a boy than an X. But if all they did was cuddle it and kiss it and tell it how *sweet* and *dainty* it was, they'd be treating it more like a girl than an X.

On page 1,654 of the *Official Instruction Manual,* the scientists prescribed: "plenty of bouncing and plenty of cuddling, *both.* X ought to be strong and sweet and active. Forget about *dainty* altogether.

Meanwhile, the Joneses were worrying about other problems. Toys, for instance. And clothes. On his first shopping trip, Mr. Jones told the store clerk, "I need some clothes and toys for my new baby." The clerk smiled and said, "Well, now, is it a boy or a girl?" "It's an X," Mr. Jones said, smiling back. But the clerk got all red in the face and said huffily, "In *that* case, I'm afraid I can't help you, sir." So Mr. Jones wandered helplessly up and down the aisles trying to find what X needed. But everything in the store was piled up in sections marked "Boys" or "Girls." There were "Boys' Pajamas" and "Girls' Underwear" and "Boys' Fire Engines" and "Girls' Housekeeping Sets." Mr. Jones went home without buying anything for X. That night he and Ms. Jones consulted page 2,326 of the *Official Instruction Manual.* "Buy plenty of everything!" it said firmly.

So they bought plenty of sturdy blue pajamas in the Boys' Department and cheerful flowered underwear in the Girls' Department. And they bought all kinds of toys. A boy doll that made pee-pee and cried, "Pa-pa." And a girl doll that talked in three languages and said, "I am the Pres-i-dent of Gen-er-al Mo-tors." They also bought a storybook about a brave princess who rescued a handsome prince from his ivory tower, and another one about a sister and brother who grew up to be a baseball star and a ballet star, and you had to guess which was which.

The head scientists of Project Baby X checked all their purchases and told them to keep up the good work. They also reminded the Joneses to see page 4,629 of the *Manual,* where it said, "Never make Baby X feel *embarrassed* or *ashamed* about what it wants to play with. And if X gets dirty climbing rocks, never say 'Nice little Xes don't get dirty climbing rocks.' "

Likewise, it said, "If X falls down and cries, never say 'Brave little Xes don't cry.' Because, of course, nice little Xes *do* get dirty, and brave little Xes *do* cry. No matter how dirty X gets, or how hard it cries, don't worry. It's all part of the Xperiment."

Whenever the Joneses pushed Baby X's stroller in the park, smiling strangers would come over and coo: "Is that a boy or a girl?" The Joneses would smile back and say, "It's an X." The strangers would stop smiling then, and often snarl something nasty—as if the Joneses had snarled at *them.*

By the time X grew big enough to play with other children, the Joneses' troubles had grown bigger, too. Once a little girl grabbed X's shovel in the sandbox, and zonked X on the head with it. "Now, now, Tracy," the little girl's mother began to scold, "little girls mustn't hit little—" and she turned to ask X, "Are you a little boy or a little girl, dear?"

Mr. Jones, who was sitting near the sandbox, held his breath and crossed his fingers.

X smiled politely at the lady, even though X's head had never been zonked so hard in its life. "I'm a little X," X replied.

"You're a *what?*" the lady exclaimed angrily. "You're a little b-r-a-t, you mean!"

"But little girls mustn't hit little Xes, either!" said X, retrieving the shovel with another polite smile. "What good does hitting do, anyway?"

X's father, who was still holding his breath, finally let it out, uncrossed his fingers, and grinned back at X.

And at their next secret Project Baby X meeting, the scientists grinned, too. Baby X was doing fine.

But then it was time for X to start school. The Joneses were really worried about this, because school was even more full of rules for boys and girls, and there were no rules for Xes. The teacher would tell boys to form one line, and girls to form another line. There would be boys' games and girls' games, and boys' secrets and girls' secrets. The school library would have a list of recommended books for girls, and a different list of recommended books for boys. There would even be a bathroom marked BOYS and another one marked GIRLS. Pretty soon boys and girls would hardly talk to each other. What would happen to poor little X?

The Joneses spent weeks consulting their *Instruction Manual* (there were 249½ pages of advice under "First Day of School"), and attending urgent special conferences with the smart scientists of Project Baby X.

The scientists had to make sure that X's mother had taught X how to throw and catch a ball properly, and that X's father had been sure to teach X what to serve at a doll's tea party. X had to know how to shoot marbles and how to jump rope and, most of all, what to say when the Other Children asked whether X was a Boy or a Girl.

Finally, X was ready. The Joneses helped X button on a nice new pair of red-and-white checked overalls, and sharpened six pencils for X's nice new pencilbox, and marked X's name clearly on all the books in its nice new bookbag. X brushed its teeth and combed its hair, which just about covered its ears, and remembered to put a napkin in its lunchbox.

The Joneses had asked X's teacher if the class could line up alphabetically, instead of forming separate lines for boys and girls. And they had asked if X could use the principal's bathroom, because it wasn't marked anything except BATH ROOM. X's teacher promised to take care of all those problems. But nobody could help X with the biggest problem of all—Other Children.

Nobody in X's class had ever known an X before. What would they think? How would X make friends?

You couldn't tell what X was by studying its clothes—overalls don't even button right-to-left, like girls' clothes, or left-to-right, like boys' clothes. And you couldn't guess whether X had a girl's short haircut or a boy's long haircut. And it was very hard to tell by the games X liked to play. Either X played ball very well for a girl, or else X played house very well for a boy.

Some of the children tried to find out by asking X tricky questions, like "Who's your favorite sports star?" That was easy. X had two favorite sports stars: a girl jockey named Robyn Smith and a boy archery champion named Robin Hood. Then they asked, "What's your favorite TV program?" And that was even easier. X's favorite TV program was "Lassie," which stars a girl dog played by a boy dog.

When X said that its favorite toy was a doll, everyone decided that X must be a girl. But then X said that the doll was really a robot, and that X had computerized it, and that it was programmed to bake fudge brownies and then clean up the kitchen. After X told them that, the other children gave up guessing what X was. All they knew was they'd sure like to see X's doll.

After school, X wanted to play with the other children. "How about shooting some baskets in the gym?" X asked the girls. But all they did was make faces and giggle behind X's back.

"How about weaving some baskets in the arts and crafts room?" X asked the boys. But they all made faces and giggled behind X's back, too.

That night, Ms. and Mr. Jones asked X how things had gone at school. X told them sadly that the lessons were okay, but otherwise school was a terrible place for an X. It seemed as if Other Children would never want an X for a friend.

Once more, the Joneses reached for their *Instruction Manual.* Under "Other Children," they found the following message: "What did you Xpect? *Other Children* have to obey all the silly boy-girl rules, because their parents taught them to. Lucky X—you don't have to stick to the rules at all! All you have to do is be yourself. P.S. We're not saying it'll be easy."

X liked being itself. But X cried a lot that night, partly because it felt afraid. So X's father held X tight, and cuddled it, and couldn't help crying a little, too. And X's mother cheered them both up by reading an Xciting story about an enchanted prince called Sleeping Handsome, who woke up when Princess Charming kissed him.

The next morning, they all felt much better, and little X went back to school with a brave smile and a clean pair of red-and-white checked overalls.

There was a seven-letter-word spelling bee in class that day. And a seven-lap boys' relay race in the gym. And a seven-layer-cake baking contest in the girls' kitchen corner. X won the spelling bee. X also won the relay race. And X almost won the baking contest, except it forgot to light the oven. Which only proves that nobody's perfect.

One of the Other Children noticed something else, too. He said: "Winning or losing doesn't seem to count to X. X seems to have fun being good at boys' skills *and* girls' skills."

"Come to think of it," said another one of the Other Children, "maybe X is having twice as much fun as we are!"

So after school that day, the girl who beat X at the baking contest gave X a big slice of her prizewinning cake. And the boy X beat in the relay race asked X to race him home.

From then on, some really funny things began to happen. Susie, who sat next to X in class, suddenly refused to wear pink dresses to school any more. She insisted on wearing red-and-white checked overalls—just like X's. Overalls, she told her parents, were much better for climbing monkey bars.

Then Jim, the class football nut, started wheeling his little sister's doll carriage around the football field. He'd put on his entire football uniform, except for the helmet. Then he'd put the helmet *in* the carriage, lovingly tucked under an old set of shoulder pads. Then he'd start jogging around the field, pushing the carriage and singing "Rockabye Baby" to his football helmet. He told his family that X did the same thing, so it must be okay. After all, X was now the team's star quarterback.

Susie's parents were horrified by her behavior, and Jim's parents were worried sick about his. But the worst came when the twins, Joe and Peggy, decided to share everything with each other. Peggy used Joe's hockey skates, and his microscope, and took half his newspaper route. Joe used Peggy's needlepoint kit, and her cookbooks, and took two of her three baby-sitting jobs. Peggy started running the lawn mower, and Joe started running the vacuum cleaner.

Their parents weren't one bit pleased with Peggy's wonderful biology experiments, or with Joe's terrific needlepoint pillows. They didn't care that Peggy mowed the lawn better, and that Joe vacuumed the carpet better. In fact, they were furious. It's all that little X's fault, they agreed. Just because X doesn't know what it is, or what it's supposed to be, it wants to get everybody *else* mixed up, too!

Peggy and Joe were forbidden to play with X anymore. So was Susie, and then Jim, and then all the Other Children. But it was too late; the Other Children stayed mixed up and happy and free, and refused to go back to the way they'd been before X.

Finally, Joe and Peggy's parents decided to call an emergency meeting of the school's Parents' Association, to discuss "The X Problem." They sent a report to the principal stating that X was a "disruptive influence." They demanded immediate action. The Joneses, they said, should be *forced* to tell whether X was a boy or a girl. And then X should be *forced* to behave like whichever it was. If the Joneses refused to tell, the Parents' Association said, then X must take an Xamination. The school psychiatrist must Xamine it physically and mentally, and issue a full report. If X's test showed it was a boy, it would have to obey all the boys' rules. If it proved to be a girl, X would have to obey all the girls' rules.

And if X turned out to be some kind of mixed-up misfit, then X should be Xpelled from the school. Immediately!

The principal was very upset. Disruptive influence? Mixed-up misfit? But X was an Xcellent student. All the teachers said it was a delight to have X in their classes. X was president of the student council. X had won first prize in the talent show, and second prize in the art show, and honorable mention in the science fair, and six athletic events on field day, including the potato race.

Nevertheless, insisted the Parents' Association, X is a Problem Child. X is the Biggest Problem Child we have ever seen!

So the principal reluctantly notified X's parents that numerous complaints about X's behavior had come to the school's attention. And that after the psychiatrist's Xamination, the school would decide what to do about X.

The Joneses reported this at once to the scientists, who referred them to page 85,759 of the *Instruction Manual.* "Sooner or later," it said, "X will have to be Xamined by a psychiatrist. This may be the only way any of us will know for sure whether X is mixed up—or whether everyone else is."

The night before X was to be Xamined, the Joneses tried not to let X see how worried they were. "What if—?" Mr. Jones would say. And Ms. Jones would reply, "No use worrying." Then a few minutes later, Ms. Jones would say, "What if—?" and Mr. Jones would reply, "No use worrying."

X just smiled at them both, and hugged them hard and didn't say much of anything. X was thinking. What if—? And then X thought: No use worrying.

At Xactly 9 o'clock the next day, X reported to the school psychiatrist's office. The principal, along with a committee from the Parents' Association, X's teacher, X's classmates, and Ms. and Mr. Jones, waited in the hall outside. Nobody knew the details of the tests X was to be given, but everybody knew they'd be *very* hard, and that they'd reveal Xactly what everyone wanted to know about X, but were afraid to ask.

It was terribly quiet in the hall. Almost spooky. Once in a while, they would hear a strange noise inside the room. There were buzzes. And a beep or two. And several bells. An occasional light would flash under the door. The Joneses thought it was a white light, but the principal thought it was blue. Two or three children swore it was either yellow or green. And the Parents' Committee missed it completely.

Through it all, you could hear the psychiatrist's low voice, asking hundreds of questions, and X's higher voice, answering hundreds of answers.

The whole thing took so long that everyone knew it must be the most complete Xamination anyone had ever had to take. Poor X, the Joneses thought. Serves X right, the Parents' Committee thought. I wouldn't like to be in X's overalls right now, the children thought.

At last, the door opened. Everyone crowded around to hear the results. X didn't look any different: in fact, X was smiling. But the psychiatrist looked terrible. He looked as if he was crying! "What happened?" everyone began shouting. Had X done something disgraceful? "I wouldn't be a bit surprised!" muttered Peggy and Joe's parents. "Did X flunk the *whole* test?" cried Susie's parents, "Or just the most important part?" yelled Jim's parents.

"Oh, dear," sighed Mr. Jones.

"Oh, dear," sighed Ms. Jones.

"*Sssh,*" ssshed the principal. "The psychiatrist is trying to speak."

Wiping his eyes and clearing his throat, the psychiatrist began, in a hoarse whisper. "In my opinion," he whispered—you could tell he must be very upset— "in my opinion, young X here—"

"Yes? Yes?" shouted a parent impatiently.

"*Sssh!*" ssshed the principal.

"Young *Sssh* here, I mean young X," said the doctor, frowning, "is just about—"

"Just about *what?* Let's have it!" shouted another parent.

" . . . just about the *least* mixed-up child I've ever Xamined!" said the psychiatrist.

"Yay for X!" yelled one of the children. And then the others began yelling, too. Clapping and cheering and jumping up and down.

"*SSSH!*" SSShed the principal, but nobody did.

The Parents' Committee was angry and bewildered. How *could* X have passed the whole Xamination? Didn't X have an *identity* problem? Wasn't X mixed up at *all?* Wasn't X *any* kind of a misfit? How could it *not* be, when it didn't even *know* what it was? And why was the psychiatrist crying?

Actually, he had stopped crying and was smiling politely through his tears. "Don't you see?" he said. "I'm crying because it's wonderful! X has absolutely no identity problem! X isn't one bit mixed up! As for being a misfit—ridiculous! X knows perfectly well what it is! Don't you, X?" The doctor winked. X winked back.

"But what *is* X?" shrieked Peggy and Joe's parents. "*We* still want to know what it is!"

"Ah, yes," said the doctor, winking again. "Well, don't worry. You'll all know one of these days. And you won't need me to tell you."

"What? What does he mean?" some of the parents grumbled suspiciously.

Susie and Peggy and Joe all answered at once. "He means that by the time X's sex matters, it won't be a secret any more!"

With that, the doctor began to push through the crowd toward X's parents. "How do you do," he said, somewhat stiffly. And then he reached out to hug them both. "If I ever have an X of my own," he whispered, "I sure hope you'll lend me your instruction manual."

Needless to say, the Joneses were very happy. The Project Baby X scientists were rather pleased, too. So were Susie, Jim, Peggy, Joe, and all the Other Children. The Parents' Association wasn't, but they had promised to accept the psychiatrist's report, and not make any more trouble. They even invited Ms. and Mr. Jones to become honorary members, which they did.

Later that day, all X's friends put on their red-and-white checked overalls and went over to see X. They found X in the back yard, playing with a very tiny baby that none of them had ever seen before. The baby was wearing very tiny red-and-white checked overalls.

"How do you like our new baby?" X asked the Other Children proudly.

"It's got cute dimples." said Jim.

"It's got husky biceps, too," said Susie.

"What kind of baby is it?" asked Joe and Peggy.

X frowned at them. "Can't you tell?" Then X broke into a big, mischievous grin. *"It's a Y!"*

14

THE EDUCATION OF
A TORTURER

Janice T. Gibson and Mika Haritos-Fatouros (1986)

In 1950, Adorno, Frenkel-Brunswik, Levinson, and Sanford published *The Authoritarian Personality*, a scientific investigation that attempted to explain how human beings could participate in such atrocities as occurred in Nazi Germany during World War II. Adorno and his colleagues suggested that certain types of personalities were more likely to be obedient and accepting of authority. This was a comforting hypothesis, because individuals could say to themselves, "*I'm* not an authoritarian so *I* could never commit such evil deeds."

Milgram's landmark 1963 study, with its strong situational explanation, removes that comfortable self-protection for most individuals. In fact, 65 percent of the subjects in Milgrams's first experiment obeyed the experimenter's requests and delivered shock at the highest level on the shock generator, at which point the victim appeared to be dead, or a least unconscious. Milgram also examined personality differences between obedient and disobedient subjects. Despite persistent efforts, the researchers could find only one personality characteristic (authoritarianism) that would predict obedience (Elms, 1972). Thus, Milgram's studies of obedient behavior strongly suggest the power of the situation. Authoritarian personality may predict obedience somewhat, but the situational constraints are powerful indeed.

In their examination of Greek military police who were trained as torturers, Gibson and Haritos-Fatouros chronicle the step-by-step process by which obedience to authority and willingness to engage in unthinkable actions can be situationally developed without too much difficulty. It turns out that examples of this are fairly easy to find; indeed, examples that Gibson and Haritos-Fatouros

Source: Reprinted from *Psychology Today,* November, 1986, 50–58. Reprinted with permission from *Psychology Today* magazine. Copyright © 1986 (Sussex Publishers, Inc.).

use range from the U.S. Marines to classroom demonstrations. The ease with which many or all of us could be trained to commit acts which we presently consider unthinkable should cause us to reflect carefully on the power of the situation and the power of other individuals' beliefs and behavior upon us. For a more optimistic angle on this issue, see the reading by Fogelman and Wiener (Reading 30).

Torture—for whatever purpose and in whatever name—requires a torturer, an individual responsible for planning and causing pain to others. "A man's hands are shackled behind him, his eyes blindfolded," wrote Argentine journalist Jacobo Timerman about his torture by Argentine army extremists. "No one says a word. Blows are showered. . . . [He is] stripped, doused with water, tied. . . . And the application of electric shocks begins. It's impossible to shout—you howl." The governments of at least 90 countries use similar methods to torture people all over the world, Amnesty International reports.

What kind of person can behave so monstrously to another human being? A sadist or sexual deviant? Someone with an authoritarian upbringing or who was abused by parents? A disturbed personality affected somehow by hereditary characteristics?

On the contrary, the Nazis who tortured and killed millions during World War II "weren't sadists or killers by nature," Hannah Arendt reported in her book *Eichmann In Jerusalem*. Many studies of Nazi behavior concluded that monstrous acts, despite their horrors, were often simply a matter of faithful bureaucrats slavishly following orders.

In a 1976 study, University of Florida psychologist Molly Harrower asked 15 Rorschach experts to examine inkblot test reports from Adolph Eichmann, Rudolf Hess, Hermann Goering and five other Nazi war criminals, made just before their trials at Nuremberg. She also sent the specialists Rorschach reports from eight Americans, some with well-adjusted personalities and some who were severely disturbed, without revealing the individuals' identities. The experts were unable to distinguish the Nazis from the Americans and judged an equal number of both to be well-adjusted. The horror that emerges is the likelihood that torturers are not freaks; they are ordinary people.

Obedience to what we call the "authority of violence" often plays an important role in pushing ordinary people to commit cruel, violent and even fatal acts. During wartime, for example, soldiers will follow orders to kill unarmed civilians. Here, we will look at the way obedience and other factors combine to produce willing torturers.

Twenty-five years ago, the late psychologist Stanley Milgram demonstrated convincingly that people unlikely to be cruel in everyday life will administer pain if they are told to by someone in authority. In a famous experiment, Milgram had men wearing laboratory coats direct average American adults to inflict a series of electric shocks on other people. No real shocks were given and the "victims" were acting, but the people didn't know this. They were told that the purpose of the study was to measure the effects of punishment on learning. Obediently, 65 percent of them used what they thought were dangerously high levels of shocks when the experimenter told them to. While they were less likely to administer these supposed shocks as they were moved closer to their victims, almost one-third of them continued to shock when they were close enough to touch.

This readiness to torture is not limited to Americans. Following Milgram's lead, other researchers found that people of all ages, from a wide range of countries, were willing to shock others even when they had nothing to gain by complying with the command or nothing to lose by refusing it. So long as someone else, an authority figure, was responsible for the final outcome of the experiment, almost no one absolutely refused to administer shocks. Each study also found, as Milgram had, that some people would give shocks even when the decision was left up to them.

Milgram proposed that the reasons people obey or disobey authority fall into three categories. The first is personal history: family or school backgrounds that encourage obedience or defiance. The second, which he called "binding," is made up of ongoing experiences that make people feel comfortable when they obey authority. Strain, the third category, consists of bad feelings from unpleasant experiences connected with obedience. Milgram argued that when the binding factors are more powerful than the strain of cooperating, people will do as they are told. When the strain is greater, they are more likely to disobey.

This may explain short-term obedience in the laboratory, but it doesn't explain prolonged patterns of torture during wartime or under some political regimes. Repeatedly, torturers in Argentina and elsewhere performed acts that most of us consider repugnant, and in time this should have placed enough strain on them to prevent their obedience. It didn't. Nor does Milgram's theory explain undirected cruel or violent acts, which occur even when no authority orders them. For this, we have developed a more comprehensive learning model; for torture, we discovered, can be taught (see "Teaching to Torment," this article).

We studied the procedures used to train Greek military police as torturers during that country's military regime from 1967 through 1974. We examined the official testimonies of 21 former soldiers in the ESA (Army Police Corps) given at their 1975 criminal trials in Athens; in addition, Haritos-Fatouros conducted in-depth interviews with 16 of them after their trials. In many cases, these men had been convicted and had completed prison sentences. They were all leading normal lives when interviewed. One was a university graduate, five were graduates of higher technical institutes, nine had completed at least their second year of high school and only one had no more than a primary school education.

All of these men had been drafted, first into regular military service and then into specialized units that required servicemen to torture prisoners. We found no record of delinquent or disturbed behavior before their military service. However, we did find several features of the soldiers' training that helped to turn them into willing and able torturers.

The initial screening for torturers was primarily based on physical strength and "appropriate" political beliefs, which simply meant that the recruits and their families were anticommunists. This ensured that the men had hostile attitudes toward potential victims from the very beginning.

Once they were actually serving as military police, the men were also screened for other attributes. According to former torturer Michaelis Petrou, "The most important criterion was that you had to keep your mouth shut. Second, you had to show aggression. Third, you had to be intelligent and strong. Fourth, you had to be 'their man,' which meant that you would report on the others serving with you, that [the officers] could trust you and that you would follow their orders blindly."

Binding the recruits to the authority of ESA began in basic training, with physically brutal initiation rites. Recruits themselves were cursed, punched, kicked and flogged. They were forced to run until they collapsed and prevented from relieving themselves for long stretches of time. They were required to swear allegiance to a symbol of authority used by the regime (a poster of a soldier superimposed on a large phoenix rising from its own ashes), and they had to promise on their knees to obey their commander-in-chief and the military revolution.

While being harassed and beaten by their officers, servicemen were repeatedly told how fortunate they were to have joined the ESA, the strongest and most important support of the regime. They were told that an ESA serviceman's action is never questioned: "You can even flog a major." In-group language helped the men to develop elitist attitudes. Servicemen used nicknames for one another and, later, they used them for victims and for the different methods of torture. "Tea party" meant the beating of a prisoner by a group of military police using their fists, and "tea party with toast" meant more severe group beatings using clubs. Gradually, the recruits came to speak of all people who were not in their group, parents and families included, as belonging to the "outside world."

The strain of obedience on the recruits was reduced in several ways. During basic training, they were given daily "national ethical education" lectures that included indoctrination against communism and enemies of the state. During more advanced training, the recruits were constantly reminded that the prisoners were "worms," and that they had to "crush" them. One man reported that when he was torturing prisoners later, he caught himself repeating phrases like "bloody communists!" that he had heard in the lectures.

The military police used a carrot-and-stick method to further diminish the recruits' uneasiness about torture. There were many rewards, such as relaxed military rules after training was completed, and torturers often weren't punished for leaving camp without permission. They were allowed to wear civilian clothes, to keep their hair long and to drive military police cars for their personal use. Torturers were frequently given a leave of absence after they forced a confession from a prisoner. They had many economic benefits as well, including free bus rides and restaurant meals and job placement when military service was over. These were the carrots.

The sticks consisted of the constant harassment, threats and punishment for disobedience. The men were threatened and intimidated, first by their trainers, then later by senior servicemen. "An officer used to tell us that if a warder helps a prisoner, he will take the prisoner's place and the whole platoon will flog him," one man recalled. Soldiers spied on one another, and even the most successful torturers said that they were constantly afraid.

"You will learn to love pain," one officer promised a recruit. Sensitivity to torture was blunted in several steps. First, the men had to endure it themselves, as if torture were a normal act. The beatings and other torments inflicted on them continued and

TEACHING TO TORMENT

There are several ways to teach people to do the unthinkable, and we have developed a model to explain how they are used. We have also found that college fraternities, although they are far removed from the grim world of torture and violent combat, use similar methods for initiating new members, to ensure their faithfulness to the fraternity's rules and values. However, this unthinking loyalty can sometimes lead to dangerous actions: Over the past 10 years, there have been countless injuries during fraternity initiations and 39 deaths. These training techniques are designed to instill unquestioning obedience in people, but they can easily be a guide for an intensive course in torture.

1) **Screening to find the best prospects:** normal, well-adjusted people with the physical, intellectual and, in some cases, political attributes necessary for the task.
2) **Techniques to increase binding among these prospects:**

- Initiation rites to isolate people from society and introduce them to a new social order, with different rules and values.
- Elitist attitudes and "in-group" language, which highlight the differences between the group and the rest of society.

3) **Techniques to reduce the strain of obedience:**

- Blaming and dehumanizing the victims, so it is less disturbing to harm them.
- Harassment, the constant physical and psychological intimidation that prevents logical thinking and promotes the instinctive responses needed for acts of inhuman cruelty.
- Rewards for obedience and punishments for not cooperating.
- Social modeling by watching other group members commit violent acts and then receive rewards.
- Systematic desensitization to repugnant acts by gradual exposure to them, so they appear routine and normal despite conflicts with previous moral standards.

became worse. Next, the servicemen chosen for the Persecution Section, the unit that tortured political prisoners, were brought into contact with the prisoners by carrying food to their cells. The new men watched veteran soldiers torture prisoners, while they stood guard. Occasionally, the veterans would order them to give the prisoners "some blows."

At the next step, the men were required to participate in group beatings. Later, they were told to use a variety of torture methods on the prisoners. The final step, the appointment to prison warder or chief torturer, was announced suddenly by the commander-in-chief, leaving the men no time to reflect on their new duties.

The Greek example illustrates how the ability to torture can be taught. Training that increases binding and reduces strain can cause decent people to commit acts, often over long periods of time, that otherwise would be unthinkable for them. Similar techniques can be found in military training all over the world, when the intent is to teach soldiers to kill or perform some other repellent act. We conducted extensive interviews with soldiers and exsoldiers in the U.S. Marines and the Green Berets, and we found that all the steps in our training model were part and parcel of elite American military training. Soldiers are screened for intellectual and physical ability, achievement and mental health. Binding begins in basic training, with initiation rites that isolate trainees from society, introduce them to new rules and values and leave them little time for clear thinking after exhausting physical exercise and scant sleep. Harassment plays an important role, and soldiers are severely punished for disobedience, with demerits, verbal abuse, hours of calisthenics and loss of eating, sleeping and other privileges.

Military training gradually desensitizes soldiers to violence and reduces the strain normally created by repugnant acts. Their revulsion is diminished by screaming chants and songs about violence and killing during marches and runs. The enemy is given derogatory names and portrayed as less than human; this makes it easier to kill them. Completing the toughest possible training and being rewarded by "making it" in an elite corps bring the soldiers confidence and pride, and those who accomplish this feel they can do anything. "Although I tried to avoid killing, I learned to have confidence in myself and was never afraid," said a former Green Beret who served in Vietnam. "It was part of the job. . . . Anyone who goes through that kind of training could do it."

The effectiveness of these techniques, as several researchers have shown, is not limited to the army. History teacher Ronald Jones started what he called the Third Wave movement as a classroom experiment to show his high school students how people might have become Nazis in World War II. Jones began the Third Wave demonstration by requiring students to stand at attention in a unique new posture and follow strict new rules. He required students to stand beside their desks when asking or answering questions and to begin each statement by saying, "Mr. Jones." The students obeyed. He then required them to shout slogans, "Strength through discipline!" and "Strength through community!" Jones created a salute for class members that he called the Third Wave: the right hand raised to the shoulder with fingers curled. The salute had no meaning, but it served as a symbol of group belonging and a way of isolating members from outsiders.

The organization expanded quickly from 20 original members to 100. The teacher issued membership cards and assigned students to report members who didn't comply with the new rules. Dutifully, 20 students pointed accusing fingers at their classmates.

Then Jones announced that the Third Wave was a "nationwide movement to find students willing to fight for political change," and he organized a rally, which drew a crowd of 200 students. At the rally, after getting students to salute and shout slogans on command, Jones explained the true reasons behind the Third Wave demonstration. Like the Nazis before them, Jones pointed out, "You bargained your freedom for the comfort of discipline."

The students, at an age when group belonging was very important to them, made good candidates for training. Jones didn't teach his students to commit atrocities, and the Third Wave lasted for only five days; in that time, however, Jones created an obedient group that resembled in many ways the Nazi youth groups of World War II (see "The Third Wave: Nazism in a High School," *Psychology Today,* July 1976).

Psychologists Craig Haney, W. Curtis Banks and Philip Zimbardo went even further in a remarkable simulation of prison life done at Stanford University. With no special training and in only six days' time, they changed typical university students into controlling, abusive guards and servile prisoners.

The students who agreed to participate were chosen randomly to be guards or prisoners. The mock guards were given uniforms and nightsticks and told to act as guards. Prisoners were treated as dangerous criminals: Local police rounded them up, fingerprinted and booked them and brought them to a simulated cellblock in the basement of the university psychology department. Uniformed guards made them remove their clothing, deloused them, gave them prison uniforms and put them in cells.

The two groups of students, originally found to be very similar in most respects, showed striking changes within one week. Prisoners became passive, dependent and helpless. In contrast, guards expressed feelings of power, status and group belonging. They were aggressive and abusive within the prison, insulting and bullying the prisoners. Some guards reported later that they had enjoyed their power, while others said they had not thought they were capable of behaving as they had. They were surprised and dismayed at what they had done: "It was degrading. . . . To me, those things are sick. But they [the prisoners] did everything I said. They abused each other because I requested them to. No one questioned my authority at all."

The guards' behavior was similar in two important ways to that of the Greek torturers. First, they dehumanized their victims. Second, like the torturers, the guards were abusive only when they were within the prison walls. They could act reasonably outside the prisons because the two prison influences of binding and reduced strain were absent.

All these changes at Stanford occurred with no special training, but the techniques we have outlined were still present. Even without training, the student guards "knew" from television and movies that they were supposed to punish prisoners; they "knew" they were supposed to feel superior; and they "knew" they were supposed to blame their victims. Their own behavior and that of their peers gradually numbed their sensitivity to what they were doing, and they were rewarded by the power they had over their prisoners.

There is no evidence that such short-term experiments produce lasting effects. None were reported from either the Third Wave demonstration or the Stanford University simulation. The Stanford study, however, was cut short when depression, crying and psychosomatic illnesses began to appear among the students. And studies of Vietnam veterans have revealed that committing abhorrent acts, even under the extreme conditions of war, can lead to long-term problems. In one study of 130 Vietnam veterans who came to a therapist for help, almost 30 percent of them were concerned about violent acts they had committed while in the service. The veterans reported feelings of anxiety, guilt, depression and an inability to carry on intimate relationships. In a similar fashion, after the fall of the Greek dictatorship in 1974, former torturers began to report nightmares, irritability and episodes of depression.

"Torturing became a job," said former Greek torturer Petrou. "If the officers ordered you to beat, you beat. If they ordered you to stop, you stopped. You never thought you could do otherwise." His comments bear a disturbing resemblance to the feelings expressed by a Stanford guard: "When I was doing it, I didn't feel regret. . . . I didn't feel guilt. Only afterwards, when I began to reflect . . . did it begin to dawn on me that this was a part of me I hadn't known before."

We do not believe that torture came naturally to any of these young men. Haritos-Fatouros found no evidence of sadistic, abusive or authoritarian behavior in the Greek soldiers' histories prior to their training. This, together with our study of Marine training and the Stanford and Third Wave studies, leads to the conclusion that torturers have normal personalities. Any of us, in a similar situation, might be capable of the same cruelty. One probably cannot train a deranged sadist to be an effective torturer or killer. He must be in complete control of himself while on the job.

15

THE TRIGGERS
OF INFLUENCE

Robert B. Cialdini (1984)

Almost as soon as people began to study social influence, research focused on ways to persuade others and ultimately to change their behavior. We now have a tradition in attitude change research, with its heyday in the 1950s by Hovland and his colleagues (e.g., Hovland, 1951; Hovland, Janis, & Kelley, 1953; Hovland, Lumsdaine, & Sheffield, 1949). These researchers focused on four major variables: the communicator (source), the recipient of the message (audience), the message itself, and the manner in which the message is communicated (see also Myers's Module 16). This area was re-energized by the work of Petty and Cacioppo in the late 1970s who developed an elegantly simple model describing and incorporating both the central and peripheral routes to persuasion.

Cialdini's interesting article adds to potential sources of influence by proposing that social behaviors may, at times, be somewhat automatic, triggered by external stimuli. Readers may note the sociobiological overtones when encountering terminology such as fixed action patterns (one popular way to describe the stereotyped and automatic behavior that sometimes occurs in animals, especially birds and fish). Whether one agrees with a biological explanation for social behaviors in humans, this article makes for stimulating reading and is appropriate to consider for all of us, who live in a culture where we are continually exposed to a vast barrage of advertising designed (often with the help of social psychologists) to influence us, persuade us, and ultimately to shape and motivate our consumer behavior. Leaf through a magazine or watch television for a while and see if you can pick up on images and ideas that are designed to trigger your behaviors. In what ways and by what means are

Source: Reprinted from *Psychology Today*, February, 1984, 40–45. Reprinted with permission from *Psychology Today* magazine. Copyright © 1984 (Sussex Publishers, Inc.).

advertisers trying to convince you that their products and services can meet your needs (or even perhaps meet needs that you heretofore did not know you had)?

I got a phone call one day from a friend who owns an Indian jewelry store in Arizona. Something fascinating had just happened, and she thought that, as a psychologist, I might be able to explain it to her. Her story involved an allotment of turquoise jewelry that hadn't sold. It was the peak of the tourist season, the store was unusually full of customers and the turquoise pieces were worth at least what she was asking; still, they hadn't moved. My friend had tried calling attention to the pieces by shifting them to a more central display area, and had told her sales staff to push the items hard—all without success.

Finally, just before leaving on a buying trip, she scribbled an exasperated note to her head saleswoman, "Everything in this case, price × ½," hoping just to be rid of the offending pieces, even at a loss. When she returned a few days later, every article had been sold. But because the saleswoman had read the "½" in her scrawled message as a "2," the entire allotment had sold at twice the original price!

That's when she called me. I thought I knew what had happened: She had unknowingly triggered a powerful automatic behavior pattern—metaphorically, a programmed tape—in her customers. Many successful salesmen and politicians, among others, use these subtle social triggers to influence our actions.

For me to explain things properly, I told my friend, she would have to listen to stories about mother turkeys and macho robins. The stories come from the relatively new science of ethology: the study of animals in their natural settings. Turkeys are good mothers—loving, watchful and protective. They spend much of their time tending, warming, cleaning and huddling the young beneath them. But all this care has an odd twist. It is triggered by just one thing, the "cheep-cheep" sound made by turkey chicks. Smell, touch and appearance seem to play minor roles. If a chick cheeps, its mother will be caring; if not, she will ignore or sometimes kill it.

Animal researchers have demonstrated dramatically how much mother turkeys rely on this one sound by bringing in a stuffed polecat. For a mother turkey, a polecat is a natural enemy she greets with squawking, pecking, clawing rage. Even a stuffed model of a polecat drawn by a string generated an immediate, furious attack. But when the same model carried inside it a small recorder that cheeped, the mother not only accepted the oncoming polecat but gathered it beneath her. When the machine was turned off, she again attacked the polecat model viciously.

How ridiculous the turkey seems under these circumstances. She will not attack a natural enemy just because it cheeps, and mistreat or murder one of her own chicks just because it does not. Ethologists tell us, however, that this sort of reaction is not unique to the turkey. They have identified such regular, blindly mechanical patterns of action in a wide variety of species. These fixed patterns can be elaborate, involving entire courtship or mating rituals. The behavior occurs in virtually the same fashion and in the same order every time, almost as if the patterns were recorded on tapes within the animal. When the situation calls for courtship, the courtship tape gets played; when the situation calls for mothering, the maternal behavior tape snaps on. Click, and the appropriate tape is activated; whirr, and out rolls the standard sequence of behavior.

The tapes are usually triggered not by an entire situation but by one aspect of it. When a male animal acts to defend his territory, for instance, it is not simply the intrusion of another male that cues the reaction of vigilance, threat and combat, but some specific feature of the intruder. Sometimes the trigger feature is a shade of color. Ethologists have found that a male robin will vigorously attack a clump of robin-red breast feathers placed in its territory, while virtually ignoring a perfect stuffed replica of a male robin without red breast feathers; in another species of bird, the bluethroat, the trigger for territorial defense is a specific shade of blue breast feathers. (Some animals pull these behavioral triggers for their own benefit.)

What do easily fooled turkeys and robins have to do with overpriced turquoise and spendthrift tourists? Two things. First, the fixed-action patterns of the birds nearly always work well. For example, because only healthy, normal turkey chicks make the peculiar sound of baby turkeys, it makes sense for mother turkeys to respond maternally to the cheep. It takes a trickster like a scientist to make her tape-like response seem silly. Second, we humans have our preprogrammed tapes, too, and although they usually work to our advantage, the trigger features that activate them can be used to dupe us into playing them at the wrong times.

Consider the jewelry store customers. It is easy to fault them for making foolish buying decisions. But a closer look offers a kinder view. They were people who had been brought up on the rule, "You get what you pay for" and had seen the rule confirmed over and over again until they had translated it into the stereo-type, "Expensive equals good." So, when they wanted good turquoise jewelry but didn't know much about turquoise, they relied on the stereotype to guide their buying decisions. Since price had become a trigger feature for quality, a dramatic increase in price led the buyers to see the turquoise pieces as more valuable and desirable.

What they were doing, without realizing it, was taking an informed gamble. Since they didn't have the time or inclination to stack the odds in their favor by studying all the factors and qualities that indicate what turquoise jewelry is worth, they counted on the one feature they always associated with quality. They were betting that price alone would tell them all they needed to know. This time, because someone mistook a ½ for a 2, they bet wrong. But in the long run, for all the past and future situations of their lives, their approach made sense.

Social psychologist Ellen J. Langer of Harvard University demonstrated another frequent trigger for reflexive human behavior: the word "because." We all know that "because" usually precedes a reason, and we all prefer to have reasons for what we do. Langer went up to people waiting to use a copying machine and explained: "Excuse me, I have five pages. May I use the Xerox machine because I'm in a rush?" Ninety-four percent of those she asked let her move ahead of them in line.

Compare this to what happened when she made the request without giving a good reason: "Excuse me, I have five pages. May I use the Xerox machine?" Under those circumstances, only 60 percent of the people stepped aside. The crucial difference between the two requests would seem to be the additional information provided by the explanation "because I'm in a rush."

But a third type of request showed that the explanation was not really the key: "Excuse me, I have five pages. May I use the Xerox machine because I have to make some copies?" This nonexplanatory stating of the obvious worked as well as the "I'm-in-a-rush" explanation. Just as the "cheep-cheep" of turkey chicks triggered an automatic mothering response, even when it came from a polecat, so did the word "because" trigger automatic compliance from nearly all the people (93 percent) in the copier line.

Although some of Langer's other studies show that there are many situations in which humans don't react in this mechanical way, it is surprising how often they do. The reason is that such automatic reactions are often the most efficient form of behavior, and at other times are virtually unavoidable. You and I exist in an extraordinarily complicated environment, and to deal with it, we need shortcuts. We can't recognize and analyze everything about each person, event and situation we encounter in even one day. We haven't the time, energy or capacity to do so. Instead, we must often use our stereotypes, our rules of thumb, to classify things according to a few key features and then respond automatically to these triggers.

Sometimes the behavior will not be appropriate; not even the best stereotypes and trigger features work every time. But we accept their imperfection because without them we would stand frozen—cataloging, appraising and calibrating—as the time for action sped by and away. And as the stimulation saturating our lives continues to grow more intricate and variable, we will have to depend increasingly on our shortcuts to handle it all.

Since we rely so much on our automatic behavior patterns, it's important that we understand them as well as we can and recognize that they make us vulnerable to others who trigger these reactions for their own purposes. Unlike the mostly instinctive response sequences of other animals, our human tapes usually develop from psychological principles or stereotypes that we have learned to accept. Although they vary in their force, some of the principles possess a tremendous ability to direct human action. We have been influenced by them since so early in our lives, and they have moved us so pervasively since then, that we rarely perceive how much real power they have or realize when they are being used to manipulate us.

Remember my friend the jewelry store owner? Although she benefited accidentally the first time, she soon began exploiting the "expensive-equals-good" stereotype regularly and intentionally during the tourist season. If an item is moving slowly, she first increases its price substantially. When this works, as it often does, the result is an enormous profit margin. If it doesn't work, she marks the article "Reduced from ____" and sells it at the original price. She thus takes advantage of the "expensive-equals-good" reaction to the inflated figure, and at the same time appeals to the human lust for a bargain.

One factor that makes these stereotypes and psychological triggers so effective is their subtlety. The person using them simply releases the great stores of influence that already exist in the situation and directs them toward the intended target. The approach is similar to that of the Japanese martial art form of judo, in which experts use their own strength only minimally against their opponents. Instead, they exploit the power inherent in such naturally present principles as gravity, leverage, momentum and inertia.

Knowing how and where to apply these principles, a judo expert can easily defeat a physically stronger rival. In the same way, people who exploit the weapons of interpersonal influence do so while exerting little personal force. This allows the exploiters an enormous additional benefit—the ability to manipulate without the appearance of manipulation. Even their victims usually see their compliance as due to the situation or their own wishes rather than to the designs of the person who profits from the compliance.

One popular form of social manipulation plays on a well-established tenet of human perception, the contrast principle. Simply put, it states that if we are presented with two things, one after the other, and the second item is somewhat different from the first, we tend to perceive it as more different than it really is. If we lift a light object first, for example, and then a heavier one, the second object seems heavier than if we had lifted it without first trying the light one.

The same principle applies to the perception of heat, as teachers in psychophysics laboratories prefer that their students discover firsthand. Each one takes a turn sitting in front of three pails of water: one cold, one room temperature and one hot. After the student places one hand in the cold water and the other in the hot, the teacher asks him to place both hands in the third pail simultaneously. The student's look of bewilderment tells the story. The hand that had been in hot water feels like it is now in cold water, and vice versa.

Many experiments have shown that the contrast principle applies to psychological as well as physical matters. For example, studies at Arizona State and Montana State universities suggest that we are likely to be less satisfied with the attractiveness of our own dates or mates because of how the media bombard us with pictures of unrealistically attractive models. In one study, college students rated a picture of an average-looking member of the opposite sex as less attractive if they had first looked through the ads in popular magazines. In another experiment, male students rated the photo of a potential blind date. Those who did so while watching the "Charlie's Angels" television show saw the blind date as less attractive than those who rated her who weren't watching television. Apparently, the contrast with the beauty of the "angels" made the blind date seem less attractive.

Influencing others by applying the contrast principle is standard procedure in many types of selling. Consider the man who walks into a fashionable clothing store and says that he wants to buy a three-piece suit and a sweater. If you were the salesperson, which should you show him first? Common sense might suggest selling the sweater first: If a man has just spent a lot of money for a suit, he may be reluctant to spend very much more in the purchase of a sweater. But good clothing salesmen know better and do what the contrast principle suggests: Sell the suit first, because when it comes time to look at sweaters, even expensive ones won't seem as costly in comparison.

A man might balk at the idea of spending $75 for a sweater, but if he has just bought a $275 suit, a $75 sweater does not seem excessive. The same principle applies when a man buys the accessories (shirt, shoes, belt and so on) to go with his new suit. As the sales motivation analysts Robert Whitney and Thomas Rubin explain in their book, *The New Psychology of Persuasion and Motivation in Selling,* "Even when a man enters a clothing store with the express purpose of purchasing a suit, he will almost always pay more for whatever accessories he buys if he buys them after the suit purchase than before."

If salespeople don't present the expensive item first, they turn the contrast principle against themselves. Offering an inexpensive product first, followed by an expensive one, makes the expensive item seem even costlier.

The contrast technique is used effectively by other kinds of salesmen, too, as I found while I was investigating the compliance tactics of real estate companies. To learn the ropes, I accompanied a salesman on a weekend of showing houses to prospective home-buyers. One thing I noticed quickly was that the salesman—let's call him Phil—would always show potential customers a couple of undesirable houses first, before getting to the ones he really hoped to sell. I asked him about it, and he laughed. They were what he called "set-up" properties, run-down houses the company maintained on its list at inflated prices. Not all of the sales staff made use of the set-up houses, but Phil did. He said he liked to watch his prospects' "eyes light up" when he showed the place he really wanted to sell after they had seen the run-down houses. "The house I have them spotted for looks really great after they've first looked at a couple of dumps."

Automobile dealers use the contrast principle in a different way, waiting until the price for a new car has been negotiated before suggesting options that might be added. In the wake of a $10,000 deal, the couple of hundred dollars required for a nicety like an FM radio seems almost trivial, as does the cost of tinted windows, dual sideview mirrors, whitewall tires, special trim and so on.

The trick is to bring up the extras individually so that each small price seems petty by contrast with the basic cost of the car. As the veteran car-buyer can attest, an originally budget-sized price can balloon remarkably from the addition of all those seemingly little options. As the customer walks out, signed contract in hand, wondering what happened, he finds no one to blame but himself. The car salesman stands quietly, smiling the knowing smile of the judo master.

16

DRUG PREVENTION IN JUNIOR HIGH: A MULTI-SITE LONGITUDINAL TEST

Phyllis L. Ellickson and Robert M. Bell (1990)

One of the exciting aspects of social psychology is our ability to take social psychological findings and apply them to bettering the world. Given the many problems in our society, the possible applications of social psychology are quite numerous. The importance of evaluating such applications is not to be underestimated, however, in that we cannot always be sure of the outcomes. This report is exceptional in the complexity of its analysis. Ellickson and Bell try an intervention with a heterogeneous population in 30 schools and test the effects of two different strategies for reducing children's usage of three drugs (alcohol, nicotine in cigarettes, and marijuana). They study the effects of their intervention with three types of users (nonusers, experimenters, and consistent users), and they examine drug usage at three intervals. Thus, Ellickson and Bell are able to comprehensively assess their inoculation/social influence model of intervention. This is the stuff good evaluations are made of.

Kurt Lewin, regarded by many as the "father of modern social psychology," believed that there is nothing so powerful as a good theory—and the test of a good theory is in its application. Can we as social psychologists put our information to work for the betterment of the human condition? Look for examples of applying social psychology in this book of reading, in your text, in your instructor's lectures, and in your own life. While you are reading this article, try to find the evidence indicating that the intervention worked, had no effect, or even "boomeranged." Then try to summarize the results. Overall, were the effects important enough to introduce this intervention in other schools' curricula?

Source: Abridged from *Science*, 1990, *247*, 1299–1305. Copyright © 1990 by the AAAS. Reprinted by permission of the publisher and the authors.

*Results from a longitudinal experiment to curb drug use during junior high
indicate that education programs based on a social-influence model can prevent or
reduce young adolescents' use of cigarettes and marijuana. This multi-site experiment
involved the entire seventh-grade cohort of 30 junior high schools drawn from eight
urban, suburban, and rural communities in California and Oregon. Implemented
between 1984 and 1986, the curriculum's impact was assessed at 3-, 12-, and
15-month follow-ups. The program, which had positive results for both low- and high-
risk students, was equally successful in schools with high and low minority
enrollment. However, the program did not help previously confirmed smokers and its
effects on adolescent drinking were short-lived.*

Although concern about adolescent drug use has grown over the past two decades, strategies for controlling use have not kept pace. Early models of drug prevention failed to make appreciable inroads against the problem. More recent approaches have been widely touted but rarely tested rigorously. Consequently, parents, schools, and community groups lack solid guidance about what "works" to keep young people from getting involved with drugs.

We describe the results of Project ALERT, a multi-site, longitudinal test of a school-based prevention program for seventh and eighth graders. The curriculum specifically targets cigarettes, alcohol, and marijuana, the so-called gateway drugs, which are the most widely used by young people and typically precede initiation of harder drugs. Use of these substances by adolescents merits public concern because each poses substantial and specific harm to their health, development, or safety. Moreover, the earlier people start using them, the longer they risk adverse effects.

Project ALERT is based on the social influence model of prevention, which has shown promise for preventing or reducing adolescent smoking. The curriculum seeks to curb adolescent drug use by motivating young people to resist drugs and helping them acquire the skills to do so. This approach differs sharply from the failed drug prevention models of the 1960s and 1970s, which were information and general skills programs. The former typically emphasized the long-term consequences of using drugs, often exaggerating their harmful effects. The latter rarely linked general skills in communication or decision making with specific situations involving drugs. In contrast, the social influence approach tries to help young people understand how drugs can affect them now, in their daily lives and social relationships. Recognizing that knowledge alone rarely changes behavior, the model also helps them identify pro-drug pressures and acquire a repertoire of strategies for resisting those pressures.

Our study was designed specifically to overcome problems that raised questions about how generalizable and credible earlier school-based studies have been. Most other evaluations have not included schools with substantial minority populations. Many have also suffered from lack of random assignment, faulty implementation, and failure to assess attrition or the accuracy of self-reported drug use measures. Even a recent large-scale study could not use randomized assignment or case controls. Moreover, studies providing student-level results have typically failed to adjust for within-school correlation of outcomes, which makes tests of significance overly liberal. When school has been the unit of analysis, the estimates have not adequately accounted for differences in individual student characteristics that could explain program effects. In the following sections, we describe how we addressed each of these challenges to research integrity.

EXPERIMENTAL DESIGN AND HYPOTHESES

We recruited 30 schools that represent a broad spectrum of communities, socioeconomic status, and racial and ethnic composition. Drawn from eight school districts in the northern and southern regions of California and Oregon, they cover urban, suburban, and rural settings. Nine have a minority population of 50% or more and 18 draw from neighborhoods with household incomes below their state median.

The 30 schools were randomly assigned to one of three experimental conditions. The ten control schools, which did not receive the Project ALERT curriculum, were allowed to continue any traditional drug information programs they might have, and four did so. In the 20 treatment schools, enrolled seventh graders received an eight-session curriculum plus three booster lessons when they reached the eighth grade. An adult health educator taught the seventh-grade program in ten of these schools; teen leaders from neighboring high schools assisted the adult teachers in the other ten schools. This variation allowed us to test whether the curriculum was more effective when older teens were involved than when it was taught solely by adults. All 30 schools refrained from actions that might have contaminated the experiment, and none dropped out.

To reduce differences in student characteristics among experimental conditions, we used three methods: blocking by district, restricted assignment, and randomized assignment of schools. In districts with only three schools, for example, exactly one school could be assigned to each condition. We restricted assignments to a subset that produced relatively little imbalance among experimental conditions in characteristics such as school test scores, language spoken at home, drug use among the schools' eighth graders, and the ethnic and income composition of school catchment areas. We then randomly selected from among the eligible assignments, giving each school a one-third probability of assignment to any particular condition. These procedures produced substantial pretreatment equivalence across experimental conditions in school-level characteristics potentially related to future drug use.

Our hypotheses about the program's effects derived from prior research on drug use patterns, antecedents, and prevention. We had four expectations: First, the program would be more effective against cigarettes and marijuana than against alcohol. Drinking is the most prevalent and socially acceptable form of substance use among both young people and adults, while substantially fewer Americans use cigarettes or marijuana or approve of doing so. Successful prevention may require a threshold level of societal disapproval. Second, the program would have a stronger impact on nonusers and experimenters than on users. Adolescent users typically have more stable, and thus more resistant, motivations to use drugs than nonusers and experimenters.

Third, program effects would be reinforced or strengthened after delivery of the eighth-grade booster curriculum. Fourth, the program would be more successful when teen leaders were included in curriculum delivery. Some evaluations have reported better results when (i) young people are included in classroom delivery or (ii) the curriculum has a booster component.

CURRICULUM CONTENT AND IMPLEMENTATION

The Project ALERT curriculum builds on and extends the social influence model underlying recent smoking prevention programs. It aims to help students develop reasons not to use drugs, identify pressures to use them, counter pro-drug messages, learn how to say no to external and internal pressures, understand that most people do not use drugs, and recognize the benefits of resistance. The seventh-grade curriculum consists of eight lessons, taught a week apart. The three eighth-grade lessons reinforce the seventh-grade program.

Features that distinguish Project ALERT from earlier antismoking programs include its attention to the beliefs and circumstances that promote use of alcohol and marijuana, its focus on "pressures from inside yourself" (as well as external pressures to use drugs), and its clearly articulated theoretical underpinnings, drawn from the health belief model and the self-efficacy theory of behavior change. The highly participatory curriculum makes extensive use of question and answer techniques, small group exercises, role modeling, and repeated skills practice. These methods allow teachers to adjust program content to diverse classrooms with different levels of information and drug exposure.

During the 2-year delivery period, 58 health educators and 75 teen leaders taught Project ALERT in the 20 treatment schools. To assess the fidelity of curriculum delivery, 17 monitors observed 950 of the 2300 lessons taught. Classroom logs and the monitor reports indicate that the curriculum was implemented and delivered as intended. Every scheduled class was presented and, in 92% of the observed classes, all lesson activities were covered.

DATA COLLECTION PROCEDURES AND VALIDITY OF REPORTED USE

Trained data collectors administered questionnaires in the classroom at four points during the program's first 2 years: before and after delivery of the seventh-grade curriculum (baseline and 3-month follow-up) and before and after delivery of the eighth-grade booster curriculum (12- and 15-month follow-ups). These questionnaires solicited information on whether, how often, and how much students had used alcohol, cigarettes, and marijuana, and on psychosocial variables related to drug use.

Few students refused to fill out the surveys (< 1%) and, because the largest group of nonrespondents closely resembled respondents, nonresponse at baseline had little effect on sample characteristics or before treatment equivalence. Total baseline nonresponse amounted to 14%, mostly attributable to parent refusals of informed consent (9%) and absence (3%).

Because the validity of self-reports is often questioned in studies of "disapproved" behavior, we used several methods to reduce incentives for distorting or concealing substance use. The data collectors followed a strict protocol that described study measures for protecting data privacy, explained that each student had the right to refuse to participate, and stressed the importance of telling the truth. As a further motivation to tell the truth, we collected a saliva sample from each student immediately before administering the survey, informing them that the samples would be tested. This procedure has been found to improve the accuracy of reported cigarette use among adolescents. To get an objective measure of the validity of reported tobacco use, we tested the specimens for cotinine.

The students appear to have told the truth. At baseline and 15 months later, 95% of students with cotinine scores that identified them as recent tobacco users ($n = 603$) reported use of cigarettes or chewing tobacco in the past month. Data on inconsistencies in student self-reports suggest that few students deliberately lied about alcohol and marijuana as well. Data from all four surveys showed the proportion of students who denied using a target substance after previously admitting use averaged about 5%, a slightly lower rate than that found in earlier research. Retractions of frequent use averaged substantially less than 1%. In addition, we found no evidence that those in the treatment schools reacted to the experiment by distorting their reports.

ANALYSIS SAMPLE AND METHODS

To ensure that differences in outcomes before and after booster lessons could not be attributed to different samples, we restricted the analysis to students who were enrolled during grades 7 and 8 and were thus eligible to receive the full 2-year curriculum. Students in the analysis sample also had to supply data on the baseline control variables and the relevant outcome variables at the three follow-up surveys. The analysis sample constitutes 60% of the baseline sample of 6527 students. Of the missing 40%, 18% moved after baseline and 22% were absent or failed to supply the relevant data at one or more of the surveys.

Students omitted from the analysis were significantly more likely to have before-treatment characteristics often cited as risk factors for drug use (for example, low grades, family disruption, and early drug use). Nevertheless, the change in composition between the baseline and analysis samples averaged only about five percentage points, with the largest gap for the percentage who had tried marijuana.

We used logistic regression at the student level to analyze a series of binary outcome measures for each target substance as a function of treatment and baseline covariates. To determine whether the curriculum's effectiveness differed for nonusers and experimenters compared to users, we divided the students into three risk levels for each substance. For cigarettes and alcohol, the levels were nonusers (never), experimenters (ever, but fewer than three times in the year before baseline and not in the month before baseline), and users (three or more times in the past year or any use in the past month). Because students who had not tried marijuana constitute a large and heterogeneous group, we subdivided them into two risk groups: those who had not smoked cigarettes by grade 7 and those who had. The third level includes all students who had already tried marijuana.

PROGRAM EFFECTS

Alcohol use. Shortly after delivery of the seventh-grade curriculum, Project ALERT produced modest reductions in drinking for all three risk levels: nonusers, experimenters, and users. Among baseline nondrinkers, the curriculum reduced the number who initiated alcohol use in the subsequent 3 months by 28% ($p = 0.04$) and cut current drinking (use in the past month) by almost one-half ($p = 0.02$). For experimenters, it produced a reduction in monthly use of 44% ($p = 0.07$). Even among users, the curriculum held down current drinking 3 months later ($p = 0.06$). These results were largely attributable to the teen leader curriculum. Although students taught solely by adults also exhibited lower use patterns than control students, the only significant seventh-grade difference was for baseline users.

After the students entered the eighth grade, however, most of these early gains disappeared. Between grades 7 and 8, student exposure to alcohol greatly increased. For example, half of the control students with no prior drinking experience at baseline initiated alcohol use within 12 months. Participation in the seventh-grade curriculum did not slow down this acceleration. Nor did the booster curriculum revive the program's earlier success.

Cigarette use. Contrary to our expectations, Project ALERT had little effect on baseline nonusers (those who had not tried cigarettes by the time they were in the seventh grade) (Table 16-1). In contrast, the curriculum produced significant reductions across all subsequent smoking levels for baseline experimenters. It also stimulated some to quit.

These favorable results typically did not show up until the students had received the three booster lessons. However, for experimenters in the health educator group, a moderate increase in quitting (no smoking for at least 1 year) emerged at 12 months, before exposure to the booster lessons ($p = 0.03$). The quitting effect increased slightly after booster program delivery ($p = 0.006$), also showing up for students in the teen leader schools ($p = 0.09$). In addition, current smoking among baseline experimenters declined after the booster program—by 17% in the teen leader schools ($p = 0.08$) and by 27% in the health educator schools ($p = 0.007$). More frequent smoking (monthly use) decreased by over one-fourth in the teen leader schools ($p = 0.03$).

Project ALERT also reduced levels of cigarette use that signal serious use, especially for baseline experimenters in the teen leader schools. After delivery of the eighth-grade booster lessons, weekly smoking declined by almost 50% in the teen leader schools ($p = 0.006$) and by one-third in the adult only group ($p = 0.09$). Daily use, which is highly likely to signify addiction among adolescents, dropped by over 50% among students in the teen leader program ($p = 0.03$).

For baseline smokers, however, Project ALERT produced negative results. Paradoxically, these boomerang effects were stronger for students in the teen leader schools. At 12 months, current smoking for baseline users had increased by 20% in these schools ($p = 0.052$), growing to almost 30% after exposure to the booster program ($p = 0.004$). Monthly and weekly use followed a similar pattern: the former was one-third higher in the teen leader schools at 12 months ($p = 0.002$), dropping only

TABLE 16-1. PROGRAM EFFECTS ON CIGARETTE USE. Where values are omitted, overall use was < 2.5% or otherwise not applicable.

Cigarette use in experimental groups	Nonusers (% of 1990) at month			Cigarette experimenters (% of 1202) at month			Cigarette users (% of 660) at month		
	3	12	15	3	12	15	3	12	15
Ever									
Teen leader	6.8	23.4	28.9						
Health educator	7.8	24.1	30.6						
Control	6.5	25.8	31.1						
In past month									
Teen leader	3.0	6.0	7.1	12.7	25.7	26.8*	51.8	58.5*	63.2***
Health educator	4.3*	7.1	9.4	13.9	23.2	23.6***	55.3	55.6	56.1
Control	2.3	8.3	8.4	15.6	26.1	32.3	52.8	48.9	48.9
Monthly†									
Teen leader				6.4	15.5	16.5**	43.1	57.4***	54.0**
Health educator				6.9	17.9	18.9	40.8	51.7*	48.8
Control				6.8	19.3	22.4	47.8	42.9	43.4

Weekly (6+ days in past month)					
Teen leader	6.0	5.7***	18.4	34.1	34.6*
Health educator	7.9	7.4*	21.0	25.8	27.4
Control	6.5	11.1	18.7	27.5	26.4
Daily (20+ days in past month)					
Teen leader	3.1	2.3**	7.8	17.1	19.0
Health educator	2.7	4.5	12.9**	15.9	18.2
Control	2.6	5.1	6.6	18.1	15.9
Quit (no use in past year)					
Teen leader	50.2	50.3*		15.1	18.6
Health educator	55.2**	54.6***		11.9	15.7
Control	47.0	44.2		15.9	18.7

* $p \leq 0.10$, compared to control.
** $p \leq 0.05$, compared to control.
*** $p \leq 0.01$, compared to control.
†Eleven or more times in the past year or three or more days in the last 3 months.

slightly after the booster program ($p = 0.02$); the latter was also higher in these schools, but significantly so only at 15 months ($p = 0.06$).

Marijuana use. Project ALERT's most consistent results, across both groups and time, were for marijuana. For students who had not tried marijuana or cigarettes at baseline, it curbed initiation by one-third and reduced current use by 50 to 60%. Project ALERT also held down more frequent (monthly) use among those who had already started smoking cigarettes, students who were three times as likely to try marijuana within a year as the baseline nonsmokers. These effects appeared 9 months after completion of the seventh-grade program and were maintained after the booster lessons.

The most substantial results occurred for students who had never used marijuana or cigarettes. About 8% of the control school students began using marijuana within a year and 12% had begun using by 15 months. In both treatment groups, however, the initiation rate was reduced by about one-third—even before they received the eighth-grade lessons ($p = 0.07$ for teen leader schools; $p = 0.03$ for health educator schools). The booster program appeared to maintain those results, keeping the reduction in the treatment schools close to one-third ($p = 0.02$ for both groups).

Project ALERT also curbed current use for this lowest risk group. Students in the schools where lessons were taught only by an adult were almost 50% less likely to have become current users by grade 8 ($p = 0.09$). That effect increased to over 60% after exposure to the booster program ($p = 0.01$). Fewer students had become current marijuana users in the teen leader schools as well, but the differences were not statistically significant.

Project ALERT's effect on students in the two higher risk groups showed a consistent pattern of reductions, but the effects were smaller and less often statistically significant. Among those who had not tried marijuana but had tried cigarettes, the program produced a 50% reduction in monthly marijuana use at 12 months ($p = 0.04$). For those who had tried marijuana at baseline, the pattern was most pronounced in the teen leader schools, where the proportion of weekly marijuana users was about half that in the control schools shortly after delivery of the seventh-grade program ($p = 0.05$). At 12 months, however, that reduction had almost disappeared. After the booster program, the effect on weekly use was partially reinstated, but the 25% difference, although significant (and larger) in the school-level analysis, was not significant at the individual level.

DISCUSSION

These results indicate that the social influence model of prevention, as implemented in Project ALERT, works. In both treatment groups, students who had not tried marijuana or cigarettes before baseline had substantially lower rates of initiation and current marijuana use than the control group. Among those who had experimented with cigarettes at baseline, the treatment groups smoked significantly less at several levels: from occasional to serious use.

The findings counter two criticisms frequently leveled at prevention programs—that they work only for children who are the least likely to become confirmed users and that they prevent trivial levels of use. In fact, Project ALERT was very effective with high-risk tobacco experimenters, who were four times as likely as baseline nonusers to become current or monthly smokers by 15 months. It also curbed smoking at levels that suggest addiction among these young adolescents.

Alcohol, however, appears to pose a different and more difficult problem. Although Project ALERT produced modest, but significant, reductions in drinking levels among all three risk groups during grade 7, it did not sustain that effect. We think this erosion occurred because the widespread prevalence of alcohol use, in society at large, as well as in the schools that participated in our experiment, undermined curriculum messages about resisting pressures to drink.

Drinking is an integral part of American social life, whereas smoking and marijuana use are considerably less common and less accepted. Among high school seniors, two-thirds report current drinking while less than 30% report smoking or using marijuana. Similarly, over 55% disapprove of trying marijuana once or twice; only 21% disapprove of trying one or two drinks (Johnston, O'Malley, & Bachman, 1988). The implication is that sustained reductions in teenage drinking are unlikely without substantial changes in society's attitudes toward alcohol and its use.

Our findings suggest that booster lessons are important for maintaining and strengthening early program results. Although it did not reinstate early program gains for alcohol, the eighth-grade booster curriculum appeared to provide the reinforcement needed for the emergence of significant smoking reductions and to prevent the erosion of seventh-grade program effects for marijuana. During the junior and senior high years, adolescents are exposed to more diverse peer networks and increased drug use among their friends and acquaintances. Providing additional lessons as they pass through this vulnerable stage may help solidify early prevention gains.

Contrary to our expectations, the findings yield no clear recommendation for using older teens in the classroom. Neither method of curriculum delivery showed a dominant pattern across all three substances. In tests for significant differences between the two treatment groups, neither stood out as superior.

The results also suggest that early cigarette smokers need a more aggressive program than that offered by the social influence model alone. Project ALERT not only failed to reduce smoking among the baseline users, but actually increased it in the teen leader schools—a boomerang effect found in other antismoking programs. For these more confirmed smokers, being told that most of their peers do not smoke and exposing them to nonsmoking teens appears to be irrelevant at best and counterproductive at worst.

The data in Table 16-2 suggest why this may be so. By the seventh grade, prosmoking attitudes were substantially more prevalent in this group than among the baseline nonusers and experimenters. Further, considerably more baseline smokers had been exposed to smoking models and pressures, particularly from their peers. Asking them to resist those pressures meant asking them to reject the values, and perhaps the company, of their chosen reference group. In retrospect, it is not surprising that few of them heeded the message.

Our results have added significance because they apply to a wide variety of school environments in California and Oregon: those with and without substantial minority

TABLE 16-2. CHARACTERISTICS OF BASELINE NONSMOKERS, EXPERIMENTERS, AND USERS.

Baseline (before intervention) characteristic	Baseline level of cigarette use		
	Nonusers (% of 1990)	Experimenters (% of 1202)	Users (% of 660)
Beliefs about cigarettes			
Intend to use in future	1	6	54
Not harmful	9	17	28
Relaxes you	8	12	44
Smoking environment			
Best friend smokes sometimes	8	22	65
Around peers who are smoking	8	25	70
Other problems			
Parents divorced, do not live together	26	41	46
Trouble communicating with parents	28	42	57
Stolen from store	9	23	42
Skipped school	8	15	34
Grades of C or lower	16	30	40

populations, those drawing from neighborhoods at the lower and higher ends of the socioeconomic spectrum, and those in urban, suburban, and rural settings. To test whether program effects were restricted to schools in a white, middle-class environment, we subdivided our sample into two groups: (i) three districts (13 schools) with high minority populations (at least 30% nonwhite enrollment in each school); and (ii) the remaining five districts (with typically 90% or more white enrollment in each school). Treatment effects were similar for both groups, and where they differed, the program generally had better effects in the high minority schools.

Project ALERT's effects indicate that school-based programs have important potential for decreasing substance use among young people. Such a decrease has positive implications for adolescent development and safety and for public health in general. Marijuana use can impair memory, distort perception, and diminish motor skills, thereby interfering with the young person's ability to learn and increasing the likelihood of driving and other accidents. The earlier people begin to smoke, the harder it is to stop and the greater the risk of illness related to tobacco use. Moreover, drug use initiation before age 15 increases the risk of dysfunctional use or abuse in later years, whereas curbing cigarette and marijuana use, particularly the latter, offers the prospect of preventing or delaying progression to other dangerous drugs. Thus, each year that adolescent use of these gateway substances can be delayed or reduced represents an important gain.

17

THE DYNAMOGENIC
FACTORS IN PACEMAKING
AND COMPETITION

Norman Triplett (1898)

This study on social facilitation (called "dynamogenic factors" in 1898) was the
first social psychological experiment to be published. While others had theorized
about social psychology (including Plato, Aristotle, and many other early
philosophers), Triplett was the first to use scientific methods to test his
hypotheses. We have included only the barest of details of Triplett's discussion
of turn-of-the-century bicycle racers, but enough remains to understand how
Triplett arrived at his hypothesis and developed it into a laboratory experiment
with a repeated-measures design and counterbalanced testing. This article is rich
with both physiological and motivational hypotheses, which are posited as
possible explanations for changes in performance due to the presence of others.
Many of these hypotheses have not stood the test of time (for example, theories
about "brain worry" and "hypnotic suggestion"). Although these hypotheses may
amuse us now, they should also make us consider whether any of our
contemporary theories will be cause for laughter 100 years hence.

The statistics in this article are not sophisticated by modern standards.
Triplett's claims rest almost entirely upon descriptions of individual cases and
what one might call "eyeball analyses," that is, finding differences that are readily
apparent to any observer without the help of statistical analyses. Although all
researchers desire group differences that are this obvious, they are rare indeed,
especially given the complexity of the questions that researchers now address.
Fortunately, advances in computer hardware and software and in statistical design
allow investigators to ask and test many questions that could not be evaluated
earlier, and to test these questions in precise and complex ways.

Thus, Triplett's article is interesting because of its historical import; it
becomes doubly interesting when combined with a recent treatment of the same

Source: Abridged from the *American Journal of Psychology*, 1898, *9*, 507–533. Copyright © 1898 by
University of Illinois Press.

issue. Module 18 in Myers details much more recent contributions to the understanding of social facilitation. Comparison of this reading to the modern research described there, separated by nearly 100 years, illustrates the rapid development of social psychological science.

THEORIES ACCOUNTING FOR THE FASTER TIME OF PACED AND COMPETITION RACES

Of the seven or eight not wholly distinct theories which have been advanced to account for the faster time made in paced as compared with unpaced competitive races and paced races against time as against unpaced races against time, a number need only be stated very briefly. They are grouped according to their nature and first are given two mechanical theories.

Suction Theory

Those holding to this as the explanation assert that the vacuum left behind the pacing machine draws the rider following along with it. Anderson's ride of a mile a minute at Roodhouse, Ill., with the locomotive as pacemaker, is the strongest argument in its favor. Those maintaining this theory believe that the racer paced by a tandem is at a disadvantage as compared with the racer paced by a quod or a larger machine, as the suction exerted is not so powerful.

The Shelter Theory

This is closely related to the foregoing. Dr. Turner accepts it as a partial explanation of the aid to be gained from a pace, holding that the pacemaker or the leading competitor serves as a shelter from the wind, and that "a much greater amount of exertion, purely muscular, is required from a man to drive a machine when he is leading than when he is following, on account of the resistance of the air, and the greater the amount of wind blowing the greater the exertion, and conversely, the greater the shelter obtained the less the exertion."

This is the theory held, in general, by racers themselves. One of the champion riders of the country recently expressed this common view in a letter, as follows: "It is true that some very strong unpaced riders do not have any sort of success in paced racing. The only reason I can give for this is just simply that they have not studied the way to follow pace so as to be shielded from the wind. No matter which way it blows there is always a place where the man following pace can be out of the wind."

Encouragement Theory

The presence of a friend on the pacing machine to encourage and keep up the spirits of the rider is claimed to be of great help. The mental disposition has been long known to be of importance in racing as in other cases where energy is expended. It is still as true as in Virgil's time that the winners "can because they think they can."

The Brain Worry Theory

This theory shows why it is difficult for the leader in an unpaced competition race to win. For "a much greater amount of brain worry is incurred by making the pace than by waiting" (following). The man leading "is in a fidget the whole time whether he is going fast enough to exhaust his adversary: he is full of worry as to when that adversary means to commence his spurt; his nervous system is generally strung up, and at concert pitch, and his muscular and nervous efforts act and react on each other, producing an ever-increasing exhaustion, which both dulls the impulse-giving power of the brain and the impulse-receiving or contractile power of the muscles."

Theory of Hypnotic Suggestions

A curious theory, lately advanced, suggests the possibility that the strained attention given to the revolving wheel of the pacing machine in front produces a sort of hypnotism and that the accompanying muscular exaltation is the secret of the endurance shown by some long distance riders in paced races.

The Automatic Theory

This is also a factor which favors the waiting rider, and gives him a marked advantage. The leader, as has been noted, must use his brain to direct every movement of his muscles. As he becomes more distressed it requires a more intense exertion of will power to force his machine through the resisting air. On the other hand, the "waiter" rides automatically. He has nothing to do but hang on. "His brain having inaugurated the movement leaves it to the spinal cord to continue it and only resumes its functions when a change of direction or speed is necessary."—(Lagrange.) When he comes to the final spurt, his brain, assuming control again, imparts to the muscles a winning stimulus, while the continued brain work of the leader has brought great fatigue.

These facts seem to have a large foundation in truth. The lesser amount of fatigue incurred in paced trials is a matter of general knowledge. It is a common experience with wheelmen, and within that of the writer, that when following a lead on a long ride the feeling of automatic action becomes very pronounced, giving the sensation of a strong force pushing from behind. Of course the greater the distance ridden the more apparent becomes the saving in energy from automatic riding, as time is required to establish the movement. It may be remembered, in this connection, that while the average gain of the paced over the unpaced record is 34.4 seconds, the difference between them for the first mile is only 23.8 seconds.

As between the pacer and the paced, every advantage seems to rest with the latter. The two mechanical factors of suction and shelter, so far as they are involved, assist the rider who follows. So the psychological theories, the stimulation from encouragement, the peculiar power induced by hypnotism, and the staying qualities of automatic action, if of help at all, directly benefit the paced rider. The element of disadvantage induced by brain action, on the contrary, belongs more especially to the rider who leads.

The Dynamogenic Factors

The remaining factors to be discussed are those which the experiments on competition, detailed in the second part hereof, attempt to explain. No effort is made to weaken the force of the foregoing factors in accounting for the better time of paced races in comparison with unpaced races of the same type, but the facts of this study are given to throw whatever additional light they may.

This theory of competition holds that the bodily presence of another rider is a stimulus to the racer in arousing the competitive instinct; that another can thus be the means of releasing or freeing nervous energy for him that he cannot of himself release; and, further, that the sight of movement in that other, by perhaps suggesting a higher rate of speed, is also an inspiration to greater effort. These are the factors that had their counterpart in the experimental study following; and it is along these lines that the facts determined are to find their interpretation.

STATEMENT OF METHOD

From the laboratory competitions to be described, abstraction was made of nearly all the forces above outlined. In the 40 seconds the average trial lasted, no shelter from the wind was required, nor was any suction exerted, the only brain worry incident was that of maintaining a sufficiently high rate of speed to defeat the competitors. From the shortness of the time and nature of the case, generally, it is doubtful if any automatic movements could be established. On the other hand, the effort was intensely voluntary. It may be likened to the 100 yard dash—a sprint from beginning to end.

Description of Apparatus

The apparatus for this study consisted of two fishing reels whose cranks turned in circles of one and three-fourths inches diameter. These were arranged on a Y shaped framework clamped to the top of a heavy table. The sides of this framework were spread sufficiently far apart to permit two persons turning side by side. Bands of twisted silk cord ran over the well lacquered axes of the reels and were supported at C and D, two meters distant, by two small pulleys. The records were taken from the course A D. The other course B C being used merely for pacing or competition purposes. The wheel on the side from which the records were taken communicated the movement made to a recorder, the stylus of which traced a curve on the drum of a kymograph. The direction of this curve corresponded to the rate of turning, as the greater the speed the shorter and straighter the resulting line.

Method of Conducting the Experiment

A subject taking the experiment was required to practice turning the reel until he had become accustomed to the machine. After a short period of rest the different trials were made with five-minute intervals between to obviate the possible effects of fatigue.

A trial consisted in turning the reel at the highest rate of speed until a small flag sewed to the silk band had made four circuits of the four-meter course. The time of the trial was taken by means of a stop-watch. The direction of the curves made on the drum likewise furnished graphic indications of the difference in time made between trials.

In the tables, A represents a trial alone, C a trial in competition.

STATEMENT OF RESULTS

In the course of the work the records of nearly 225 persons of all ages were taken. However, all the tables given below, and all statements made, unless otherwise specified, are based on the records of 40 children taken in the following manner: After the usual preliminaries of practice, six trials were made by each of 20 subjects in this order: first a trial alone, followed by a trial in competition, then another alone, and thus alternating through the six efforts, giving three trials alone and three in competition. Six trials were taken by 20 other children of about the same age, the order of trials in this case being the first trial alone, second alone, third a competition trial, fourth alone, fifth a competition, and sixth alone.

By this scheme, a trial of either sort, after the first one, by either of the two groups, always corresponds to a different trial by the opposite group. Further, when the subjects of the two groups come to their fourth and sixth trials, an equal amount of practice has been gained by an equal number of trials of the same kind. This fact should be remembered in any observation of the time made in trials by any group.

During the taking of the records, and afterwards in working them over, it was seen that all cases would fall into two classes:

First. Those stimulated—

1 to make faster time in competition trials,
2 in such a way as to inhibit motion.

Second. The small number who seemed little affected by the race.

The tables which follow are made up from records of the subjects mentioned. The classification was in general determined by the time record as taken by the watch.

The first table gives the records of 20 subjects who, on the whole, were stimulated positively. The second table contains 10 records of subjects who were overstimulated. In the tables, A represents a trial alone, C a trial in competition. The 20 subjects given in Group A and Group B, of Table 17–1, in nearly all cases make marked reductions in the competition trials. The averages show large gains in these trials and small gains or even losses for the succeeding trials alone. The second trial for Group A is a competition, for Group B a trial alone. The gain between the first and second trials of the first group is 5.6 seconds, between the first and second trials of the second group, 2.52 seconds. The latter represents the practice effect—always greatest in the first trials, the former the element of competition plus the practice. The third trial in Group A—a trial alone—is .72 seconds slower than the preceding race trial. The third trial in Group B—a competition—is 4.48 seconds faster than the preceding trial alone. The fourth tri-

TABLE 17-1 SUBJECTS STIMULATED POSITIVELY

Group A

	Age.	A.	C.	A.	C.	A.	C.
Violet F.	10	54.4	42.6	45.2	41.0	42.0	46.0
Anna P.	9	67.0	57.0	55.4	50.4	49.0	44.8
Willie H.	12	37.8	38.8	43.0	39.0	37.2	33.4
Bessie V.	11	46.2	41.0	39.0	30.2	33.6	32.4
Howard C.	11	42.0	36.4	39.0	41.0	37.8	34.0
Mary M.	11	48.0	44.8	52.0	44.6	43.8	40.0
Lois P.	11	53.0	45.6	44.0	40.0	40.6	35.8
Inez K.	13	37.0	35.0	35.8	34.0	34.0	32.6
Harvey L.	9	49.0	42.6	39.6	37.6	36.0	35.0
Lora F.	11	40.4	35.0	33.0	35.0	30.2	29.0
Average	11	47.48	41.88	42.6	39.28	38.42	36.3
P.E.		6.18	4.45	4.68	3.83	3.74	3.74
Gains			5.6	.72	3.32	.86	2.12

Group B

	Age.	A.	A.	C.	A.	C.	A.
Stephen M.	13	51.2	50.0	43.0	41.8	39.8	41.2*
Mary W.	13	56.0	53.0	45.8	49.4	45.0	43.0*
Bertha A.	10	56.2	49.0	48.0	46.8	41.4	44.4
Clara L.	8	52.0	44.0	46.0	45.6	44.0	45.2
Helen M.	10	45.0	45.6	35.8	46.2	40.0	40.0
Gracie W.	12	56.6	50.0	42.0	39.0	40.2	41.4
Dona R.	15	34.0	37.2	36.0	41.4	37.0	32.8
Pearl C.	13	43.0	43.0	40.0	40.6	33.8	35.0
Clyde G.	13	36.0	35.0	32.4	33.0	31.0	35.0
Lucile W.	10	52.0	50.0	43.0	44.0	38.2	40.2
Average	11.7	48.2	45.68	41.2	42.78	39.0	39.82
P.E.		5.60	4.00	3.42	3.17	2.89	2.84
Gains			2.52	4.48	1.58	3.78	.82

*Left-handed.

als in these two groups are on an equality, as regards practice, from an equal number of trials of the same kind. In the first case the gain over the preceding trial is 3.32 seconds. In the latter there is a loss of 1.58 seconds from the time of the preceding competition trial. In like manner there is an equality of conditions in regard to the sixth trial of these groups, and again the effect of competition plainly appears, the competition trial gaining 2.12 seconds, and the trial alone losing .82 seconds with respect to the preceding trial. These are decided differences.

The 10 subjects whose records are given in Table 17–2 are of interest. With them stimulation brought a loss of control. In one or more of the competition trials of each subject in this group the time is very much slower than that made in the preceding trial alone. Most frequently this is true of the first trial in competition, but with some it was

TABLE 17-2   SUBJECTS STIMULATED ADVERSELY

Group A

	Age.	A.	C.	A.	C.	A.	C.
Jack R.	9	44.2	44.0	41.8	48.0	44.2	41.0
Helen F.	9	44.0	51.0	43.8	44.0	43.0	41.2
Emma P.	11	38.4	42.0	37.0	39.6	36.6	32.0
Warner J.	11	41.6	43.6	43.4	43.0	40.0	38.0
Genevieve M.	12	36.0	36.0	32.6	32.8	31.2	34.8
Average	10.4	40.84	43.32	39.72	41.48	39.00	37.40
P.E.		2.41	3.57	3.25	3.85	3.55	2.52

Group B

	Age.	A.	A.	C.	A.	C.	A.
Hazel M.	11	38.0	35.8	38.2	37.2	35.0	42.0
George B.	12	39.2	36.0	37.6	34.2	36.0	33.8
Mary B.	11	50.0	46.0	43.4	42.0	48.0	36.8
Carlisle B.	14	37.0	35.4	35.0	33.4	36.4	31.4
Eddie H.	11	31.2	29.2	27.6	27.0	26.8	28.8
Average	11.8	39.08	36.48	36.36	34.76	34.40	34.56
P.E.		4.61	4.07	3.89	3.71	5.33	3.45

characteristic of every race. In all, 14 of the 25 races run by this group were equal or slower than the preceding trial alone. This seems to be brought about in large measure by the mental attitude of the subject. An intense desire to win, for instance, often resulted in over-stimulation. Accompanying phenomena were labored breathing, flushed faces and a stiffening or contraction of the muscles of the arm. A number of young children of from 5 to 9 years, not included in our group of 40, exhibited the phenomena most strikingly, the rigidity of the arm preventing free movement and in some cases resulting in an almost total inhibition of movement. The effort to continue turning in these cases was by a swaying of the whole body.

This seems a most interesting fact and confirmatory of the probable order of development of the muscles as given by Dr. Hall and others. In the case of those sufficiently developed to have the fast forearm movement, fatigue or overstimulation seemed to bring a recurrence to the whole arm and shoulder movement of early childhood, and if the fatigue or excitement was sufficiently intense, to the whole body movement, while younger children easily fell into the swaying movement when affected by either of the causes named.

CONCLUDING STATEMENT

From the above facts regarding the laboratory races we infer that the bodily presence of another contestant participating simultaneously in the race serves to liberate latent energy not ordinarily available. This inference is further justified by the difference in time between the paced competition races and the paced races against time, amounting to an average of 5.15 seconds per mile up to 25 miles. The factors of shelter from the wind, encouragement, brain worry, hypnotic suggestion, and automatic movement, are common to both, while the competitors participate simultaneously in person only in the first. In the next place the sight of the movements of the pacemakers or leading competitors, and the idea of higher speed, furnished by this or some other means, are probably in themselves dynamogenic factors of some consequence.

18

EXCERPT FROM CULTURE AND SOCIAL BEHAVIOR

Harry C. Triandis (1994)

Myers's text addresses the issue of social loafing wherein people exert lessened effort in the presence of coactors. Comparison to our Triplett reading (17) demonstrates how social psychology has improved our understanding of group processes over the last century. Social facilitation is a good example of a research area that was productive but for which interest subsided and then blossomed again (see also Reading 9). The advice given to individuals about mental sets is also useful for a research area as a whole: If you cannot make headway in solving a problem, put it away for a while and return to it later with a fresh look.

Another important issue is addressed in the following reading. The issue is that of cultural influences on social behavior. Myers makes several references to cultural differences in social loafing. Sometimes the behavior of North American subjects is like the behavior of people from other cultures, and sometimes it is not. One must be careful not to fall into the all-too-easy trap of ethnocentrism from which one assumes that one's social world is the yardstick by which all other societies should be measured. When as children we looked at *National Geographic* magazine and saw strange people eating weird foods, living in bizarre housing, dressing in clothes we wouldn't be caught dead in, we felt as though our way of being human was the norm. Would others feel the same way if they had a *National Geographic* published by their culture and we were the strange ones? We suspect so. What kind of person would you be if you were born to parents who were members of the Ik tribe in Uganda (Turnbull, reading 12)? Very different than you are now, but we suspect you would have fit in well with the prevailing culture.

In a world made closer by high-speed travel and instantaneous communication (you can watch news events as they occur from around the planet, and even in outer space, live on CNN), Triandis reminds us that cultural relativity still exists. Would the findings on social loafing change in countries that convert from communism toward privatization? Will there be changes in the collective farm of the former Soviet Union, the Israeli kibbutz, the workers in China, with the end of the Cold War and the further shrinking of the world?

Culture is to society what memory is to individuals. In other words, culture includes traditions that tell "what has worked" in the past. It also encompasses the way people have learned to look at their environment and themselves, and their unstated assumptions about the way the world is and the way people should act.

The most inclusive definition of culture—that culture is the human-made part of the environment—was given by Herskovits in his book *Cultural Anthropology* (1955). Since I learned my first cultural anthropology from that book, I am still partial to that definition. Granted, it is very broad, but we can break it down. By distinguishing objective aspects of culture (tools, roads, radio stations) from subjective aspects (categorizations, associations, norms, roles, values), we can examine how subjective culture influences behavior.

When we analyze subjective culture, we learn how people perceive, categorize, believe, and value entities in their environment. In short, we discover the unique ways in which people in different cultures view their social environment.

The elements of subjective culture are organized into patterns. Although in each culture these patterns have unique configurations, we can identify some general schemas that apply to all cultures: These are *cultural syndromes*. A cultural syndrome is a pattern of beliefs, attitudes, self-definitions, norms, and values that are organized around some theme that can be identified in a society. There are four such syndromes:

- *Complexity*. Some cultures are more complex than others.
- *Individualism*. Some cultures structure social experience around autonomous individuals.
- *Collectivism*. Some cultures organize their subjective cultures around one or more collectives, such as the family, the tribe, the religious group, or the country.
- *Tightness*. Some cultures impose many norms, rules, and constraints on social behavior, while others are rather loose in imposing such constraints.

Culture influences our behavior in subtle ways. In reading this selection you will discover quite a lot about yourself, your culture, and other cultures. In addition, you will see that your understanding of social behavior has been shaped by Western culture, because social psychology is the product of Europe and North America. Almost all social psychologists are from that part of the world, as are almost all the data. The West is an increasingly shrinking part—approximately 27 percent—of humankind, whereas 35 percent of all humans live in China and India! This reading is designed to provide a broader view of social behavior by paying attention to the impact of culture on social behavior.

Although culture shapes social behavior, it is not the single most important factor. Biology and ecology also play a crucial role. Their relative importance varies with the situation. Certainly, if we found ourselves in an environment with too little oxygen, our behavior would primarily be determined by the fact that we couldn't breathe. But as we will see, culture too is very important.

We are not aware of our own culture unless we come in contact with another one. To illustrate this point, let me tell you what happened to me the first time I went to India in 1965. I wrote to the only Western hotel in Mysore and asked the hotel to reserve a room for me for certain dates. I received a reply card that had two lines, one of which read: "We are unable to provide a room for the dates indicated." There was an X next to that statement. Assuming that the hotel had no room, I wrote to A. V. Shanmugam (my coauthor in Triandis, 1972) and asked him to find me another place. He did not bother to check with the hotel, because he knew that a large group of movie actors making a film in the nearby jungle were staying there. When I arrived in Mysore, I found the alternative accommodation unsatisfactory. In the hope that someone might have canceled a reservation, I went to the Western hotel to see if a room was available. When I gave my name, the desk clerk was astonished and said they had been expecting me! I pointed out that the card they sent had an X next to the words "We are unable . . ." and the astonished clerk replied: "Of course! We cross out the categories that do *not* apply."

Our habitual patterns of thought are so well entrenched that it never occurred to me that the way we do things in the West, placing a check (or an X) next to the category that *does* apply, is not done universally. It is important to note that the system used in that hotel is as efficient as our system of placing a mark next to the category that does apply. Our culture is not superior; it is just different.

While this anecdote is amusing and instructive, it raises an important issue: How much of the content of psychology may in fact be a distortion when applied to other cultures?

During my travels to Africa, Asia, and Latin America, I met many psychologists and was especially impressed by the fact that many of them had an inferiority complex. The West is the standard, especially in psychology. Many of these psychologists assume that if their own data do not match the Western theories, something is wrong with the data, not the theories.

I also encountered another type of problem: In most traditional cultures, modesty is a much greater virtue than in the West. Thus, most of these social psychologists consider it in bad taste to say: "Your theory is wrong"; they would rather keep quiet. Among the non-Western cultures, only the Japanese (e.g., Iwao, 1988) feel sufficiently sure of themselves to tell us: "*You* are wrong." However, they do it so politely that most Western social psychologists fail to notice!

One of the cultural differences that I have investigated more than others, because I suspect it is the most important kind of difference, is the difference between cultures that are individualistic and cultures that are collectivist. Individualists think of themselves as autonomous, independent of groups, and believe that it is okay to do what they want to do, regardless of their groups' wishes. Collectivists, on the other hand, tend to see themselves as appendages or aspects of a group, such as the family, the tribe, the corporation, the country; they feel interdependence with members of this group; and they are willing to subordinate their personal goals to the goals of the group. For example, during World War II the Japanese used kamikaze pilots, who crashed their planes into American naval vessels. Such suicide missions clearly subordinate personal goals to those of the group. Such behavior is rare in individualistic cultures.

In collective cultures people are often more concerned about acting appropriately than about doing what they would like to do. As a result, there is less consistency between attitudes and behavior than is likely to be found in individualistic cultures. This results in differences in the importance of attitudes as predictors of social behavior and places less emphasis on consistency between what is "inside" the person and that person's behavior. The Japanese often say: "You can think what is in your mind, but shouldn't say that. It's rude" (Kidder, 1992, p. 387). In other words, even expressing a thought that does not match the norms is inappropriate.

Iwao (1988) has pointed out that the Japanese are much less concerned with consistency than are Westerners. Yet much of Western social psychology deals with consistency. We in the West think that "if X is true, non-X cannot be true." But this view makes relatively little sense in cultures such as India, where philosophical monism is widely used; i.e., "Everything is one" and "The opposite of a great truth is also a great truth." For instance, Ghandhi (Ghandhi Museum in Ahmedabad, India) said: "All religions reflect the same great truth."

While some aspects of social psychology are universally valid, others apply only in the West. If we want a universal social psychology, we need to find out what is universal, what is culture specific, and how various dimensions of cultural variation change the phenomena that we are studying. This universal social psychology will include the social psychology that is in your textbook, but it will include it as "a special case" of the universal social psychology.

A TASTE OF CULTURAL DIFFERENCES

Most readers are likely to have been exposed to only one culture. As the example of what happened in the Mysore hotel suggests, even after exposure to many cultures we are most likely to use the framework of our own cultural region (e.g., the West, the East) in interpreting events. To broaden your perspective, let me describe some surprising cultural differences.

Among the Karaki of New Guinea a man is "abnormal" if he has not engaged in homosexual behavior prior to marriage; the "missionary" coital position we consider "normal" is used only in about a quarter of the societies of the world; in cultures where hunger is endemic, fat women are much more attractive than slender ones; hissing is a polite way to show deference to superiors in Japan. There are also culture-specific disorders that occur just in one culture and can be understood only if one knows the myths and legends of that culture. Kluckhohn (1954, pp. 927–940) provides an extensive set of interesting examples of such cultural differences.

If you read ethnographies about Asian and African cultures, or about nonliterate cultures, you will get a picture of ordinary life that is very different from the picture you get talking with Europeans or North Americans. For example, Phillips (1965) described the village of Bang Chan in Thailand. In this culture affability, gentleness, and good humor are typical attributes of the villager's social behaviors. Face-to-face conflict must be avoided to the point of not saying something important that happens to be unpleasant. For example, you would not say: "Your house is burning." Instead you would say: "Why don't you go see your house?" Detailed interviews with women whose husbands had taken additional wives indicated that although the women were greatly disturbed, they said nothing to their husbands (p. 69). They did not want to put anyone on the spot!

In this culture, conflict is usually followed by one of the parties' leaving the scene without explanation, confrontation, or argument. As a result, many families are dissolved with little ceremony. The polite way to say "no" to a request is to giggle; that communicates the person's intentions perfectly.

Throughout the world, religion governs the life of most people. However, the extent that this is true varies enormously from culture to culture. In Japan, for instance, only about a fifth of the population takes religion seriously. In fact, some baptize their children the Shinto (traditional Japanese religion) way, marry the Christian way, and have Buddhist funerals. It is a matter of taste, similar to eating Chinese food or pizza. By contrast, about two-thirds of the population in the United States and six-sevenths of the population in India take religion very seriously (Gallup International Research Institute survey, 1977).

The ideas of the world's main religions are often mixed with traditional beliefs, and frequently scientific beliefs are mixed in as well. For example, people will recognize that lightning is caused by electricity but will explain that phenomenon by saying that it is discharged by such and such a god. Common traditional beliefs are often animistic: The event is explained by a spirit that was mad, happy, angry, disturbed, satisfied. Illness is not considered in terms of the germ theory but is viewed as a spiritual event. For example, enemies have bewitched the sick person.

There are traces of magical thinking, not only in traditional cultures but also in the United States. For example, the belief that "once in contact, always in contact" (known as the law of contagion) and the idea that the image equals the object (known as the law of similarity) were identified as the essence of magic by Frazer (1890–1959) and have been demonstrated to be active among American undergraduates (Rozin, Millman, & Nemeroff, 1986). Specifically, Rozin et al. (1986) showed that drinks that have been in contact with a sterilized dead cockroach become extremely undersirable (law of contact), even when people are certain that the sterilization made the cockroach perfectly clean. A well-laundered shirt worn by a disliked person is less desirable than one worn by a neutral person (again the law of contact). Desirable foods (e.g., fudge) are disgusting when they come in the shape of disgusting objects (dog feces), showing the operation of the law of similarity. People are less accurate in throwing darts at the faces of people they like than at those they dislike, again showing the operation of the law of similarity.

The strong association of emotions with magic indicates that some very basic, possibly universal, processes are in operation. Since we all use a bit of magical thinking, we should have no trouble understanding how African ideas about illness occur. Following are some of these ideas. They are presented to give you a taste of a very different culture and to introduce you to a world that is different from the West.

Traditional healing is much more widely used in Africa than is modern medicine, and the obvious question is why? Vontress (1991) did fieldwork in Africa and also conducted interviews with African traditional healers and those who use their services, to answer this question. On a continent where there are only about 100 psychiatrists for 342 million people, where transportation to remote communities is difficult (80 percent of the population lives in such communities), and where there is little Western medicine (75 percent of the population is illiterate), it is not surprising that the vast majority of the population depends on traditional healing methods.

These methods are derived from animism, the belief that all things have spirits in them. Stones, leaves, trees, rivers, even the earth itself, are considered inhabited by spirits, and people believe that illness occurs when a spirit has been offended or when some of the natural relationships among the spirits have been disturbed. It thus is up to a traditional healer, who has the ability to "control" the spirits, to intervene.

Do *not* look down on these healers; they are by no means ineffective. They have studied their craft for as long as nine years. In some cases they have their own "association" that awards certificates and makes them swear that they will not harm their patients—a form of the Hippocratic oath! During their studies, traditional healers generally learn to be exceptionally good observers and to become familiar with the medicinal properties of plants. They learn how to see what is wrong with their patients, and they take extensive medical histories. They also know how to identify and use botanical substances. Botanists have classified about 350,000 known plants, but the systematic study of the effects of touching, eating, or inhaling such plants has only just begun.

In fact, modern historians of pharmacology are discovering that ancient peoples effectively used some plants for medicinal purposes. An interesting example is a plant called silphion that is now extinct but used to grow on the Cyrene coast of North Africa. Greek and Roman women used it for birth control. It was "the pill" of the ancient world (Riddle & Estes, 1992). While this plant was harvested to extinction, plants that are genetically related to it still exist and do have contraceptive effects when used on laboratory animals.

African healers learn about plant attributes and uses from their teachers, who in turn learned from traditions developed over millennia of trial and error. They are quite skilled in their use of plants for healing, though they do make occasional mistakes with dosage. Through careful observation and through a broad knowledge of the patient's environment, healers are in a better position to detect psychosomatic disturbances and to use shock treatments (such as immersing their patients in cold water, or scaring them with masked invaders who threaten to kill them) than are modern psychiatrists (Torrey, 1986) who typically can take little time to work with patients who have no money. Traditional healers can ask countless questions and talk to the patients and their relatives to obtain clues that can lead to useful cures. They can impress their patients with colorful costumes and a variety of objects (e.g., roots, insects, monkey skulls, shells) and deal effectively with a wide range of problems (e.g., from impotence to depression). They are a combination of physician, priest, and psychologist. Torrey (1986), an iconoclastic American psychiatrist, doubts that the cure rates of such healers for psychological problems are different from the cure rates of modern psychiatrists. In observing other cultures it is useful to keep in mind that we see the world less "as it is" and more "as we are."

19

DEINDIVIDUATION AND VALENCE OF CUES: EFFECTS OF PROSOCIAL AND ANTISOCIAL BEHAVIOR

Robert D. Johnson and Leslie L. Downing (1979)

This study on deindividuation pits two hypotheses against each other. The earliest studies on deindividuation (Festinger, Pepitone, & Newcomb, 1952; Singer, Brush, & Lublin, 1965; Zimbardo, 1970) hypothesize that deindividuation is associated with antisocial behavior. Gergen, Gergen, and Barton (1973), however, hypothesize that deindividuation leads to greater sensitivity to external cues, which may influence individuals to be either more *antisocial* or more *prosocial*. Thus, they agree that the subjects in Zimbardo's (1970) study who wore deindividuating costumes became less self-aware and more disinhibited, but that the direction of their actual behavior was evoked by the "Ku Klux Klannishness" of their costumes. This important methodological point has substantial theoretical implications; we should always be on the lookout for the nonobvious or hidden implications in the operational definitions of our psychological constructs.

Zimbardo and most researchers consider that deindividuation includes at least some degree of anonymity. But deindividuation also includes diffusion of responsibility, group versus individual awareness, and lack of evaluation apprehension. Johnson and Downing help to clarify these ingredients in deindividuation and propose a two-step process involved in leading to antisocial or prosocial action. Future research will hopefully continue the process of clarification.

Source: Abridged from the *Journal of Personality and Social Psychology*, 1979, *37*, 1532–1538. Copyright © 1979 by the American Psychological Association. Reprinted by permission of the publisher and the authors.

ABSTRACT

Deindividuation has been shown to relate to increases in antisocial behavior. Typical manipulations, however, have confounded deindividuation with the presence of negatively valenced cues, such cues being inherent in the costumes or situations used to produce deindividuation. The present study manipulated deindividuation and valence of costume cues in a 2 × 2 factorial design. Zimbardo's theory of deindividuation suggests that deindividuation should disinhibit antisocial behavior, independent of cue valence, and should reduce any influence due to cues. Gergen, however, suggests that cues may have increasing influence, given deindividuation, and that deindividuation may increase prosocial behavior, given positive cues, and increase antisocial behavior, given negative cues. Results supported Gergen's position. Given options to increase or decrease shock level received by a stranger, no main effect was found for deindividuation. There was a main effect for costume cues, and an interaction of cues with deindividuation, with deindividuation facilitating a significant increase in prosocial responses in the presence of positive cues and a nonsignificant increase in antisocial responses in the presence of negative cues. Also cues interacted with trial blocks, prosocial behavior increasing with positive cues and antisocial behavior increasing with negative cues over trial blocks.

The construct deindividuation was first systematically investigated by Festinger, Pepitone, and Newcomb (1952). In their view, one consequence of an individual's involvement and identification with a group is a reduction of individual responsibility for individual behavior. They believed that deindividuation was a phenomenon on which groups would differ and that degree of deindividuation in a group could be indexed by the rate of failure of individuals to identify correctly the group members who had contributed different behaviors. It was expected that previously inhibited behaviors (i.e., saying negative things about one's parents) would be disinhibited as a result of deindividuation. As predicted, groups scoring highest on deindividuation did say more negative things about their parents. This was, however, a correlational study in which the direction of causality between deindividuation and disinhibition is unclear. Later studies (Singer, Brush, & Lublin, 1965; Zimbardo, 1970), using lab coats and hoods to obscure the identifiability of individuals, have shown that such a manipulation increases disinhibition of socially undesirable behaviors (i.e. speaking, obscene words and administering electrical shock to another person).

Theoretical Issues

Exactly which behaviors will be disinhibited in a given situation is not yet clear. Nor is it clear how situational cues affect the type or amount of disinhibition that occurs. Two major positions on these issues have been advanced.

Zimbardo's View In Zimbardo's theory of deindividuation (1970), anonymity, along with other input variables, produces a state of the organism, *deindividuation,* that in turn produces a general disinhibition of previously inhibited behavior. Negative comments about parents, college women's use of obscene words, and subjecting others to pain are all behaviors inhibited by prior experience, possibly by expectation of punishment. Deindividuation disinhibits such behaviors by means of a general weakening of inhibitory mechanisms. Which behaviors will be disinhibited depends upon which ones have been inhibited. Inhibited behaviors, once initiated, will tend to increase in frequency and intensity because they are intrinsically reinforcing. According to this theory, because the real source of the behavior is its intrinsically self-rewarding nature, deindividuation should lead to decreasing influence of external cues.

These hypotheses were subjected to an experimental test using what is perhaps the best-known deindividuation paradigm (Zimbardo, 1970). Groups of subjects were individuated (with identifying name tags) or deindividuated (with lab coats and hoods obscuring their identity) and were then given a sanctioned opportunity to administer electrical shocks to another person. Zimbardo has interpreted the increased duration of shocks given by deindividuated subjects to be a result of the deindividuating experience disinhibiting aggressive behavior.

Gergen's View   The prediction that antisocial behavior is most likely to be disinhibited by deindividuation was questioned by Gergen, Gergen, and Barton (1973). In their study, darkness- and anonymity-induced deindividuation led not to increased aggression but to increases in touching, caressing, and other affectionate behaviors. These workers advanced the notion that either prosocial or antisocial behavior could be enhanced by deindividuation, depending upon valence of situational cues. In this view, the darkness manipulation may have been more suggestive of intimacy than of aggression, hence anonymity-induced deindividuation increased the frequency of intimacy behaviors.

Experimental Confounds

A more important question is whether the disinhibition observed in prior research was in fact due to deindividuation and not to some unintentionally manipulated variable. One such variable relates to the cue value of the deindividuating costumes, which may be reminiscent of Ku Klux Klan outfits or perhaps of some Halloween ghouls, either of which might be considered cues eliciting aggression (Berkowitz, 1974). It is noteworthy that even without differential identifiability, Berkowitz and his colleagues have demonstrated increased duration of shocks to a target person due to the presence of cues previously associated with aggression (Berkowitz, 1974). A similar line of reasoning could serve as an alternative explanation for differential levels of the use of profanity in the Singer et al. (1965) study. Old clothes (deindividuated condition) may have provided cues for lowered restraints against obscene language, whereas dressy clothes (individuated condition) may have provided cues to a number of learned associations of verbal restraint and propriety. Finally, the dark chamber used by Gergen et al. (1973) to deindividuate subjects may have provided cues (e.g., darkness, the awareness of the presence of others through the sense of smell, the sounds of breathing, and the sense of touch, even if at first accidental) suggestive of intimacy and thus facilitating intimate behavior. In this study, however, a control condition indicated that darkness cues did not disinhibit intimacy if subjects were not anonymous.

The major question addressed by the present study is whether the direction of behavior change induced by nonidentifiability is influenced by the valence of situational cues. Given an influence of cues, Zimbardo's (1970) theory would predict that nonidentifiability will disinhibit aggressive behavior and that any effect of cues should be less than the effect for identifiable subjects. On the other hand, the reasoning of Gergen et al. (1973) predicts that nonidentifiability will lead to increases in antisocial behavior if antisocial cues are present and to increases in prosocial behavior if prosocial cues are present. A third possibility is that anonymity per se has no effect, but that prior demonstrations of anonymity effects actually resulted from confounded differences in situational cues.

METHOD

Subjects

Sixty female subjects were recruited from introductory psychology, sociology, and child development courses to participate in a study described as concerned with changes in group evaluations of a stranger. Most subjects were given extra credit in their course as an incentive to participate.

Procedure

Subjects were randomly assigned, 15 to each of four conditions, in a 2×2 factorial design that manipulated individuation (identifiable) versus deindividuation (nonidentifiable) and prosocial versus antisocial cues. Each subject was informed by phone, at the time she was recruited, that the experiment was to be run in groups of four, and that it was therefore very important for her to appear on time. Upon arrival, subjects were informed that each student had been asked to report to a different room in order to preclude interaction with others prior to the experiment. It was also explained that Polaroid pictures of the other group members would be used to establish the essential feeling of being part of a group and that disguises would be worn in the pictures to obscure individual difference characteristics that might be influential. In fact, although as many as four subjects were run in each session, each subject was treated completely independently of the others, and all subjects at any one time were in different treatment conditions. No subject had any contact with any other subject during the experimental session.

It was explained to each subject that the paid nonstudent male volunteer whom they would be evaluating was taking part in a verbal learning experiment and that it was important for them to become involved with the stranger. Involvement was to be established by their participation in selecting the level of shock that this person received for failure to respond correctly in the learning task. Subjects were instructed that it was an exploratory study on the effect of arousal on learning and that the experimenters did not know what effect different shock levels would have. Following each error the learner would be given a shock the base level of which could be increased or decreased by the responses of the subjects. The actual shock level received following an error would be the base level adjusted by the average adjustment selected by the four group members. Each subject would select high, moderate, or slight increases (+ 3,

+ 2, + 1) or decreases (− 3, − 2, − 1) in the shock to be administered. It was explained that following each trial the subject would see on her console the shock selections of the other three subjects plus her own, that these would be averaged to determine the level of shock increase or decrease to be administered on that trial, and that no record would be kept of individual responses but only of the group average for each trial. Thus all subjects' responses, regardless of condition, were to be nonidentifiable to the experimenter and to any others who might see the data. The "learning task" ended when the subject had made 15 errors. The number of correct responses made prior to the 15th error was the measure of successful learning that subjects were to try to facilitate by their shock selections.

Cue Manipulation   The costume manipulation of cues was produced by having each subject wear either a robe resembling those of the Ku Klux Klan or a nurse's uniform. The ostensible purpose of the costumes was to obscure individual differences. The nature of the specific costume given to each subject was presented as an accident of convenience (i.e., "I'm not much of a seamstress; this thing came out looking kind of Ku Klux Klannish." or "I was fortunate the hospital *recovery room* let me borrow these nurses' gowns to use in the study.") A Polaroid picture was taken of each subject in her costume, and pictures of others in the group, in similar costumes, were attached to the subjects' consoles. Each subject was told that copies of her picture had been placed on the consoles of others in the group.

Deindividuation Manipulation   In the individuation condition, consoles were labeled so that each subject could identify the shock level set by each person in the group and the person by whom it was set. Also, large name tags were attached to the costumes of the individuals in the Polaroid pictures. In the deindividuation condition, pictures of others in costume were attached to subject consoles, but no name tags were worn, and subjects were provided with no means of identifying the person who made any given response.

Following the interview, subjects filled out a preliminary evaluation of the confederate. Learning trials were then begun, errors being indicated by the lights on the subjects' consoles, signaling to them to select + 3, + 2, or + 1 levels of increase or − 1, − 2, or − 3 levels of decrease in intensity of the shock the confederate was to receive. After all subjects in the group had responded, feedback of the choices of others was displayed and shock was supposedly administered. Feedback was preprogrammed to average 0 across each of three blocks of trials. Following the learning task, subjects were asked to fill out a postexperimental questionnaire, after which they were probed for suspicion, debriefed, asked not to divulge the deceptions to others, and dismissed.

RESULTS

Evaluation of the Stranger

Five bipolar scales for evaluating the stranger were administered immediately following the interview, prior to the learning task. The experimental conditions did not significantly differ from each other, the means for each condition being on the *insincere, dishonest, cold, phony,* and *unkind* side of the midpoint. It appears that the confederate was perceived to be obnoxious, as planned, in all conditions.

Manipulation Checks

Perception of Cues   Four bipolar scales on the postexperimental questionnaire were used to assess subjects' perception of costume cues. As intended, the Ku Klux Klan costumes were rated as significantly more tough, harmful, unkind, and cold than were the nurses' costumes, $p < .01$, for each scale. Composite totals of responses to these four scales indicated that the Ku Klux Klan costumes were perceived as significantly more negative than the nurses' costumes, $F(1, 56) = 24.95, p < .01$. This difference reflects the negative ratings of the Ku Klux Klan costumes, $M = 5.59$, versus the slightly positive ratings of the nurses' costumes, $M = 3.71$ on a 1 (extremely compassionate) to 7 (extremely aggressive) scale.

Perceived Sense of Deindividuation   As expected, deindividuated subjects, compared to individuated subjects, indicated on the postexperimental questionnaire that it would be more difficult to identify shock selections of other individuals in their group, $F(1, 6) = 15.84, p < .01$, and that it would be more difficult to distinguish members of their group from nongroup members following the experiment, $F(1, 56) = 19.55$, $p < .01$. These measures suggest that in fact deindividuation was manipulated as intended.

Shock Selections

The primary dependent variable, shock selection, was analyzed by a $2 \times 2 \times 3$ analysis of variance, individuation versus deindividuation, and prosocial versus antisocial cues between subjects and trial blocks within subjects. This analysis revealed a significant main effect for cues, $F(1, 56) = 46.28, p < .01$, with shock decrease the mean response for prosocial cues and shock increase the mean response for antisocial cues. The main effect for individuation versus deindividuation was not significant, $F(1, 56) = 2.92$, but there was a significant Cues $\times$ Deindividuation interaction, $F(1, 56) = 8.21, p < .01$. The interaction (see Table 19-1) is a result of an increasing effect of cues on behavior in deindividuated versus individuated conditions.

A Newman-Keuls test revealed that each condition was significantly different from each other condition, each at the $p < .01$ level, except the simple effect of deindividuation within antisocial cues. This comparison is essentially a conceptual replication of Zimbardo (1970). It was directionally consistent with that effect but only achieved $p < .15$ even by a one-tailed simple t test.

DISCUSSION

The experimental manipulations appear to have been effective. The prosocial costumes, though closer to neutral than had been intended, were rated as significantly less negative than the antisocial costumes. The manipulation of deindividuation was as-

TABLE 19-1 MEAN SHOCK SELECTION AS A
FUNCTION OF CUE AND
DEINDIVIDUATION CONDITIONS

	Condition	
Cue	Individuated	Deindividuated
Prosocial	$-.35_a$	-1.47_b
Antisocial	$.76_c$	$.95_c$

Note: Possible range of scores was from -3 (the prosocial choice of maximally reducing shock level) to $+3$ (the antisocial choice of maximally increasing shock level). Means without a common subscript were significantly different from each other ($p < .01$).

sessed by self-reports of ability to identify behaviors of specific group members (cf. Festinger et al., 1952) and perceived anonymity of group members (cf. Zimbardo, 1970). Both measures demonstrated that deindividuation was manipulated as intended.

Of primary interest in this research were the effects of cues and of deindividuation on shock selection. In the presence of Ku Klux Klan costume cues, subjects were likely to increase shock levels, whereas in the presence of prosocial cues, subjects were likely to decrease shock levels. This finding by itself suggests alternative interpretations of the Singer et al. (1965) study and the Zimbardo (1970) study presented in this paper's introduction. In those studies costume cues were completely confounded with the manipulations of deindividuation. It is entirely possible that the increased antisocial behavior observed in those studies (i.e., frequency of obscene words and duration of electrical shocks) was a function of the costume cue manipulation alone and depended less on anonymity than has been widely believed.

In contrast to the previous research, the present study allows us to look at the effects of deindividuation independent of costume cues. According to Zimbardo, (a) deindividuation should have resulted in more aggressive, antisocial behavior for both costume variations, and (b) any effect of cues should have been attenuated as a function of deindividuation. According to Gergen et al. (1973), however, cues should interact with deindividuation, deindividuation leading to more antisocial behavior in the presence of antisocial cues and to more prosocial behavior in the presence of prosocial cues. The interaction obtained in the present study (see Table 19-1) is consistent with Gergen's position.

Conceptually, most theorists (cf. Zimbardo, 1970) have viewed deindividuation as a state of the organism that can be induced by a variety of input variables, including but not limited to anonymity. Experimentally, however, deindividuation has nearly always been manipulated by varying some aspect of identifiability. This is true of the research discussed in the introduction and is true of the present research. More recently (cf. Diener, 1979), deindividuation has been manipulated by means of complexes of input variables including a sense of group unity, group cohesiveness, group responsibility, and even kinesthetic feedback from physical activity. These inputs may in fact induce a sense of anonymity, but very likely they have additional influences beyond those related to identifiability.

20

EXCERPT FROM THE PSYCHOLOGY OF ATTITUDE CHANGE AND SOCIAL INFLUENCE

Philip G. Zimbardo and Michael R. Leippe (1991)

In Module 20, Myers discusses how group decisions can become quite different from the sum of individuals' decisions, and discusses group polarization and group think as two social cognitive processes that influence group decision making. Zimbardo and Leippe (1991) answer a similar question in a specific applied setting—the courtroom. We often think of the courtroom setting as an impartial situation; after all our legal system is designed to make sure that everything is fair and that justice is served. But is it? Psychology has been used increasingly in choosing jurors, developing angles from which to argue a case, and preparing witnesses (nonverbal behavior and clothing choices). And, of course, once the jurors are sequestered for the final decision, group processes occur freely. Because both sides use social psychological processes, Zimbardo and Leippe suggest that when pitted against each other they cancel out; thus, legal decisions are still ultimately based on the evidence itself. Do you agree, and why?

As this introduction was being written, two trials were underway which have attracted wide public attention—the trials of the two Melendez brothers who killed their parents in California and the trial of Lorena Bobbitt who used a kitchen knife to sever her husband's penis in Virginia. Since both these trials will be over by the time you read this, may we suggest that it might be very interesting, in light of the Zimbardo and Leippe reading, to go back and read posttrial comments by the jurors who were faced with deciding these cases. We suspect that issues related to the group processes described in this reading may have arisen.

Source: Excerpted from *The psychology of attitude change and social influence* by P. G. Zimbardo and M. R. Leippe, 1991, New York: McGraw-Hill. Copyright © 1991 by McGraw-Hill. Reprinted by permission of the publisher and the authors.

THE JURY ROOM

We now come to the topic of the deliberation of juries. The jury is the ultimate symbol of democratic justice in our society. In film and television, the jury usually delivers the punch line: Did the hero-lawyers's brilliant defense and impassioned summation persuade the jury to acquit the innocent accused? Will the jury send the evil mob leader "up the river?"

Juries usually consist of twelve citizens who have two highly interrelated tasks. First, they must listen to the evidence presented at trial and evaluate it. Second, they must communicate their impressions to other jurors, with the goal of reaching a unanimous agreement about guilt. During their first task, jurors are targets of many influence attempts, some of which we've discussed. Once in the jury room, however, they are both sources and targets of interpersonal influence—active ingredients in an influence-rich stew of opinion and discussion that hopefully will congeal into a verdict.

Most of the time it does, and quickly. Verdicts are reached in 95 percent of all American trials, by juries that typically deliberates less than 2 hours (Kalven and Zeisel, 1966). Furthermore, most jury verdicts are highly sensitive to the evidence (Saks and Hastie, 1978; Visher, 1987). The defendant may be beautiful and nice, or the weird victim may be hard to relate to. Yet, laboratory simulations and reviews of real court cases suggest that biasing factors like these are usually overridden by legitimate admitted evidence, *provided the evidence is clear.*

It is heartening to know that at times evidence controls inference and generalizations. Does this mean that jury deliberations are uninteresting from an influence perspective? The answer is "No." First, there is the issue of *how* twelve people manage to agree on a basically good decision most of the time. Second, there is the situation in which the evidence is very mixed. That's where the psychological action is.

Majorities Rule Most of the Time

In the 1957 movie *Twelve Angry Men,* eleven jurors quickly conclude that a boy is guilty of murdering his father. One juror, played by Henry Fonda, holds out for acquittal and suffers through the kind of focused and eventually hostile group pressures to "come around." But in the end, this courageous minority of one eventually turns around the others, saving the defendant from hanging. Is this a common scenario? Though not unheard of, such persuasive influence by a single dissenting juror is extremely rare. Most often, the eventual verdict is the one favored by the majority of jurors when they *entered* deliberation, especially if the majority consists of at least two-thirds of the jurors (Davis, 1980; Kalven and Zeisel, 1966). This majority-rule relationship concurs with our earlier observation that the weight of the admitted trial evidence is usually decisive. If, say, ten of twelve jurors vote not guilty on the first ballot taken before deliberations, it is likely that defense evidence was stronger than prosecution evidence.

But *how* do majorities usually get their way? According to surveys of former jurors, as well as mock trials in which the investigators eavesdrop on mock juries, minority members do not immediately give in when they discover that they are outnumbered (Stasser et al., 1982). Rather, they must be won over through social influence processes. There are two generic forms of influence: *informational influence,* in which people adopt the behavior or attitudes of others because they perceive that the others have more, and more valid, information; and *normative influence,* in which people conform or comply in order to maintain harmonious social relations. Both influence processes are operative in jury deliberations.

More People, More Arguments   First consider informational influence. During deliberation, the individual jurors present their opinions and their arguments for it. Assume that ten jurors favor a guilty verdict, while two believe that there is enough reasonable doubt to acquit the defendant. Will the ten members of the majority all present the same argument? Probably not. Each proponent of guilt may contribute his or her own angle on the evidence, perhaps adding information that the others do not remember. Of course, the two holdouts may have somewhat separate arguments as well. But each of those minority members with only one new set of supportive arguments must go head to head against ten opposing sets. What we have is a *persuasion* situation in which the message with a greater number of reasonable arguments creates the attitude change. This is usually the message of the majority.

To Hang Is to Fail   Normative influence may result from the minority's "selfish attempt to gain social approval and avoid social disapproval" (Stasser et al., 1982). Members of a large majority become disgruntled when their calm attempts at persuasion fail to move a dissenting minority, and their communications become tinged with hints of rejection, dislike, and incredulity. It takes a brave, firmly convinced, and almost heroic type of person to bear the brunt of such sustained social pressure. Normative influence may work at another level as well (Stasser et al., 1982). A jury's goal is to reach a verdict. If it does not, if it becomes a hung jury, it has failed to reach that goal. It has frustrated justice—and, in a sense, wasted everyone's time except, of course, the defendant's. The desire to avoid this failure to reach a socially desirable group goal may compel many minority members to become increasingly receptive to the majority viewpoint.

As a member of a jury who needed to do some persuading, would you pitch your appeals to the informational or normative concerns of those who oppose you? Your characteristic style surely matters here. You could be a moralizer or a "just the facts" sort of person. Beyond preferred style, however, the case itself may determine which basis of social influence you exploit. In one study, mock jurors deliberated in groups of six after reading a civil case involving injuries caused when a poorly constructed furnace exploded (Kaplan and Miller, 1987). Jurors were told that another jury had reached a verdict against the defendant (the furnace manufacturer) and in favor of the plaintiff (the injured home owner). Their task was to agree on a damage award. Half the juries were to decide *compensatory damages,* which are to compensate the plaintiff for actual losses resulting from the defendant's negligence. The remaining juries were to decide on *exemplary damages,* awarded over and beyond compensation with the intent of punishing the defendant and deterring others from similar indiscretions.

Note that an award for compensatory damages more or less involves looking at the facts. How much did this unfortunate accident cost the plaintiff? In contrast, the award for exemplary damages is more subjective and judgmental; it reflects social values (pro- or antibusiness), sense of moral responsibility, and the like. Given these differences, we might expect more attempts at informational persuasion (stating the facts) in the former (compensatory damages) case and more attempts at normative pressure (moralizing) in the latter (exemplary damages) case. This is exactly what the researchers found when they studied the content of the juries' deliberations. Jurors faced with a fact-based decision (compensatory damages) appealed to facts and evidence in most of their statements ("Just the hospital bills alone would be enormous"), whereas jurors faced with a values-based decision (exemplary damages) most often made statements suggestive of social approval and disapproval ("It is wrong to . . ." "Do what the majority thinks is right"). In general, then, we can expect a majority to focus on whatever "pressure points" are most relevant to winning others over to "their side" of a case.

Group Polarization   The preceding example reminds us that jury decisions are not always dichotomous guilty or not guilty choices. Juries may also make quantitative decisions. In civil suits, the jury may decide how much money to award. In criminal cases, it may have the task of deciding what the defendant is guilty of, if at all. Often the alternatives are ordered according to increasing seriousness and corresponding punishment: for example, manslaughter (a prison term), second-degree murder (a longer prison term), and first-degree murder (life imprisonment or death). Research suggests that, in these situations, it is quite possible that from the first to the last ballot the jury may grow more extreme in its judgments. The majority itself may move—toward greater extremity. *Group polarization* occurs.

To get a better feel for this phenomenon, let us briefly review some observations about how groups become more extreme over time in settings other than those involving injuries, and then turn to jury settings. Polarization was discovered in the early 1960s in studies of business decisions (Stoner, 1961) and was later verified in other studies in which subjects were asked to advise a person or business in the throes of a dilemma (Myers and Lamm, 1976). For example, should Charlie quit that safe and comfortable, but dead end, job and start the business he always wanted? Subjects read background information about the case and then indicated privately what minimal probability of success Charlie should require before he makes his move. The lower the required probability, the riskier they are in encouraging Charlie to be daring. Subjects then got together in a group to discuss Charlie's dilemma, after which they again expressed their opinion of the minimal probability for making a change.

The typical result can be summarized as follows: If, at first, the members of the group individually all tend to favor a risky course of action ("Charlie, go for it even if you've only got a 30 percent chance of making it"), group discussion makes them even riskier ("Go for it if you've only got a 20 percent chance"). If the trend is toward caution at first ("You'd better be 70 percent sure"), discussion makes them even more cautious ("Make that 80 percent"). Group discussion moves the group further out in the direction it was leaning toward initially.

The same effect has been found for attitude issues. French students who at first only mildly liked their president liked him more after talking about him, while their original dislike for Americans was intensified by discussion (Moscovici and Zavalloni, 1969).

Why does group polarization occur? There are two major reasons. First, if all group members are leaning on one side of the issue, most of the ideas and arguments they voice during discussion will also favor that side (Burnstein and Vinokur, 1973). The individual who liked something for two reasons may have five good reasons after hearing others express their views—informational influence again. Second, many people value being a little more extreme—in the right direction of course—than the average person. To be a little extreme is to appear unique, an often desirable quality. As opinions are exchanged in the group, individuals learn that they are not noticeably more extreme, and they shift to become so (Brown, 1965; Goethals and Zanna, 1979). You may recognize this as a special case of normative influence (again) in which those who want to individuate themselves from similar others in a given group setting must behave in ways that are more extreme, if not qualitatively different.

Can polarization occur in juries? It would seem so. Mock jurors in one study deliberated over traffic cases that contained either strong or weak evidence against the defendant. When the case was weak, jurors entered deliberation leaning toward "not guilty" and became further convinced of innocence during deliberation. When the case was strong, jurors' initial leanings toward "guilty" became stronger during deliberation (Myers and Kaplan, 1976).

The propensity for groups to polarize makes the huge damages awarded in some malpractice and personal injury cases seem less surprising. A solid majority, sympathetic to the permanently injured plaintiff, gets on a roll as it discusses how much it should punish the negligent physician or corporation while perhaps sending a message to other potential wrongdoers. This is majority rule—in no moderate terms.

When Things That Shouldn't Influence Do Influence

With so much information and so many participants in the courtroom and jury room, there is always the possibility that a jury's decision will be affected by factors that, ideally, should not matter. Such factors are called "extralegal" because they are outside the realm of legal evidence and procedure. As we've noted, if extralegal factors do influence jurors, it is mainly when the evidence is unclear. Let's briefly examine two of these variables.

Inadmissible Evidence   We have all watched courtroom dramas on television in which the judge instructs the jury to disregard a witness's statement or a piece of evidence that the lawyer slips in—on the grounds that it is legally inadmissible. And you may have asked yourself: "Come on! How can they possibly ignore, let alone forget, what they saw or heard?" You're right, they cannot. Mock trial studies suggest that disallowed evidence influences jury decisions, perhaps *even more* than it would if it hadn't been disallowed (Sue et al., 1973; Wolf and Montgomery, 1977). By disallowing it, the judge calls attention to the legal evidence, makes it salient, and thus gives it a special memory tag when the jurors are encoding all the massive amount of trial information for later retrieval. The judge may also arouse psychological reactance: jurors may feel that their freedom to consider all evidence of importance is being constrained and may respond by affording the disallowed evidence more weight than it deserves.

Not All Jurors Are Created Equal   Not infrequently, two or three jurors dominate deliberations. If we can trust highly realistic and involving simulations, complemented by recollections of actual jurors, it appears that, in most twelve-person juries, three jurors do more than half of the talking while three others may do no talking at all (Stasser et al., 1982, 1989; Strodtbeck et al., 1957). This unevenness in participation, in fact, is evident in all types of small group interactions (Bales, 1958). In the jury, it allows the occasional Andrew Choa (or Henry Fonda)—a single individual—to have basically a "single-handed" impact on the verdict. It also means that the unique biases of one or a few jurors could dictate a verdict.

To improve on your chances of having a bigger say in the deliberations, you must get elected foreperson. This isn't so hard: either speak first, get nominated first, or simply volunteer. Take your pick; that is enough to get you elected. To really cinch election, if the deliberation table is rectangular, sit in the "power seat"—the end, or head of the table. Even if sitting there does not get you elected foreperson, you may be able to wield extra influence through nonverbal dynamics. The person at the end is visible to all others and can speak to everyone while also looking at them. Not surprisingly, jurors at the end of the table both initiate and receive the most communicative acts (Strodtbeck and Hook, 1961). Part of this relationship, though, is probably due to the fact that jurors already experienced at taking control (such as managers and entrepreneurs) *choose* the end seats in the first place. Some people, you might say, can take power sitting down.

Our point here is that there is always the possibility that a jury verdict will reflect the bias and orientation of a few jurors who wield extraordinary influence. The chances of this happening are increased in more ambiguous cases that are open to alternative interpretations.

Jury Selection: Can Juries Be "Stacked"?   The possible power of just a few jurors raises the issue of influence through jury selection. The opposing attorneys in a case are allowed to question potential jurors during a pretrial selection hearing. If either one feels that a potential juror may be predisposed against his or her client or case, the attorney can reject the person as a juror. Thus, to an extent, lawyers have a say about *who* is on a jury during this process, known as voir dire. Can the sharp attorney gain an influence advantage by choosing the audience—by "stacking" a jury with people sympathetic to his or her cause?

It certainly is possible under some circumstances to identify jurors with traits and backgrounds that make it likely they will be biased toward a certain verdict. For example, people with rigid, authoritarian views might be predisposed to see as guilty an accused murderer of a well-respected police officer (Mitchell, 1979). Politically liberal jurors may have a bias that favors acquittal of antigovernment demonstrators accused of inciting a riot. Studies indicate that if you get the people with the relevant traits on the jury, your side might enjoy an advantage in some cases (Horowitz, 1980; Wrightsman, 1987). However, the odds are that your opposing lawyer will also be trying to select the "right" juror. Together, your efforts may cancel each other out. Moreover, it isn't always easy to intuit which kind of person will be sympathetic to what side. These factors limit the likelihood that lawyers, on their own, can select a jury that is especially partial to their side.

Scientific jury selection may fare somewhat better. This is a consulting service provided by some social scientists. They survey people with various backgrounds and traits and ask them their opinions about the upcoming case. From the responses they get, they find out which traits are related to the verdict the attorney seeks and advise the attorney to select as jurors those who appear to share those traits (Schulman et al., 1973).

Even when attorneys use scientific methods, though, the number of cases that can be influenced by jury selection probably is small. Unless the case is very close, it is the weight of the solid evidence that rules judgments. Most jurors—regardless of their backgrounds, traits, and prejudices—let the evidence be their main decision-making guide.

21

ANTIPOLLUTION MEASURES AND PSYCHOLOGICAL REACTANCE THEORY: A FIELD EXPERIMENT

Michael B. Mazis (1975)

Everyday, in ways that are subtle and in ways that are not so subtle, you and I try to get other people to do what we want them to do. Sometimes our best efforts do not work. This can be especially frustrating when it's in others' own best interest to do what we ask of them. Parents try to shape and mold children's behavior in socially acceptable ways. But children often don't like to be told what to do. And it's not just children. None of us enjoy having our freedom of choice removed. And yet we realize that there are behaviors which take extra effort on our part which are worth the extra effort when we consider the greater good of society at large. Littering is one example. Recycling is another. It would be easier to toss the empty soft drink can out the car window, and some people still do. But increasingly, people are holding onto the can and then recycling it. Deposit laws in most states provide an economic incentive as well.

Seat belt laws in most states mandate that passengers "buckle up— it's the law." New York was the first state to mandate use by all front-seat passengers in 1985. Just having the seat belts in cars has been federally mandated for decades, but people don't always use them. A 1994 Department of Transportation (DOT) report found that national seat belt use in the United States was 66 percent in 1993, up from 62 percent in 1992 and 59 percent in 1991. The DOT has established a goal of 75 percent seat belt usage by 1997. For whatever reason, women are about 50 percent more likely than men to wear their seat belts. One reason for increased compliance with seat belt laws that the DOT cited was an increase in states enacting "primary laws" where police can stop a driver simply for failure to wear a seat belt versus "secondary laws" where police can issue a

Source: Abridged from the *Journal of Personality and Social Psychology,* 1975, *31,* 654–660. Copyright © 1975 by the American Psychological Association. Reprinted by permission of the publisher and the author.

ticket for not using a seat belt only when they have stopped a driver for another reason, such as speeding. The DOT also estimates that the 4 percent rise in seat belt use from 1992 to 1993 resulted in 500 lives saved and 14,000 serious injuries avoided on the highways of the United States. Interestingly, in Germany seat belt use is 95 percent, and insurance companies there are allowed by law to cut payments made to unbelted drivers involved in accidents. But do you always buckle up when you drive or when you are a passenger in a car? Do you resent, even a little bit, being told what to do by the government?

Mazis addressed the process of resisting social influence and psychological reactance to the loss of options in a field study examining public reaction to the enactment of antiphosphate laws in Miami, Florida, in the early 1970s. Miami consumers had been accustomed for many years to buying high-phosphate detergents, in spite of their proven environmentally harmful effects. Similar laws are now fairly uniform nationwide. Not surprisingly, the banned detergents were seen more positively by those who could no longer buy them. That should not surprise you. Remember the tale of Romeo and Juliet, Shakespeare's pair of star-crossed lovers, whose desire for each other increased as obstacles, such as feuding parents, were placed in their way? Have you ever wanted to read a book or see a movie because someone else said it should be banned? How many people suddenly became interested in the Robert Maplethorpe collection of photographs after they were banned by a museum in Cincinnati, Ohio, a few years ago? If you were staying at a friend's house and told you could absolutely not, under any circumstances, look in one particular drawer in the kitchen, what would you do the first chance you had?

Psychological reactance theory asserts that when a person believes himself free to engage in a given behavior and his freedom is eliminated or threatened with elimination, the individual experiences psychological reactance, a motivational state directed toward reestablishment of the threatened or eliminated freedom (Brehm, 1966). One major determinant of reactance, external pressure applied through social influence or persuasive communications, has been studied extensively. Laboratory experiments have typically manipulated social influence by having confederates restrict subjects' freedom of choice through freedom threatening statements (Brehm & Sensenig, 1966; Worchel & Brehm, 1971).

Research exploring the influence of persuasive communications has focused on factors attenuating reactance effects. Conformity pressures (Grabitz-Gniech, 1971; Pallack & Heller, 1971), the involvement of peers in eliminating alternatives (Worchel & Brehm, 1971), and individual difference variables, including manipulated felt competence (Wicklund & Brehm, 1968), feelings of inadequacy (Grabitz-Gniech, 1971), and locus of control (Biondo & MacDonald, 1971) have been found to influence reactivity.

While the loss of options may be a major determinant of psychological reactance also, it has not been fully explored in reactance research. Grabitz-Gniech (1971) and Brehm, Stires, Sensenig, and Shaban (1966) examined the effect of reducing the choice of records and paintings, respectively, among college students in laboratory experiments. While statistically significant reactance effects were found, both experiments failed to present an ego-involving situation in which subjects lost an important freedom. The possibility of demand characteristics producing a reactive response must be considered. Perhaps a more appropriate laboratory for experimentation is the marketplace where consumers' freedom of choice has been frequently restricted through governmental action such as requiring safety devices on automobiles; recalling soups, cranberries, tuna, drugs, and automobiles; and restricting the use of energy.

The elimination of free choice by authority sources has been explored in reactance research, but the only authority source studied has been the psychological experimenter (Hammock & Brehm, 1966). For research involving authority sources to have generalizability, particularly for social issues, a wider sampling of authority sources is needed. For example, Davis and Eichhorn (1963) have studied the issue of compliance and noncompliance with physicians' regimens. The current experiment is directed toward determining if responses to the imposition of a "socially beneficial" governmental action (antiphosphate ordinance) might be predicted from psychological reactance theory.

Obviously, not all individuals react against all restrictions of free choice. It remains for research to specify which subjects and under which restrictions psychological reactance is manifested when options are eliminated or curtailed by authority sources.

The principal consequence of reactivity needs to be specified more precisely also. The present study explores two major manifestations of reactivity, enhanced attractiveness of restricted alternatives and reduced desirability of alternatives forced upon subjects. Most reactance studies have failed to separate these two effects.

The present investigation concerns response to an event affecting many households throughout the United States—imposition of an antiphosphate law. On January 1, 1972, Dade County (Miami), Florida, began prohibiting the sale, possession, or use of laundry detergents and other cleaning products containing phosphates. Since only a small number of popular brands were available in no-phosphate formulations, shoppers found their choice of laundry detergent drastically diminished. These dramatic changes in the number of choice alternatives provided an opportunity to examine psychological reactance theory predictions in a field setting.

According to reactance theory, Miami households would be motivationally aroused due to the phosphate restrictions and feel an increased desire to have the forbidden detergent as contrasted with households in a control city (Tampa) whose freedom of choice was unrestricted. The reactance aroused in Miami subjects should result in higher effectiveness attributed to phosphate detergents as compared with Tampa subjects and more negative attitudes toward governmental regulation of environmental matters which should influence the product evaluations of Miami consumers.

Since Miami households could be classified into three major subgroups, additional reactance theory predictions may be made. The first group consisted of housewives who were able to continue purchasing products labeled by their favorite brand names, but which were now being sold without phosphates; these households are referred to as "nonswitchers." Since one leading detergent manufacturer quickly began distributing no-phosphate reformulations of all its existing laundry detergent brands, users could continue to purchase their regular brands after the anti-phosphate law went into effect.

Several other detergent manufacturers did not begin distribution of no-phosphate reformulations for several months and therefore users were forced to switch brands after the phosphate restrictions went into effect. These consumers, who were forced to switch from their regular brands, are referred to as "switchers."

Based on their dissimilar motivational states, it is anticipated that (a) switchers would express more negative attitudes about the effectiveness of no-phosphate products and/or more positive attitudes about the effectiveness of phosphate products than would nonswitchers and (b) switchers would have a more negative attitude toward the antiphosphate law than would nonswitchers.

Switchers should feel a greater restriction of their freedom of choice than should non-switchers as a result of being unable to purchase a laundry detergent sold under their favorite brand label. It must be remembered that both switchers and nonswitchers were using a totally new product; however, in one case consumers were using a product with a "new" label or brand name, while in the other they were able to use a re-formulated product being sold under their favorite brand name.

The third group of Miami households are those who defied the antiphosphate ordinance by smuggling detergent into Miami from surrounding counties or who accumulated large amounts of phosphate detergent before the January enforcement date. Since these smugglers and hoarders may have had very favorable attitudes toward phosphate detergents before the enactment of the no-phosphate restrictions, no predictions can be made concerning their attitudes about the effectiveness of phosphate brands based on reactance theory. Their predisposition toward phosphate brands may have been instrumental in their being categorized as "violators." On the other hand, switchers and nonswitchers were placed into those categories as a result of detergent manufacturers' decisions about whether to produce no-phosphate reformulations of detergent brands.[1]

TABLE 21-1   MEANS AND STANDARD DEVIATIONS FOR EFFECTIVENESS RATINGS OF PHOSPHATE DETERGENTS

Characteristic	Miami (n = 76)		Tampa (n = 45)	
	M	SD	M	SD
Whiteness	8.68	1.87	8.27	1.56
Freshness	8.77	2.08	7.87	1.51
Cleans in cold water	8.52	2.15	7.47	1.83
Brightness	8.31	2.09	7.84	1.80
Stain removal	8.00	2.43	6.96	2.05
Pours easily	9.45	2.05	9.07	1.77
Gentleness	8.81	1.80	8.71	1.51

Note: Based on an 11-point scale with 11 labeled "absolutely perfect" and 1 labeled "poor."

[1]No subjects classified as nonswitchers switched to another manufacturer's brand after enactment of the antiphosphate ordinance.

METHOD

An instrument was designed to determine attitudes about laundry detergents and related products, opinions about laws regulating the use of phosphates, and demographic characteristics. Seventy-six interviews were completed by four female interviewers in Miami and 45 completed questionnaires were returned by the two female interviewers in Tampa. Nine questionnaires were discarded as a result of incomplete responses. Interviews were conducted from a period from 7 to 9 weeks after the anti-phosphate statute became effective.

Since only limited funding was available to defer the cost of interviewing, sample selection in both Tampa and Miami emphasized subject homogeneity to restrict the impact of extraneous variables. To enhance the similarity between Tampa and Miami samples, all respondents interviewed were: (a) English-speaking Caucasian women; (b) with family incomes of $7,500 to $15,000 per year; (c) who had at least one child under 16 years of age living at home; (d) who resided in single-family dwellings; and (e) who used primarily phosphate detergent brands during the preceeding 6 months. Comparisons between Tampa and Miami samples revealed no significant income, age, or educational differences.

Two middle-income census tracts were chosen in both cities and blocks were randomly selected within tracts. Two sampling points were randomly designated within each block and interviewing commenced from each point in a clockwise direction until two respondents were found who met the criteria enumerated above.

RESULTS

Miami versus Tampa

At the beginning of each interview, subjects were asked to rate the effectiveness of the phosphate laundry detergent they had used most during the previous 6 months. Seven brand characteristics were evaluated on an 11-point scale labeled "absolutely perfect" and "poor" at the end points. Salient characteristics were determined through a free association procedure similar to that used by Fishbein (1967).

Reactance theory predictions are supported by the data in Table 21-1. On all seven characteristics, Miami subjects gave higher mean effectiveness ratings to phosphate brands than did Tampa subjects.

The two way Groups × Trials analysis of variance provides statistical support for the proposition that Miami housewives were in a reactive motivational state. Overall, Miami subjects rated phosphate detergents as being more efficacious than did Tampa subjects ($F = 5.42, p < .05$).

Miami subjects expressed a less optimistic view about the success of governmental action in solving water pollution problems and toward the usefulness of phosphate content regulation than did Tampa subjects.

Tampa residents stated a stronger degree of agreement with the statement, "The government should play an important role in protecting our water from pollution," than did Miami subjects (Tampa = 1.61, Miami = 2.39; $t = 3.62, p < .01$). In addition, Tampa housewives had greater expectations about the usefulness of laws restricting the sale of detergents containing phosphates than did Miami respondents (Tampa

$= 2.20$, Miami $= 2.76$; $M = 2.72$, $p < .01$), thereby sustaining the view that Miami housewives were experiencing psychological reactance.

Switchers versus Nonswitchers

Brand Ratings   According to psychological reactance theory, the amount of freedom eliminated directly influences psychological reactance. Since switchers were experiencing more psychological choice deprivation, they should provide lower mean effectiveness ratings to no-phosphate brands than should nonswitchers.

The data in Table 21-2 shows that of the 76 Miami households responding (9 of which had incomplete data), the 44 switchers provided lower average effectiveness ratings across all seven detergent attributes than did the 23 nonswitchers. The Groups $\times$ Trials analysis of variance reveals significantly lower attractiveness estimates for no-phosphate products by switchers than by nonswitchers ($F = 4.48$, $p < .05$).

The greater degree of psychological reactance being experienced by switchers may take the form of increased attractiveness of the restricted alternative (phosphate detergent), as well as decreased attractiveness of the alternative forced upon subjects (no-phosphate detergent).

DISCUSSION

While student subjects in laboratory experiments have often behaved as predicted by psychological reactance theory, the current study provides strong support for the theory's predictions among housewives in a field setting. As predicted, Miami subjects rated phosphate detergents as being more effective than did Tampa subjects. Hypotheses derived from psychological reactance theory concerning Miami versus Tampa subjects' attitudes toward government's role in protecting the public from wa-

TABLE 21-2   MEANS FOR EFFECTIVENESS RATINGS OF DETERGENTS

Characteristic	No-phosphate detergents		Phosphate detergents	
	Switchers M	Nonswitchers M	Switchers M	Nonswitchers M
Whiteness	7.07	7.87	8.59	8.61
Freshness	7.11	7.85	8.75	8.78
Cleans in cold water	6.36	7.61	8.72	8.43
Brightness	6.30	7.43	8.41	8.17
Stain removal	6.14	7.41	7.79	8.13
Pours easily	8.45	9.17	9.30	9.78
Gentleness	7.23	8.04	8.93	8.74

Note: Based on an 11-point scale labeled "absolutely perfect" and "poor" at end points.

ter pollution and in imposing legal restrictions against the sale of products containing phosphates were sustained as well.

Since adaptation effects (Helson, 1964) may have contributed to the enhanced attractiveness of phosphate detergent as a result of expanded use of the less effective no-phosphate brands, the most compelling evidence supporting a reactance theory interpretation is found in the attitudinal differences of switchers and nonswitchers. Analysis of effectiveness ratings revealed that there were no significant mean differences in the evaluation of alternative brands of no-phosphate detergent. As a result, the differential attitudes expressed by switchers and nonswitchers can be attributed to psychological reactance rather than to physical differences in the brands used.

This research does make several contributions to the psychological reactance literature. First, it demonstrates that psychological reactance is not solely a laboratory phenomena. Housewives did feel more psychological choice deprivation when they were forced to switch from their favorite phosphate brands to unfamiliar brands of no-phosphate laundry detergent.

Second, greater insight into the consequences of reactance was obtained. Negative attitudes about the effectiveness of the alternative forced upon housewives rather than enhancement of the eliminated alternative was found.

Since most subjects expressed satisfaction with their laundry detergents, psychological reactance would be less likely to take the form of increased desirability of the eliminated alternative as compared with decreased attractiveness of the forced alternative due to ceiling effects. The mean rating for control group (Tampa) subjects was 8.02 on an 11-point scale. While the circumstances surrounding this experiment may be unique, it is possible that reactance often takes the form of a reduction in the attractiveness of the forced alternative since people are satisfied with the products they use as a result of dissonance reduction. More valuable than such speculation would be further research on this topic.

Third, public policy implications of psychological reactance research have been made apparent. From a societal perspective, the most appropriate laboratory for psychological reactance research might be the consumer market. While governmental agencies and legislators issue administrative decisions and enact ordinances which restrict freedom of choice, consumer assessment after restriction is rarely undertaken. Too much restriction may result in extensive noncompliance. However, additional research is needed to assess the degree of consumer reactivity as a result of: (a) the issue, (b) the proportion of choice alternatives remaining and number of substitutes available, (c) the authority sources (e.g., federal vs. local and state government; legislative vs. executive decisions) used to eliminate freedom of choice, and (d) the permanence of a reactive motivational state.

SOCIAL RELATIONS

22

THE WHEELCHAIR
REBELLION

John Gliedman (1979)

In Module 22, Myers sets the stage for an in-depth discussion on prejudice and describes in some detail the pervasiveness of racial and gender prejudice. But what other kinds of prejudice are there, and which kinds are *you* guilty of? Most of us are self-aware enough to know some of our own prejudices, but we may well have others about which we are not even aware. Written over 15 years ago, John Gliedman's exposé of our prejudices against the handicapped still holds true for most children and adults in our society.* Since 1979, there have been a number of significant social and legal changes in the United States. In 1990, the U. S. Congress passed what has become known as the Americans with Disabilities Act, which became fully effective two years later, in July of 1992. There continues an ongoing debate over the "political correctness" of different labels applied to diverse groups (my favorite is calling looters "nontraditional shoppers" [SLE]).

Furthermore, Gliedman identifies our acceptance of the *medical model* as one cause for our continued well-meaning but nonetheless paternalistic and discriminatory "treatment" of handicapped individuals. Gliedman calls for a more respectful sensitivity to differences among people. Given the norms in our present culture, developing an appreciation for diversity will probably require rethinking and refeeling many of the old lessons we have acquired in our culture, some of which are discussed in the next module.

Source: Reprinted from *Psychology Today,* 1979, 59, 101. Reprinted with permission from *Psychology Today* magazine. Copyright © 1979 (Sussex Publishers, Inc.).

*The use of inclusive pronouns here is deliberate—being a member of a group (e.g., minority race, female, homosexual, handicapped) that receives the prejudice of and discrimination by others does not protect one from those very same prejudices.

By the early 1970s, many of the nation's black leaders, political activists, and liberal reformers had been exhausted by a decade of confrontation and violence. Undaunted, or perhaps too desperate to care, people with various kinds of handicaps nevertheless began to organize a civil rights movement of their own. A new generation of groups for the disabled was born, such as the American Coalition of Citizens with Disabilities and Mainstream, Inc. Like older and more established groups, they lobbied for better social services and protested the endless Catch-22 provisions in the welfare laws that hurt the severely disabled. But they also demanded something more: they called for significant structural changes in housing, public buildings, and transportation that have long posed barriers to their mobility; and they began working for an end to the prejudice and job discrimination that had proved far more obstructive to an active life than such handicaps as blindness, deafness, or paraplegia.

Even today, the civil rights movement for the disabled is relatively small. The impetus for change comes from the top. A sympathetic Congress (many of whose members themselves have disabled relatives), the efforts of diligent lobbyists, the initiative of legal advocates, and a federal bureaucracy receptive, at least in principle, to the idea of treating the disabled as another disadvantaged minority group—all contributed to the relatively unpublicized passage of landmark legislation in the 1970s. Nevertheless, Frank Bowe, director of the American Coalition, sized up the status of the movement this way: "It is possible to legislate rights, and this has been done. But rights become reality only after political struggle."

Bowe says more than half of all working-age disabled adults who could work are jobless. There is systematic discrimination against those who do work, according to Bowe and others, which keeps them in menial or futureless jobs; across the United States, a network of "sheltered workshops" employs 200,000 handicapped people whose wages average under $1 an hour—far less than the minimum wage. Little energy goes to inventing, producing, or marketing products specially designed for the disabled, and what is marketed generally goes through the medical or social-service system as mediator. Thus are the handicapped barred from behaving as independent producers, consumers, and citizens in the economy.

Along with those tangible disadvantages, the disabled must also cope with a kind of paternalism from their able-bodied allies that has long been discredited in race relations. Even today, many unprejudiced Americans accept traditional stereotypes about different kinds of handicaps. However, instead of reacting cruelly because of the fears and anxieties aroused by those disabilities, we take a more humane approach. We extend to handicapped people what seems to be an enlightened model of medical tolerance. Rather than blame them for their pitiful condition, we say that their social and mental incompetence is produced by a disease or a disease-like condition beyond their control to alter. We believe that, in a social sense, they are chronic patients; and that we owe them the same struggle with our fears and prejudices, the same understanding and tolerance, that we owe victims of any serious disease or injury.

The problem with this analysis, from the disabled person's point of view, is that it allows him or her no scope whatsoever for leading an adult social life. As Talcott Parsons first noted, the role of a patient in middle-class society is functionally very similar to that of a child. We expect the patient to be cheerful and accepting, to obey doctors' orders, and, in general, to devote all his energies to getting well. When an able-bodied person falls sick, he ceases to be judged as an adult; in return, he is expected to work actively to get well. The area defined as his to control shifts to the sickbed. But in America a person labeled handicapped is assigned a specially destructive variant of the sick role. Not merely powerless because he is sick, he is defined as doubly powerless because he cannot master the job of "getting well." Unable to fill that role obligation, he is seen as socially powerless, deprived of a political identity— until he chooses to assert one.

Many members of the civil rights movement for the disabled have told me that the annual cerebral palsy telethon symbolizes for them the deeply humiliating paternalism of society's medical tolerance toward handicapped people. Michael Poachovis, a political organizer on the West Coast, said, "It's absolutely degrading. Watching those telethons you might think that all palsied adults are mentally retarded, pathetically trusting, asexual children." Others find little comfort in the usual image of disabled people presented in the media. Ron Whyte, a writer in New York City, summed up his feelings this way: "You don't learn about Harlem by listening to 'Amos 'n' Andy.'" Only rarely are we forced to confront the paternalism that lurks behind our attempts to deal fairly with the handicapped. Witness the discomfort of audiences watching Jon Voight as a demanding, rebellious, and unabashedly erotic crippled veteran in the recent film *Coming Home*.

Over the past five years, I have studied the problems of disability while on the research staff of the Carnegie Council on Children. Handicapped children were the point of departure for my work. But, along with my colleague William Roth, I eventually devoted as much time to adults as to children, since the problems of the different age groups tend to be closely related.

In the 1960s and 1970s, about 20 million people of working age described themselves as disabled. Those estimates might easily be 50 percent too high or too low. They might be too low because they do not include most people whom a psychologist would classify as mildly retarded; most people who have experienced a major mental illness; or those with speech or learning disabilities. The figures might be too high because they are based upon answers to the question. "Do you have any medical condition or other impairment lasting three months or longer that limits the kind or amount of work that you can do? Answers given to this kind of question are highly unreliable. On the other hand, it is perfectly possible that these contradictory factors cancel out, and that the figure of 20 million is not too far off after all.

Accepting this estimate provisionally, it seems reasonable to assume that disabled people comprise between 5 and 10 percent of the total working-age population. This is a huge number, at least as large as the number of able-bodied hispanics in this age range and quite possibly as large as the number of able-bodied blacks.

Disabilities are, of course, much more common among the elderly. The best guess is that between one-third and one-fourth of all people 60 years or older are currently disabled. But the sociological relationships between disability and old age require further study; it is quite possible that the social experiences of most elderly people in possession of their mental faculties can also be described by the minority-group model of disability which views the social stigma as attached to the condition of being aged rather than a result of any actual disability.

It is even more difficult to assess the number of children with real disabilities. Many kinds of handicap that pass unnoticed among adults may be blown up out of proportion by parents, teachers, and a child's peers. A host of clinical findings also suggests that perceptions of the severity of a handicap are exquisitely sensitive to social milieu. What some people in one social stratum treat as a minor or negligible disability may be considered severely disabling in another. At the present, one can only guess that the total number of disabled children and youths lies somewhere between five and 10 million.

Members of an oppressed social group have little in common apart from the fact that society singles them out for systematic oppression. Examples abound: European Jews in the 1920s and 1930s, many of whom did not consider themselves primarily Jewish; and closer to home, women, homosexuals, the elderly. Similarly, handicapped people are beginning to see themselves as an oppressed minority because society exposes most of them to a common set of pressures that violate their civil rights. Long ago, the social psychologist Kurt Lewin called the defining characteristic of a minority group an "interdependence of fate." Discrimination—much of it in the economic marketplace—constitutes the sociological fate of the disabled. This discrimination imposes a minority-group identity upon a collection of adults and children, each of whom has, in most respects, as much in common with able-bodied people as with one another.

Two or three decades ago, sociologists often studied the phenomenon of "passing"—the attempt of light-skinned blacks to pass as whites, of Jews to pass as gentiles. That phenomenon helps to clarify the relevance of minority-group analysis to disabled people. The first group of disabled people who fit the minority-group model are those who can rarely pass as able-bodied. They include the deaf, the blind, the physically disabled, the cosmetically disfigured, the very short, and individuals with chronic diseases whose symptoms are unpleasant and obtrusive. Another group of disabled people encounters many of the same problems as the black who passed as white in the 1930s or 1940s. They can usually come off as able-bodied, but they often pay a high psychological price for their successful strategies of concealment. The passers include many people once institutionalized in mental hospitals or custodial institutions for the mildly retarded; many epileptics; many people with severe reading disabilities; many with concealable but socially stigmatizing medical conditions or chronic diseases.

For most people with cancer, heart disease, diabetes, and back ailments, the minority-group analysis is probably of secondary importance. Still, even those with such disabilities would benefit greatly from an end to job discrimination against disabled persons, improvement in the quality of the nation's social and health services, and, in many instances, elimination of architectural and transportation barriers to mobility. One other group of disabled adults requires mention—those who are so incapacitated by their mental or emotional limitations that they could not lead normal lives even if society's considerable prejudice against them were to melt away. That group includes the severely (and intractably) psychotic, and somewhere between one-tenth and one-fourth of all mentally retarded people.

In making its case to the able-bodied mainstream, the central obstacle confronted by the movement is the widespread acceptance of the medical model. Even when it is invoked out of a genuine desire to help the disadvantaged—for instance, as when homosexuality is defined as a disease—this set of assumptions can be damaging. Regardless of whether the economy is growing or contracting, the disabled have a right to their fair share of jobs, goods, and services. But the moment any group is defined as a collection of ill or defective people, social priorities insensibly change. Questions of stigma and systemic discrimination fade into the background: the first priority goes to *treating* the putative inferiority.

As in the case of other disadvantaged groups, the professionals who work with the disabled are often among the worst offenders. Most workers in the human services still acquire in their training a basically medical view of social problems, what the historian Christopher Lasch has recently called the social-pathology model. The disease metaphor is far more pervasive in care of the disabled than in most other areas. It influences not only the policymakers and the care-givers, but also the social scientists who are doing the very research that could bring about changes in attitudes.

Most often, such researchers will postulate the presence of a single diseaselike entity that colors the attitudes of the majority of able-bodied people—a maladjustment in relating to disabled people—and then proceed to measure the prevalence of the disease among the groups studied. Even the best of this work suffers from the failing of so much social science: the discovery of striking facts whose exact significance is unclear because the underlying social phenomenon is far more complex than the experimenters' theories admit. Studies of the attitudes of able-bodied people toward the handicapped usually report what they say about the disabled, not how they act toward them. Virtually none of the research sorts out the relative roles of fear, ignorance, inexperience, or prejudice.

Jerome Siller, professor of educational psychology at New York University, has done extensive studies on able-bodied people's expressed attitudes toward different disability groups. Siller asked his subjects what characteristics they attribute to different sorts of disability (for instance, amputees may be seen as more intelligent, aggressive, or kind than people with other handicaps).

He uncovered a hierarchy of acceptability. The most acceptable disabilities were the relatively minor ones, like partial vision or hearing loss, a speech impediment or a heart condition. Amputees were a rung lower on the acceptability hierarchy. The deaf and the blind ranked somewhere in the middle, then came the mentally ill; below them stood people with epilepsy, cerebral palsy, or total paralysis.

When ranking included blacks, they usually ended up in the middle of the hierarchy, near the deaf and the blind. In some studies, such as one of employer attitudes made in the early 1970s by clinical psychologist James A. Colbert and his associates, blacks were preferred above all disability groups. Here, too, the sociological implications of these results are unclear. For instance, many investigators have found that the most negative attitudes of all expressed are about obese people. Yet it is hard to believe that we actually equate the stigma attached to being fat, crushing as it may be, with the kinds of stigma experienced by inner-city blacks, epileptics, or people with cerebral palsy. Some important distinctions among those stigmata are being missed by the research design.

Similar ambiguities cloud the interpretation of what is still the most important finding in the field: Stephen A. Richardson of Albert Einstein College of Medicine discovered that as children age, there are significant changes in their expressed attitude toward physical disabilities. Richardson found that a stable preference-ladder first appeared around age six. Asked their feelings about six pictures of children—all but one of them disabled—six-year-olds tended to rank slight facial disfigurement as most acceptable, second only to normalcy. Eight- to 10-year-olds ranked those with crutches and leg braces as most acceptable after the able-bodied child, followed by a child in a wheel-chair, one with amputated forearm, one with facial disfigurement, and finally, an obese child. By senior year, girls set facial disfigurement as least acceptable while boys ranked it fourth out of six in acceptability. (Male and female adults tend to follow the same pattern.) Again, there was the paradoxical finding that race was less stigmatizing than disability, and obesity often more stigmatizing.

Basic research into the psychology of disabled people themselves suffers from a similar medical bias. Because of the stigmata of disability, for example, handicapped people often move through a different social world from the one the rest of us inhabit; many of them do so in bodies that place important constraints on the way they obtain information about the world around them. Researchers frequently appear to assume that the developmental theories proposed by Piaget and others, elaborated from observations of able-bodied children, will work for the handicapped. But it may be that the cognitive and emotional growth of handicapped children follows its own healthy logic. A disabled child who is physically dependent may be putting his most sophisticated cognitive skills into learning how to charm, manipulate, or otherwise enlist the aid of others; to keep safe from harm; to deal with the split between his social worlds: the home, where he is loved and respected, and the street, where he is viewed as a biological fact. The able-bodied child at the same age may be spending the same energy on working free of his dependence on parents and building his sense of competence by developing skills.

Here and there, voices have called for a reexamination of traditional assumptions about the development of disabled people. During the 1960s, Cherise Gouin-Décarie, professor of psychology at the University of Montreal, studied Canadian children who were born with deformities because their mothers had taken the drug thalidomide during pregnancy. She was struck by the failure of conventional psychological theories to shed light on the children's development, and proposed instead "the methods of analysis . . . used to treat the problems of minorities." André Lussier came to similar conclusions in his case history of an English child born with severe limb deformities. Lussier, a psychoanalyst, reported that he was consistently played false by his theoretical framework. Behavior that he first interpreted as pathological and harmful to the child's development frequently turned out to be an essential ingredient in the child's conquests of his physical limitations. For example, when the child boasted that he could learn to play the trumpet, Lussier interpreted it as unrealistic fantasy—until the boy actually succeeded in doing it. All manner of actions that seemed pathological when assessed by the norms of standard psychoanalytic theory turned out to have a different functional meaning in the disabled child's life. Lussier concluded, "We must look beyond pathological mechanisms for a comprehensive explanation." Twenty years after the appearance of Lussier's report, that attempt has still not been made.

Very similar kinds of medical biases compromise the value of much present-day theory and research in education for the handicapped. A generation ago, educators assessed the academic needs of black children and handicapped children in the same way, by measuring the disadvantaged child's academic behavior against what was assumed to be normal for a white, middle-class, able-bodied child. After determining the ways in which the child deviated from these presumably universal norms, the educator devised special compensatory programs to cure or to lessen the child's academic deviance.

Increasingly, this conception of minority education has come under sharp attack. As Frank Riessman, professor of education at Queens College, notes, "If one analyzes the approaches that have been successful in improving the educational performance of inner-city children, one realizes that they are rooted in the strengths and the cognitive styles of the children rather than in a compensatory emphasis on deficiencies." Sadly, the deviance approach so common in minority education in the 1960s continues to go unchallenged in special education.

By far the greatest abuses of the medical model of disability occur in the technical literature that discusses the economic needs of disabled people. Most of this literature simply assumes that the employment problems of disabled people are caused by their physical limitations, rather than by the interaction of their limitation with job discrimination, environmental obstacles to mobility, and other forms of discrimination. The assumption has the unhappy ring of arguments that the economic problems of black Americans are caused by inherited genes that make them biologically inferior.

For society at large, the "therapeutic state" (to recall Nicholas N. Kittrie's term) is a threat, not a reality. But millions of disabled Americans already live within the invisible walls of a therapeutic society. In this society of the "sick," there is no place for the ordinary hallmarks of a present or future adult identity, no place for choice between competing moralities, no place for politics, no place for work, and no place for sexuality. All political, legal, and ethical issues are transformed into questions of disease and health, deviance and normal adjustment, proper and improper "management" of the disability. To recall political scientist Sheldon S. Wolin's fine phrase, the "sublimation of politics" has proceeded furthest of all with handicapped people. Of all America's oppressed groups, only the handicapped have been so fully disenfranchised in the name of health.

23

THE CONTEXT OF ANTI-GAY VIOLENCE: NOTES ON CULTURAL AND PSYCHOLOGICAL HETEROSEXISM

Gregory M. Herek (1990)

Humans seem to have an endless ability to single out others for prejudice and hatred. How do we learn how to hate? And why is violence a likely outcome of that hatred? The phenomenon of "gay bashing," where random homosexuals (or even people who in some way "look" or "act" like they might be homosexuals) are targeted for physical violence by heterosexuals, is a disturbing part of the current social scene in the United States. The targets are usually solitary males, the bashers are typically groups of males. What is going on here?

The following reading describes the cultural and psychological roots of what Herek calls "heterosexism" (antigay bias and the presumption that the heterosexual life is the only valid way of living). This chapter was first published in 1990. Some of the specific information contained in it concerning the legal and social status of lesbians and gay men has changed slightly since its original publication. Nonetheless, 1993 saw a year of debate over the stated Pentagon policy toward gays in the military ("don't ask, don't tell"), and supporters of gay rights continue to argue that Americans have yet to come to terms with the issue of sexual orientation. Many heterosexuals still feel queasy about homosexuality. They do not approve of the behavior, do not know what to think about it, do not want to hear about it, and become upset when finding out that a friend or relative is gay. Not many parents look at the newborn baby and hope that the child will grow up to be gay. Homosexuality and issues of sexual orientation force us to think about and talk about sex, an issue that is emotionally loaded with moral baggage from our childhood. Our society has traditionally regarded even heterosexual sex as a taboo issue, perhaps even unclean and certainly not

Source: Abridged from the *Journal of Interpersonal Violence*, 1990, *5,* 316–333. Copyright © 1990 by Sage Publishing Co. Reprinted by permission of the publisher and the author.

something to be discussed openly. You just didn't ask grandma at the holiday dinner table if she had been multiply orgasmic lately!

Like racism, anti-Semitism, or sexism, antigay bias may serve a purpose in society by preserving privilege for some people, limiting access to the job market for potential rivals, and filling some need that people have to put others on a rung below themselves on the social ladder (see Readings 14, 19, 20, 22, 25 for other causal influences). Some gay-rights activists have argued that the type of bigotry against homosexuals most closely resembles sexism. The argument is that people are much more likely to express animosity toward gay men than toward homosexual women, and that a reason for this is a distaste for anything even closely resembling effeminate behavior in men. A 1993 National Gay and Lesbian Task Force study found that over 25 percent of gay men have experienced some form of overt harassment compared to less than 10 percent for lesbians. When attackers of gay men are asked what provoked their hostility, they frequently describe "the womanly qualities in the men." It may be that heterosexual men become very nervous about the idea of being objects, especially if they are the type of men who are used to viewing their own sexual partners (women) as objects. Such a man might not be able to conceptualize that a gay man would not be feeling the same way toward them—predatory. Striking out first toward such a threat becomes a viable alternative to a threatened male. The issue is complex and made even more so with the established link between AIDS and high-risk male homosexual behavior. Herek's reading provides many interesting ideas for understanding the context of violence, both in thought and in behavior, against homosexuals.

Hate crimes against lesbians and gay men in the United States must be understood in context: Anti-gay violence is a logical, albeit extreme, extension of the heterosexism that pervades American society. *Heterosexism* is defined here as an ideological system that denies, denigrates, and stigmatizes any nonheterosexual form of behavior, identity, relationship, or community. Like racism, sexism, and other ideologies of oppression, heterosexism is manifested both in societal customs and institutions, such as religion and the legal system (referred to here as *cultural heterosexism*) and in individual attitudes and behaviors (referred to here as *psychological heterosexism*).

INSTITUTIONAL MANIFESTATIONS OF CULTURAL HETEROSEXISM

Cultural heterosexism is like the air that we breathe: It is so ubiquitous that it is hardly noticeable. Even a cursory survey of American society reveals that homosexuality is largely hidden and, when publicly recognized, is usually condemned or stigmatized. This alternation between invisibility and condemnation is readily apparent in four major societal institutions: religion, the law, psychiatry and psychology, and mass media.

In prescribing guidelines for moral living, modern Christian and Jewish religious institutions stress the inherent virtue of committed marital relationships through which children are conceived and raised in the faith. Marriages are heterosexual by definition; homosexual behavior is widely condemned; same-sex relationships and families are not recognized (see Boswell, 1980, for historical background). Some denominations and congregations recently have adopted more accepting positions concerning homosexuality. They have opposed discrimination, allowed gay people to join the clergy and, in rare cases, blessed gay relationships (e.g., Diamond, 1989; Fernandez, 1990; Goldman, 1989; Lattin, 1988). Others, however, have reaffirmed and even intensified their rejection. The Catholic church, for example, officially opposed extending civil rights protection to gay people in a Vatican statement which also was widely interpreted as condoning anti-gay violence: "When civil legislation is introduced to protect behavior to which no one has any conceivable right, neither the Church nor society at large should be surprised when other distorted notions and practices gain ground, and irrational and violent reactions increase" (Congregation for the Doctrine of the Faith, 1986, paragraph 10). In the third paragraph of that document, homosexual feelings are described as "ordered toward an intrinsic moral evil," which leads to the conclusion that homosexuality "itself must be seen as an objective disorder."

Gay men and lesbians also remain largely outside the law (Melton, 1989). Except in two states (Wisconsin and Massachusetts) and a few dozen municipalities (e.g., San Francisco, New York City, Chicago), legal protections do not exist for gay people in employment, housing, or services. Gay relationships have no legal status, and lesbian and gay male parents often lose legal custody of their children when their homosexuality becomes known (Falk, 1989). The right of states to outlaw homosexual behavior was upheld by the U.S. Supreme Court in 1986 (*Bowers v. Hardwick,*1986). In a clear illustration of the linkage between legal philosophies and religious teachings, Justices White and Burger refused to find a constitutional right for adults to engage privately in consenting homosexual behavior, based on the fact that legal proscriptions against sodomy have very "ancient roots" and that condemnation of homosexuality "is firmly rooted in Judeo-Christian moral and ethical standards" (*Bowers v. Hardwick,* 1986).

In contrast to other institutions, the mental health field has made homosexuality highly visible; this visibility, however, has been within a discourse of pathology. Despite Freud's refusal to label homosexuality a sickness, mainstream American psychiatry and psychoanalysis spent much of the 20th century seeking its "cure" (Bayer, 1987). When finally subjected to rigorous scientific testing, however, the linkage of homosexuality with psychopathology proved to be wrong (Gonsiorek, 1982; Gonsiorek & Weinrich, in press; Hooker, 1957). Consequently, the American Psychiatric Association finally dropped homosexuality as a diagnosis from its Diagnostic and Statistical Manual in 1974 (Bayer, 1987). Since then, the American Psychological Association (APA) has led other scientific and professional organizations in removing the stigma so long associated with homosexuality (e.g., APA, 1975). Nevertheless, the International Classification of Diseases (ICD) continues to label homosexuality as a mental illness, and the language of pathology still infuses popular perceptions.

A fourth institution that reflects and perpetuates cultural heterosexism is the electronic mass media. Mirroring society, media portrayals of homosexuality are relatively infrequent and typically are negative when they occur. Russo's (1981) study of Hollywood films, for example, demonstrated that most homosexual characters die before the end of the movie, usually from suicide or murder. In children's cartoons, characters whose homosexuality is implied through their violation of gender roles long have been targeted for ridicule, contempt, and violence (Russo, 1989). Even when gay characters have been portrayed positively in more recent films and television programs, they almost always appear in a story *because* they are gay (i.e., because their homosexuality is important to the plot; Gross, 1984). Thus all characters are heterosexual unless explicitly identified as homosexual, in which case the story focuses on their sexuality rather than their day-to-day nonsexual lives.

As these examples show, homosexuality is alternately rendered invisible and condemned by cultural institutions. Psychological heterosexism parallels this process: Most heterosexuals perceive the world entirely in heterosexual terms until confronted with evidence of homosexuality, at which time they respond with some combination of discomfort, confusion, condemnation, hostility, and disgust. In the next section, the ideological systems that underlie this dual negation are explored.

PSYCHOLOGICAL HETEROSEXISM

The foundation of *psychological heterosexism*—the individual manifestation of anti-gay prejudice—is laid down early in life. Long before children know anything about homosexuality or heterosexuality per se, they learn to prize what their parents and peers define as "good" and "normal." They learn moral values, attitudes toward the body and sexuality, and the distinction between private and public. They develop a gender identity and internalize negative feelings and stereotypical beliefs about those who violate gender roles. They learn to value acceptance from peers and adults, and acquire strategies for winning it. They learn the benefits and costs associated with multiple social roles, including those of the "normal" and its counterpart, the deviant. They learn the social attitudes associated with race, gender, and those who are different or "queer," long before they understand that *queer* is an epithet for homosexuals (Goffman, 1963; Katz, 1976).

Because of homosexuality's cultural invisibility, relatively few children are likely to have personal contact with someone who is openly gay while learning these concepts (Schneider & Lewis, 1984). Consequently, rather than defining homosexuality as a characteristic associated with flesh-and-blood human beings, most people respond to it primarily as a symbol: the embodiment of such concepts as "sin," "sickness," "predator," "outsider," or whatever else an individual considers to be the opposite of her- or himself, or set apart from her or his community. Whereas attitudes toward people with whom one has direct experience function primarily to organize and make sense of that experience, attitudes toward symbols serve a variety of expressive needs. At least three functions are served by psychological heterosexism (Herek, 1986b, 1987).

First, anti-gay prejudice may serve a *value-expressive* function, helping individuals to affirm who they are by expressing important personal values. For example, a fundamentalist Christian may express hostile attitudes toward gay people as a way of affirming her or his own Christianity. She or he opposes homosexuality because such opposition is an integral part of being a good Christian, which is of central importance to feeling good about oneself. The same individuals would express similar hostility toward other groups if they were similarly defined in religious terms. Violence also may serve a value-expressive function for the perpetrator. For example, members of hate groups such as the Ku Klux Klan appeal to moral authority in their anti-gay rhetoric (see Segrest & Zeskind, 1989).

Anti-gay prejudice can also serve a *social-expressive* function by helping individuals to win approval from important others (e.g., peers, family, neighbors) and thereby increase their own self-esteem. As with the value-expressive function, lesbians and gay men are treated as abstract concepts. With social-expressive prejudice, they are the epitome of outsiders; attacking them solidifies one's own status as an insider, one who belongs to the group. Expressing anti-gay attitudes or violently attacking gay people thus leads to being accepted and liked, which are of central importance to the individual. For example, some assailants in anti-gay street assaults view the attack primarily as a way of demonstrating their loyalty and increasing group solidarity (Weissman, 1978). Perpetrators in male-male rapes and sexual assaults also have been observed to be motivated by needs to maintain status and affiliation with peers (Groth & Burgess, 1980).

Anti-gay prejudice also may serve a *defensive* function by reducing the anxiety that results from unconscious psychological conflicts (e.g., those associated with one's own sexuality or gender). The defensive function is summarized in the popular notion that people who express anti-gay prejudice actually are revealing their own latent homosexuality. For people with defensive attitudes, lesbians or gay men symbolize unacceptable parts of the self (e.g., the feminine man, the masculine woman). Expressing anti-gay hostility is a strategy for avoiding an internal conflict by externalizing it to a suitable symbol which then is attacked. Anti-gay assaults, for example, may provide a means for young males to affirm their masculinity (consciously or not) by attacking someone who symbolizes an unacceptable aspect of their own personalities (e.g., homoerotic feelings or tendencies toward effeminacy). Similarly, some perpetrators in male-male sexual assaults apparently wished to punish the victim as a way of dealing with their own unresolved and conflictual sexual interests (Groth & Burgess, 1980).

Anti-gay hostility thus functions to define who one *is* by identifying gay people as a symbol of what one is *not* and directing hostility toward them. With the value-expressive function, prejudice defines the world according to principles of good and evil, right and wrong; by opposing the embodiment of evil (gay people), one affirms one's own goodness. With the social-expressive function, prejudice defines the ingroup and outgroup; by denigrating outsiders (lesbians and gay men), one affirms one's own status as an insider. With the defensive function, prejudice defines the self and the "not-self"; by attacking gay people, one symbolically (and unconsciously) attacks the unacceptable or bad aspects of self.

Gay people can fulfill these symbolic roles only so long as they remain abstract concepts for the prejudiced heterosexual person, rather than flesh-and-blood human beings. Having a close friend, coworker, or family member who is openly gay can eventually change a prejudiced person's perception of homosexuality from a value-laden symbolic construct to a mere demographic characteristic, like hair color or political party affiliation. By coming out to others, lesbians and gay men disrupt the functions previously served by anti-gay attitudes. When heterosexuals learn that someone about whom they care is gay, formerly functional prejudice can quickly become dysfunctional: The untruth in stereotypes becomes obvious, social norms are perceived to have changed, and traditional moral values concerning sexuality are challenged by their juxtaposition against the heterosexual person's past experience with, knowledge about, and feelings of love for the specific gay man or lesbian. Thus, as with other forms of prejudice, interpersonal contact between gay people and heterosexuals under favorable conditions is one of the most effective ways of reducing psychological heterosexism (Allport, 1954; Amir, 1976; Herek, in press; Schneider & Lewis, 1984).

Coming out, however, is difficult and possibly dangerous. It requires making public an aspect of oneself that society perceives as appropriately kept private. It can mean being defined exclusively in terms of sexuality by strangers, friends, and family. It also can mean being newly perceived as possessing some sort of disability or handicap, an inability to be what one should be as man or woman. In the worst situations, it means being completely rejected or even attacked by those to whom one has come out.

Many gay people remain in the closet because they fear these negative interpersonal consequences, as well as discrimination and stigmatization. Additionally, having continually to overcome invisibility is itself a frustrating experience; allowing others to assume that one is heterosexual often is the path of least resistance. Consequently, most heterosexuals' attitudes and behavior toward gay people remain uninformed by personal interactions and instead are driven by the cultural ideologies of sexuality and gender.

Symbolism and Attitudes

As a consequence of the gay political movement, heterosexuals now can have positive attitudes toward gay people that are psychologically functional in ways not previously possible. Because of its identification with movements for racial equality and women's rights, as well as the rights of privacy and free speech, the movement for gay civil rights increasingly has become a respectable progressive political cause. Consequently, heterosexuals who identify themselves as liberals, feminists, and civil libertarians can express support for gay rights as a way of affirming their social identities (a value-expressive function). This equation of the gay community with notions of political progressivism receives impetus when bigoted individuals and hate groups identify gay people as targets comparable to Blacks and Jews (Segrest & Zeskind, 1989). Ironically, such attacks may permit positive attitudes toward gay people to serve both value-expressive and social-expressive functions as many members of society express their distaste for such bigotry and distance themselves from the groups that promulgate it. If uncoupling of gender and sexuality becomes widespread, the cultural basis for defensive anti-gay prejudice also may diminish as gay people become less suitable symbols for externalizing anxiety about one's own gender identity.

Additionally, AIDS has affected the symbolic status of homosexuality in American culture in both negative and positive ways. By linking stigmatized sexual behavior with death, the popular view of AIDS in the United States reinforces both a moralistic condemnation of homosexuality and individual feelings of defensiveness. Gay people (lesbians have not been differentiated from gay men in popular discourse on AIDS) are viewed by many as receiving just punishment for their sins, and homosexuality is equated with death (Herek & Glunt, 1988). Yet, the AIDS epidemic also has led many heterosexuals to confront their own attitudes toward homosexuality for the first time. Because AIDS has made gay people more visible, more heterosexuals have had to articulate their own feelings about homosexuality, often in relation to a gay loved one.

CONCLUSION

Anti-gay violence and victimization in the United States today cannot adequately be understood apart from cultural heterosexism. By alternately denying and stigmatizing homosexuality, this ideology fosters the individual anti-gay prejudice that makes victimization of lesbians and gay men possible. The analysis presented here highlights the neccessity of a comprehensive approach to eliminating anti-gay violence. Interventions that focus specifically on violence and victimization clearly are needed. These efforts, however, will not be sufficient to eliminate the ultimate causes of anti-gay violence. Making lesbians and gay men visible and removing the stigma that has so long been attached to homosexual orientation will require institutional changes as well as personal interventions. Societal transformations have begun in the past few decades that eventually may shake the foundations of cultural and psychological heterosexism. Perhaps most important of these has been the widespread emergence of lesbians and gay men from invisibility into public life. By discouraging and directly punishing this emergence, anti-gay violence functions to perpetuate heterosexism as well as express it. Eradicating heterosexism, therefore, inevitably requires confronting violence against lesbians and gay men. Eliminating anti-gay violence, in turn, requires an attack upon heterosexism.

24

EXCERPT FROM
CIVILIZATION AND ITS DISCONTENTS

Sigmund Freud (1930)

Humans are able to be loving and caring but can also be remarkably violent and aggressive. Much debate has focused on the origins of violence in humans. This debate crosses broad disciplinary lines involving biologists, ethologists, anthropologists, sociologists, philosophers, theologians, as well as social psychologists. The debate also affects public policy and is incorporated into our legal system's attempt to control crime and violence.

And yet, our responses to violence as a culture appear to be somewhat inconsistent; while we value peace and tranquility, we are fascinated by the darker side of human social behaviors. Graphically violent movies do well at the box office. We have penalties in our sporting events for unnecessary roughness, implying that certain levels of roughness are tolerable (or even desirable). We worry over whether this or that political leader is a "wimp." The debates over gun control and the death penalty often evoke images and statements about revenge and violence. Eldridge Cleaver is credited with stating that "Violence is as American as apple pie." Is he right? If he is, is it inevitable?

Although many social psychologists now give only a passing reference to Freud, his writings have been extremely influential in twentieth-century thought and are rich in social psychological hypotheses. In this excerpt, Freud develops his ideas on aggression. For Freud, aggression is an instinctive response, but a response that can nevertheless be held under control by civilization's persistent efforts. The integrative nature of Freud's work makes it delightful to read even for those who do not accept the thrust of psychoanalysis. Freud builds a case

Source: Excerpted from *Civilization and its discontents. Edited and translated by J. Strachey.* Copyright © 1974 by Norton, New York. Reprinted by permission of the publisher.

from not wanting to love his neighbor to the meaning of the evolution of civilization. Whereas hypotheses about the origins of civilization are inherently untestable, there is much heuristic value even in this brief segment, including hypotheses regarding attitudes toward strangers, ingroup and outgroup processes, and whether happiness is related to the freedom to be aggressive.

[Freud begins his discussion of civilization and aggression by examining the well-known imperative:] 'Thou shalt love thy neighbor as thyself.' It is known throughout the world and is undoubtedly older than Christianity, which puts it forward as its proudest claim. Yet it is certainly not very old; even in historical times it was still strange to mankind. Let us adopt a naive attitude towards it, as though we were hearing it for the first time; we shall be unable then to suppress a feeling of surprise and bewilderment. Why should we do it? What good will it do us? But, above all, how shall we achieve it? How can it be possible? My love is something valuable to me which I ought not to throw away without reflection. It imposes duties on me for whose fulfilment I must be ready to make sacrifices. If I love someone, he must deserve it in some way. He deserves it if he is so like me in important ways that I can love myself in him; and he deserves it if he is so much more perfect than myself that I can love my ideal of my own self in him. Again, I have to love him if he is my friend's son, since the pain my friend would feel if any harm came to him would be my pain too—I should have to share it. But if he is a stranger to me and if he cannot attract me by any worth of his own or any significance that he may already have acquired for my emotional life, it will be hard for me to love him. Indeed, I should be wrong to do so, for my love is valued by all my own people as a sign of my preferring them, and it is an injustice to them if I put a stranger on a par with them. But if I am to love him (with this universal love) merely because he, too, is an inhabitant of this earth, like an insect, an earthworm or a grass-snake, then I fear that only a small modicum of my love will fall to his share—not by any possibility as much as, by the judgement of my reason, I am entitled to retain for myself. What is the point of a precept enunciated with so much solemnity if its fulfilment cannot be recommended as reasonable?

On closer inspection, I find still further difficulties. Not merely is this stranger in general unworthy of my love; I must honestly confess that he has more claim to my hostility and even my hatred. He seems not to have the least trace of love for me and shows me not the slightest consideration. If it will do him any good he has no hesitation in injuring me, nor does he ask himself whether the amount of advantage he gains bears any proportion to the extent of the harm he does to me. Indeed, he need not even obtain an advantage; if he can satisfy any sort of desire by it, he thinks nothing of jeering at me, insulting me, slandering me and showing his superior power; and the more secure he feels and the more helpless I am, the more certainly I can expect him to behave like this to me. If he behaves differently, if he shows me consideration and forbearance as a stranger, I am ready to treat him in the same way, in any case and quite apart from any precept. Indeed, if this grandiose commandment had run 'Love thy neighbour as thy neighbour loves thee', I should not take exception to it. And there is a second commandment, which seems to me even more incomprehensible and arouses still stronger opposition in me. It is 'Love thine enemies'. If I think it over, however, I see that I am wrong in treating it as a greater imposition. At bottom it is the same thing.[1]

I think I can now hear a dignified voice admonishing me: 'It is precisely because your neighbour is not worthy of love, and is on the contrary your enemy, that you should love him as yourself.'

Now it is very probable that my neighbour, when he is enjoined to love me as himself, will answer exactly as I have done and will repel me for the same reason. I hope he will not have the same objective grounds for doing so, but he will have the same idea as I have. Even so, the behaviour of human beings shows differences, which ethics, disregarding the fact that such differences are determined, classifies as 'good' or 'bad'. So long as these undeniable differences have not been removed, obedience to high ethical demands entails damage to the aims of civilization, for it puts a positive premium on being bad.

The element of truth behind all this, which people are so ready to disavow, is that men are not gentle creatures who want to be loved, and who at the most can defend themselves if they are attacked; they are, on the contrary, creatures among whose instinctual endowments is to be reckoned a powerful share of aggressiveness. As a result, their neighbour is for them not only a potential helper or sexual object, but also someone who tempts them to satisfy their aggressiveness on him, to exploit his capacity for work without compensation, to use him sexually without his consent, to seize his possessions, to humiliate him, to cause him pain, to torture and to kill him. Who, in the face of all of his experience of life and of history, will have the courage to dispute this assertion? As a rule this cruel aggressiveness waits for some provocation or itself at the service of some other purpose, whose goal might also have been reached by milder measures. In circumstances that are favourable to it, when the counter-forces which ordinarily inhibit it are out of action, it also manifests spontaneously and reveals man as a savage beast to whom consideration towards his own kind is something alien. Anyone who calls to mind the atrocities occurring [human recorded history] will have to bow humbly before the truth of this.

The existence of this inclination to aggression, which we can detect in ourselves and justly assume to be present in others, is the factor which disturbs our relations with our neighbour and which forces civilization into such a high expenditure [of energy]. In consequence of this primary mutual hostility of human beings, society is perpetually threatened with disintegration. The interest of work in common would not hold it together; instinctual passions are stronger than reasonable interests. Civilization has to use its utmost efforts in order to set limits to man's aggressive instincts and to hold the manifestations of them in check by psychical reaction

[1]A great imaginative writer may permit himself to give expression — at least in jest — to psychological truths that are severely proscribed. Thus Heine confesses: 'Mine is a most peaceable disposition. My wishes are: a humble cottage with a thatched roof, but a good bed, good food, the freshest milk and butter, flowers before my window, and a few fine trees before my door; and if God wants to make my happiness complete, he will grant me the joy of seeing some six or seven of my enemies hanging from those trees. Before their death I shall, moved in my heart, forgive them all the wrong they did me in their lifetime — one must, it is true, forgive one's enemies — but not before they have been hanged.' (Heine, *Gedanken und Einfälle*. [section I].)

formations. Hence, therefore, the use of methods to incite people into identifications and aim-inhibited relationships of love, hence the restriction upon sexual life, and hence too the ideal's commandment to love one's neighbour as oneself—a commandment which is really justified by the fact that nothing else runs so strongly counter to the original nature of man. In spite of every effort, these endeavours of civilization have not so far achieved very much. It hopes to prevent the crudest excesses of brutal violence by itself assuming the right to use violence against criminals, but the law is not able to lay hold of the more cautious and refined manifestations of human aggressiveness. The time comes when each one of us has to give up as illusions the expectations which, in his youth, he pinned upon his fellowmen, and when he may learn how much difficulty and pain has been added to his life by their ill-will. At the same time, it would be unfair to reproach civilization with trying to eliminate strife and competition from human activity. These things are undoubtedly indispensable. But opposition is not necessarily enmity; it is merely misused and made an *occasion* for enmity.

The communists believe that they have found the path to deliverance from our evil. According to them, man is wholly good and is well-disposed to his neighbour; but the institution of private property has corrupted his nature. The ownership of private wealth gives the individual power, and with it the temptation to ill-treat his neighbour; while the man who is excluded from possession is bound to rebel in hostility against his oppressor. If private property were abolished, all wealth held in common, and everyone allowed to share in the enjoyment of it, ill-will and hostility would disappear among men. Since everyone's needs would be satisfied, no one would have any reason to regard another as his enemy; all would willingly undertake the work that was [...] have no concern with any economic criticisms of the communist system; I [...] into whether the abolition of private property is expedient or advanta[...] to recognize that the psychological premises on which the system [...] illusion. In abolishing private property we deprive the human [...] of its instruments, certainly a strong one, though certainly [...] in no way altered the differences in power and influence [...] siveness, nor have we altered anything in its nature. [...] property. It reigned almost without limit in primi[...] scanty, and it already shows itself in the nurs[...] up its primal, anal form; it forms the basis [...] among people (with the single exception, [...] child). If we do away with personal [...] rogative in the field of sexual rela[...] strongest dislike and the most vi[...] equal footing. If we were to [...] sexual life and thus abolish[...] true, easily foresee what [...] ng we can expect, and there.

[...] nclination to aggres[...] ble to bind together a [...] r people left over to receive the manifestation of their aggressiveness. I once discussed the phenomenon that it is precisely communities with adjoining territories, and related to each other in other ways as well, who are engaged in constant feuds and in ridiculing each other. In this respect the Jewish people, scattered everywhere, have rendered most useful services to the civilizations of the countries that have been their hosts; but unfortunately all the massacres of the Jews in the Middle Ages did not suffice to make that period more peaceful and secure for their Christian fellows. When once the Apostle Paul had posited universal love between men as the foundation of his Christian community, extreme intolerance on the part of Christendom towards those who remained outside it became the inevitable consequence. [Also,] the dream of a Germanic world-dominion called for anti-Semitism as its complement; and it is intelligible that the attempt to establish a new, communist civilization in Russia should find its psychological support in the persecution of the bourgeois. One only wonders, with concern, what the Soviets will do after they have wiped out their bourgeois.

In all that follows I adopt the standpoint, therefore, that the inclination to aggression is an original, self-subsisting instinctual disposition in man, and I return to my view that it constitutes the greatest impediment to civilization. At one point in the course of this enquiry, I was led to the idea that civilization was a special process which mankind undergoes, and I am still under the influence of that idea. I may now add that civilization is a process in the service of Eros, whose purpose is to combine single human individuals, and after that families, then races, peoples and nations, into one great unity, the unity of mankind. Why this has to happen, we do not know; the work of Eros is precisely this. These collections of men are to be libidinally bound to one another. Necessity alone, the advantages of work in common, will not hold them together. But man's natural aggressive instinct, the hostility of each against all and all against each, opposes this programme of civilization. This aggressive instinct is the derivative and the main representative of the death instinct which we have found alongside of Eros and which shares world-dominion with it. And now, I think, the meaning of the evolution of civilization is no longer obscure to us. It must present the struggle between Eros and Death, between the instinct of life and the instinct of destruction, as it works itself out in the human species. This struggle is what all life essentially consists of, and the evolution of civilization may therefore be simply described as the struggle for life of the human species.

25

THE RAPE CULTURE

Dianne F. Herman (1989)

Watching television has taken precedence over leisure activities such as reading, sewing, gardening, and other family- and community-oriented activities that occupied previous generations in our society. That fact alone is a value choice. Herman's chapter highlights how our value choices perpetuate rape through our images of masculinity. She suggests that two very important relationships to be considered are the relationships between rape and the construction of masculinity in our society, and between rape and our cultural acceptance of violence.

   Although many of the statistics that you will read about have changed somewhat by the time you read this selection, the issues are unfortunately the same. In one of the best studies of rape incidence in the United States surveying 6159 students from 32 representative colleges and universities, approximately 28 percent of college women reported experiencing and 8 percent of college men reported perpetrating "an act that met legal definitions of rape, which includes attempts" (Koss, Gidycz, & Wisniewski, 1987, p. 168). That is a lot of people. Further, this rape victimization rate is 10 to 15 times greater than rates reported by the U. S. government's 1984 *National Crime Survey*. Even using the lower rate admitted by these college men produces rates that are 2 to 3 times greater than those from the *National Crime Survey*. These rates must cause us to pause. And add to those findings the fact that researchers have found that 52 percent of college males answered "yes" when asked "If you could rape a woman and absolutely be sure of getting away with it, would you?" and 84 percent agreed "Some women look like they're just asking to be raped" (Greendlinger & Byrne, 1987).

   Source: Excerpted from *Women: A feminist perspective* (4th edition), edited by J. Freeman, 1989, Palo Alto, CA: Mayfield. Copyright © 1989 by Mayfield Publishing Co. Reprinted by permission of the publisher and the author.

That there are so few personality characteristics associated with rapists suggests that there must be something in the situation that allows or drives aggression against women (read Myers's Modules 24 and 25 for ideas about situational causes). That there are so few behavioral correlates associated with the women who are raped also suggests something beyond the particular individuals involved. Herman hypothesizes that it is the broader value of masculinity that is the culprit, as portrayed in our media and our culture.

When Susan Griffin wrote, "I have never been free of the fear of rape," she touched a responsive chord in most women. Every woman knows the fear of being alone at home late at night or the terror that strikes her when she receives an obscene telephone call. She knows also of the "minirapes"—the pinch in the crowded bus, the wolf whistle from a passing car, the stare of a man looking at her bust during a conversation. Griffin has argued, "Rape is a kind of terrorism which severely limits the freedom of women and makes women dependent on men."

Women live their lives according to a rape schedule.

> There is what might be called a universal curfew on women in this country. Whenever a woman walks alone at night, whenever she hitchhikes, she is aware that she is violating well-established rules of conduct and as a result, that she faces the possibility of rape. If in one of these situations she *is* raped, the man will almost always escape prosecution and the woman will be made to feel responsible because she was somehow "asking for it."

Underlying this view of rape is a traditional concept of male and female sexuality, one that assumes that males are sexually aggressive and females are sexually passive. Those sharing these assumptions conclude that rape is a natural act that arises out of a situation in which men are unrestrained by convention or threat of punishment. However, animals in their natural habitat do not rape, and many societies have existed where rape was not known. According to Margaret Mead in *Sex and Temperament,* the Arapesh do not have "any conception of the male nature that might make rape understandable to them." Among the Arapesh, men and women are both expected to act with gentleness and concern. Thus, there is no reason to maintain the assumption that rape is a natural act. Certain social conditions do seem to contribute to a higher incidence of rape. Peggy Sanday, in a cross-cultural study of 186 tribal societies, found rape to be more frequent in male-dominated and violent societies.

Anthropological studies like those of Margaret Mead have demonstrated that sexual attitudes and practices are learned, not instinctual. In this country people are raised to believe that men are sexually active and aggressive and women are sexually passive and submissive. Since it is assumed that men cannot control their desires, every young woman is taught that she must be the responsible party in any sexual encounter. In such a society, men and women are trained to believe that the sexual act involves domination. Normal heterosexual relations are pictured as consisting of an aggressive male forcing himself on a female who seems to fear sex but unconsciously wants to be overpowered.

Because of the aggressive–passive, dominant–submissive, me-Tarzan–you-Jane nature of the relationship between the sexes in our culture, there is a close association between violence and sexuality. Words that are slang sexual terms, for example, frequently accompany assaultive behavior or gestures. "Fuck you" is meant as a brutal attack in verbal terms. In the popular culture, "James Bond alternately whips out his revolver and his cock, and though there is no known connection between the skills of a gun-fighter and love-making, pacificism seems suspiciously effeminate." The imagery of sexual relations between males and females in books, songs, advertising, and films is frequently that of a sadomasochistic relationship thinly veiled by a romantic facade. Thus, it is very difficult in our society to differentiate rape from "normal" heterosexual relations. Indeed, our culture can be characterized as a rape culture because the image of heterosexual intercourse is based on a rape model of sexuality.

HOW COMMON IS RAPE?

Victimization surveys indicate that for every reported rape, an additional one to three rapes have occurred but have not been reported. Diana E. H. Russell's 1978 study of 930 San Francisco women found that 44 percent reported at least one completed or attempted rape. Only 8 percent, or less than one in twelve, of the total number of incidents were ever reported to the police. Using Russell's findings, the actual incidence of rape is 24 times higher than F.B.I. statistics indicate.

In addition, a woman is probably less safe from rape in this country than she is in any other developed nation. The United States has one of the highest rape rates in the world. In 1984, the United States had 35.7 rapes per 100,000 people. The Bureau of Justice Statistics found European nations had an average of 5.4 rapes per 100,000 inhabitants in that same year.

VICTIMS OF RAPE

There is considerable evidence to suggest that a most likely assailant is someone who is trusted, and even loved, by the victim. In Russell's survey of San Francisco women, only 115 out of 606 rapists were strangers to their victims. In addition, whereas 70 percent of stranger rapists were not reported to the police, 89 percent were not reported when the attacker was a boyfriend, and 99 percent were not when the rapist was a date. *Cosmopolitan* magazine found in its September 1980 survey that, of the more than 106,000 women who responded, 24 percent stated thay they had been raped at least once: 51 percent of those had been raped by friends, 37 percent by strangers, 18 percent by relatives, and 3 percent by husbands.

Once it is understood that rape occurs quite commonly between people who are acquainted, other findings about this crime start to make sense. Most studies, for example, report that about half of all rapes occur in the victim's or rapist's home. Another 15 percent occur in automobiles. Car rapes are especially likely to involve participants who are intimate. Many rapes occur on dates.

In 1982, *Ms.* magazine reported a series of studies on college campuses confirming that, even given new and more liberal attitudes about premarital sex and women's liberation, date rape and other forms of acquaintance rape may be reaching epidemic proportions in higher education. In some cases, women have even been assaulted by men ostensibly acting as protective escorts to prevent rape. A 1985 study of over 600 college students found that three-quarters of the women and more than one-half of the men disclosed an experience of sexual aggression on a date. Nearly 15 percent of the women and 7 percent of the men said that intercourse had taken place against the woman's will. The victim and offender had most likely known each other almost one year before the sexual assault. Date rape occurred most frequently when the man initiated the date, when he drove to and from and paid for the date, when drinking took place, and when the couple found themselves alone either in a car or indoors. In these instances, it appears that college men may feel they have license to rape.

The tendency to dismiss rape allegations when victim and offender know each other has contributed to the silence that surrounds marital rape. Finkelhor and Yllo in their study of marital rape found that only one textbook on marriage and the family of the thirty-one they surveyed mentioned rape or anything related to sexual assault in marriage. These authors cite studies that indicate that at least 10 percent of all married women questioned on this topic report that their husbands have used physical force or threats to have sex with them. Marital rape may be the most common form of sexual assault: more than two times as many of the women interviewed had been raped by husbands as had been raped by strangers.

For most people, forced sex in marriage has little to do with what they would call "real" rape. When they think of real rape, they think of a stranger, a weapon, an attack, or a threat to a woman's life. Forced marital sex, on the other hand, conjures up an unpleasant, but not particularly serious, marital squabble over sex. On the contrary, marital rape frequently involves *more* serious physical injury and psychological trauma than do stranger rapes. Russell found that 19 percent of all marital rapes involved beating, and another 16 percent involved hitting or kicking. Finkelhor and Yllo cite, for example, a case where a woman suffered a 6-centimeter gash in her vagina when her husband attempted to rip out her vagina. These authors found that disagreements over sex were not the reason husbands rape their wives. Husbands' desires to frighten, humiliate, punish, degrade, dominate, and control their spouses were found to be the most common motivations for the sexual assaults. In their 1980–1981 study of Boston area mothers, Finkelhor and Yllo found that about half of the marital rape victims were also battered. Many cases were uncovered in which wives were tortured through sadistic sexual assaults involving objects. Many more were humiliated by being forced to engage in distasteful or unusual sexual practices. One-quarter of the victims in their survey were sexually attacked in the presence of others—usually their children. Many times, the rape was the final violent act in a series of physical and emotional abuses or the payback when a woman filed for separation or divorce. Sadly, many women suffer years of abuse thinking that the assaults are caused by their failure to be good wives or feeling that they have no way out and that this is the lot of the married woman. Too often, their husbands justify their attacks on their wives by blaming the wives for causing their loss of control, or by saying that they are entitled to treat their spouses any way they choose.

Because rape so frequently involves people who know each other, most rapists and their victims are of the same race and age group. In 1985, approximately 80 percent of all rapes and attempted rapes were intraracial. One reason that the myth that rapes are interracial dies hard is that cases of this type frequently receive the most publicity. In a study of rape in Philadelphia, researchers discovered that the two major newspapers, when they reported on rape cases, mentioned mainly interracial offenses. Intraracial rapes were only occasionally mentioned. Gary LaFree examined the effect of race in the handling of 881 sexual assaults in a large midwestern city. He found that black males who assaulted white women received more serious charges, longer sentences, and more severe punishment in terms of executed sentences and incarceration in the state penitentiary. Although black women are three times more likely to be raped than are white women, rape is least prosecuted if the victim is black. The rape of poor, black women is not an offense against men of power.

WHY MEN RAPE

Russell has stated, "rape is not so much a deviant act as an overconforming one. It is an extreme acting out of qualities that are regarded as masculine in this and many other societies: aggression, force, power, strength, toughness, dominance, competitiveness." In a 1979 study of high-school students, one group of researchers found that 50 percent of high-school males who were interviewed believed it was acceptable "for a guy to hold a girl down and force her to have sexual intercourse in instances such as when 'she gets him sexually excited' or 'she says she's going to have sex with him and then changes her mind.'" When questioning college males, a 1981 study by Briere, Malamuth, and Ceniti found that 60 percent of the sample indicated that if no one knew and they would not be punished, there was some likelihood that they would use force to obtain sex. In this study, the authors believed that attitudes about sex and women were more important in explaining these pro-rape responses than were sexual frustration or sexual maladjustment. Russell concludes from studies such as these that

> The considerable percentage of men who acknowledge some likelihood that they might rape if they could get away with it, plus the widespread prevalence of actual rape victims . . . suggest that continued efforts to explain rape as a psychopathological phenomenon are inappropriate. How could it be that all of these rapes are being perpetrated by a tiny segment of the male population? Clearly, rape must be seen as primarily a social disease.

One of the most surprising findings of studies on rape is that the rapist is normal in personality, appearance, intelligence, behavior, and sexual drive. Empirical research has repeatedly failed to find a consistent pattern of personality type or character disorder that reliably discriminates the rapist from the nonrapist. What is clear is that the rapist is not an exotic freak. Rather, rape evolves out of a situation in which "normal" males feel a need to prove themselves to be "men" by displaying dominance over females.

Nothing supports more convincingly the premise that rape in our society is the act of a male attempting to assert his masculinity than the studies that have been conducted on homosexual rapes in prisons. Interestingly, researchers have discovered that aggressors in prison-rape cases usually have little or no prior history of homosexual behavior. They do not consider themselves homosexuals, and neither do the other inmates. Rather, they equate their actions with those of an aggressive, heterosexual male. They are often called "jockers" or "wolves" by other inmates, terms that characterize them as males.

Aside from the need to demonstrate "masculine" competence, rapists tend to hold certain values. The rapist's attraction to dominance and violence stems from his interpretation of sexuality—"man ravishes, woman submits." Many rapists believe that women enjoy sadomasochistic sex.

Interviews with convicted rapists often reveal that these men subscribe to what Pauline Bart has labeled the notion of male entitlement. "The assumption is that a woman's body is a man's *right,* and if violence occurs while the rapist is exercising that right (the act itself not being defined as violence, remember) it is because the woman attempts to deny him his due."

Psychologists David L. Mosher and Ronald D. Anderson, in a study of college males, found that men who scored high on a hypermasculinity questionnaire also tended to score high on a questionnaire designed to measure sexually coercive behaviors. Callous sexual attitudes appear to go in hand with sexually coercive acts. When asked to imagine a rape scene, the macho males were more likely to report sexual arousal, but they also reported feelings of anger, distress, fear, guilt, shame, and disgust.

Nicholas Groth, in his book *Men Who Rape,* has stated that rape is a pseudosexual act in which components of power, anger, and sexuality are fused. Different offenders will display these factors with different intensities. For the rapist, sex becomes a weapon used to express his aggression and his needs to dominate and control. Studies of relapsed sexual aggressives have found that 75 percent of repeated sexual assaults committed by rapists after treatment were precipitated by situations that evoked negative emotional states, such as frustration, anger, anxiety, or depression. Another 20 percent of a group of relapsed clients involved situations of interpersonal conflict.

American culture produces rapists when it encourages the socialization of men to subscribe to values of control and dominance, callousness and competitiveness, and anger and aggression, and when it discourages the expression by men of vulnerability, sharing, and cooperation. In the end, it is not only the women who become the victims of these men, but also the offenders themselves, who suffer. These men lose the ability to satisfy needs for nurturance, love, and belonging, and their anger and frustration from this loss expresses itself in acts of violence and abuse against others. The tragedy for our society is that we produce so many of these hardened men.

SOCIETY'S RESPONSE TO RAPE

Women have often complained that their veracity is questioned when they report charges of rape. The first public agency with which a woman makes contact when she reports a rape is usually the police department, and it has often been less than sympathetic to rape complaints.

According to many studies, one of the most frequent causes of unfounded rape is a prior relationship between the participants. In the Philadelphia study, 43 percent of all date rapes were unfounded. *Unfounding* simply means that the police decide there is no basis for prosecution. The police, according to the researcher, seemed to be more concerned that the victim had "assumed the risk" than they were with the fact that she had not given consent to intercourse.

Another common reason police unfound cases is the apparent lack of force in the rape situation. The extent of injuries seems to be even more important in the decision to unfound than is whether the offender had a weapon. There is no requirement that a male businessperson must either forcibly resist when mugged or forfeit protection under the law. But proof of rape, both to the police and in court, is often required to take the form of proof of resistance, substantiated by the extent of injuries suffered by the victim. Yet local police departments frequently advise women not to resist if faced with the possibility of rape.

For many women, the experience of having their account of the events scrutinized, mocked, or discounted continues in the courtroom. Women have often said that they felt as though they, not the defendants, were the persons on trial. According to Burgess and Holmstrom, "Going to court, for the victim, is as much of a crisis as the actual rape itself." They quote one victim shortly after she appeared in district court: "I felt like crying. I felt abused. I didn't like the questions the defense was asking. I felt accused—guilty 'til proven innocent. I thought the defense lawyer made it a big joke." They relate how one twelve-year-old girl had a psychotic breakdown during the preliminary court process.

The victim, by taking the case to court, incurs extensive costs, both psychological and financial. Expecting to testify just once, she is likely to have to repeat her story at the hearing for probable cause, to the grand jury, and in superior-court sessions. To convey the discomfort of such a process, feminists have recommended that individuals imagine having to tell an audience all the details of their last sexual experience. In addition to exposing themselves to public scrutiny, rape victims may be subject to harassment from the friends or family of the perpetrator.

Financially, the time away from work nearly always stretches beyond expectations. According to Burgess and Holmstrom, the victims they accompanied to court were often forced to sit three to four hours in the courthouse, only to be told that the case had been continued. After they and their witnesses had taken time off from work and, in some cases, traveled great distances, they were less than enthusiastic about the idea of seeing justice done. Wood has said, "Due to the traumatic experience which a victim must go through in order to attempt to secure the attacker's successful prosecution, it is amazing any rape cases come to trial."

Even if the victim is resilient enough to pursue her case, she may encounter prejudicial attitudes from judges and juries. Kalven and Zeisel conducted an analysis of jurors' reactions to many crimes, including rape, in over 3,500 trials. They found that in rape cases the jury does not consider solely the issue of consent during intercourse but also includes as relevant to conviction any suggestions of contributory behavior on the part of the victim. The jury convicted defendants of rape in only three of forty-two cases of nonaggravated rape, whereas the judge would have convicted in twenty-two of these. Shirley Feldman-Summers and Karen Lindner investigated the perceptions of victims by juries and found that, as the respectability of the victim decreased, the jury's belief that the victim was responsible for the rape increased. In a sense, juries have created an extralegal defense. If the complainant somehow "assumed the risk" of rape, juries will commonly find the defendant guilty of some lesser crime or will acquit him altogether. "A seventeen-year-old girl was raped during a beer-drinking party. The jury probably acquitted, according to the judge, because they thought the girl asked for what she got." In one case, according to Medea and Thompson, "a woman who responded with 'fuck off' when approached lost her case because 'fuck' is a sexually exciting word." If the victim knew the offender previously, especially as an intimate, juries will be reluctant to convict.

In one case of "savage rape," the victim's jaw was fractured in two places. The jury nevertheless acquitted because it found that there may have been sexual relations on previous occasions, and the parties had been drinking on the night of the incident.

As a consequence of these practices, rape is a crime that is very rarely punished, though there is some evidence to suggest that legal reform has improved the rate of convictions for rape. Michigan was one of the states where there was a significant attempt to treat rape complainants with fairness and in the same manner as other victims of crime are treated. The result has been an improvement in prosecutions from 10 percent in 1975 to 19 percent of rape arrests leading to convictions in 1985.

Most individuals convicted of rape serve a sentence of no longer than four years, except when the victim is white and the offender is black. Of the 455 men executed for rape from 1930 to 1967, 405 were black. Black males, however, do not uniformly receive the most severe punishment. If their victims are black females, they are likely to receive the most lenient sentences. According to a study of rape convictions in Baltimore in 1967: "Of the four categories of rapist and victim in a racial mix, blacks received the stiffest sentences for raping white women and the mildest sentences for raping black women."

During the 1986–1987 school year, a survey was taken of over 1500 sixth to ninth graders who attended the Rhode Island Rape Crisis Center's assault-awareness program in schools across the state. The results of the survey strongly indicated that even the next generation of Americans tends to blame the victim of sexual assault. For example, 50 percent of the students said a woman who walks alone at night and dresses seductively is asking to be raped. In addition, most of the students surveyed accepted sexually assaultive behavior as normal. Fifty-one percent of the boys and 41 percent of the girls stated that a man has a right to force a woman to kiss him if he has spent "a lot of money" on her. Sixty-five percent of the boys and 57 percent of the girls in junior high schools said it is acceptable for a man to force a woman to have sex if they have been dating for more than six months. Eighty-seven percent of the boys and 79 percent of the girls approved of rape if the couple were married. Interestingly, 20 percent of the girls and 6 percent of the boys taking the survey disclosed that they had been sexually abused.

In cases of rape, judges, juries, police, prosecutors, and the general public frequently attribute blame and responsibility to the victim for her own victimization. Unfortunately, these negative responses are often compounded by reactions from family and friends. Encounters with parents, relatives, friends, and spouses many times involve either anger at the victim for being foolish enough to get raped or expressions of embarrassment and shame that family members will suffer as a result of the attack.

Much of the psychological harm of rape comes from the lack of support the victim receives and the tendency of victims to blame themselves. Women frequently ask themselves why they "let it happen." "There is a strong desire for the victim to try and think of how she could undo what has happened. She reports going over in her mind how she might have escaped from the assailant, how she might have handled the situation differently." For many women, the aftermath of the rape is worse than the physical pain and psychological trauma of the actual rape. These women are plagued by feelings of guilt, shame, loss of self-esteem, and humiliation. Many rapes go unreported because victims have been unjustifiably convinced that they were guilty of precipitating the attack. This is even more probable in cases where the victim knows the offender.

In a rape culture, even the victims believe that men are naturally sexual aggressors. Their response to the rape is to blame themselves for not taking proper precautions, rather than to demand a change in the behavior of men.

THE RAPE CULTURE

Exposure to sexual violence in the media has been shown to increase male acceptance of rape. Unfortunately, violent descriptions of male and female sexual encounters are all too common. In a content analysis of adult paperbacks published between 1968 and 1974 that *were not pornographic,* Don Smith found that one-fifth depicted sexual episodes involving a completed rape. In addition, almost 100 percent of these rape scenes portrayed the victim as sexually stimulated to the point of orgasm. Perhaps most men are educated through nonpornographic, but violent, depictions of sex in the common culture to become aroused at a description of a rape scene. It is little wonder that Malamuth and his colleagues find that "there are considerable data showing that within the general population a substantial percentage of men show arousal patterns similar to those of known rapists."

As long as sex in our society is construed as a dirty, low, and violent act involving domination of a male over a female, rape will remain a common occurrence. The erotization of male dominance means that whenever women are in a subordinate position to men, the likelihood for sexual assault is great. We are beginning to see that rape is not the only way in which women are sexually victimized, and that other forms of sexual exploitation of women are rampant in our society. Feminists have raised our consciousness about rape by developing rape crisis centers and other programs to assist victims and their families, by reforming laws and challenging politicians, by training professionals in medicine and in the criminal-justice system, and by educating women and the general public on the subject. They are also enlightening us about pornography; sexual harassment on the job and in higher education; sexual exploitation in doctor, dentist, and therapist relations with patients; and sexual assault in the family, such as incest and rape in marriage.

Rape is the logical outcome if men act according to the "masculine mystique" and women act according to the "feminine mystique." But rape does not have to occur. Its presence is an indication of how widely held are traditional views of appropriate male and female behavior, and of how strongly enforced these views are. Our society is a rape culture because it fosters and encourages rape by teaching males and females that it is natural and normal for sexual relations to involve aggressive behavior on the part of males. To end rape, people must be able to envision a relationship between the sexes that involves sharing, warmth, and equality, and to bring about a social system in which those values are fostered.

26

THE TRAGEDY
OF THE COMMONS

Garrett Hardin (1968)

The social dilemma proposed by ecologist Garrett Hardin in 1968 is still a serious concern 25 years later. The story of the tragedy of the commons examines the tendency for humans to look at short-term personal gains and neglect long-term social consequences. It becomes a problem because many of the resources on the planet are nonrenewable or will become nonrenewable if humans exploit them in such a manner as to pervert their renewability. Consider the rain forests of the Amazon, the steady cutting and burning of all timber and vegetation, and the impact on the animal species and on the indigenous human groups who live there. This rush to strip and mine natural resources or convert rain forest into farming lands is removing from the planet one of its vital resources. What makes sense for industry and the small number of people who become wealthy in the short term may have disastrous consequences for many of us in the long term. And not just governments and industry act as if there's no tomorrow. We, as individuals, are faced with many personal instances that test our ability to see the broader picture and deal with the fear of exploitation by others. Any number of social dilemmas, such as presented in the Prisoner's Dilemma or Julian Edney's Nut Game, require humans to cooperate, not compete; to communicate, not assume; to think in terms of the long term, not the immediate future. When conflict is defined as the perceived incompatibility of actions or goals, perceptions may have to change for order to exist (see also Reading 27 for conflict negotiation).

It wasn't that long ago that Malthus and others warned us of overpopulation with dire predictions that a finite world could only support a finite population. Any increase in world population must also coincide with increased production of

Source: Abridged from *Science,* 1968, *162,* 1243–1248. Copyright © 1968 by the AAAS. Reprinted by permission of the publisher and the author.

food, drinkable water, etc. The good news is that with advances in food production there is plenty of food to go around on this planet; the bad news is that poverty, politics, and inadequate distribution have not allowed our planet's people to be adequately fed. For reasons having nothing to do with limited resources, people starve and crops rot in fields. Does that mean we can or cannot rely on technology to alleviate the long-term consequences of adding more and more people to the planet? Laboratory studies and naturalistic observations of crowding in animals other than humans do not provide reassurance. Even with ample food and water supplies, the social behavior of animals has a tendency to fall apart in very high density environments. We cannot create more land. And yes, these problems may be long term, so long term that you and I and our grandchildren will not be directly affected. Can we rely on the technology of the future to solve the future "tragedy of the commons" which we may not even comprehend at this point in human history? That's a difficult question and one which has no answer in the present. Your answer is probably a reflection of your ability to hope for the best in the future. As we have seen before (see Reading 7), hope is fine, but active solutions and long-range planning to potential problems are more effective strategies.

The tragedy of the commons develops in this way. Picture a pasture open to all. It is to be expected that each herdsman will try to keep as many cattle as possible on the commons. Such an arrangement may work reasonably satisfactorily for centuries because tribal wars, poaching, and disease keep the numbers of both man and beast well below the carrying capacity of the land. Finally, however, comes the day of reckoning, that is, the day when the long-desired goal of social stability becomes a reality. At this point, the inherent logic of the commons remorselessly generates tragedy.

As a rational being, each herdsman seeks to maximize his gain. Explicitly or implicitly, more or less consciously, he asks, "What is the utility *to me* of adding one more animal to my herd?" This utility has one negative and one positive component.

1 The positive component is a function of the increment of one animal. Since the herdsman receives all the proceeds from the sale of the additional animal, the positive utility is nearly $+1$.

2 The negative component is a function of the additional overgrazing created by one more animal. Since, however, the effects of overgrazing are shared by all the herdsmen, the negative utility for any particular decision-making herdsman is only a fraction of -1.

Adding together the component partial utilities, the rational herdsman concludes that the only sensible course for him to pursue is to add another animal to his herd. And another; and another. . . . But this is the conclusion reached by each and every rational herdsman sharing a commons. Therein is the tragedy. Each man is locked into a system that compels him to increase his herd without limit—in a world that is limited. Ruin is the destination toward which all men rush, each pursuing his own best interest in a society that believes in the freedom of the commons. Freedom in a commons brings ruin to all.

Some would say that this is a platitude. Would that it were! In a sense, it was learned thousands of years ago, but natural selection favors the forces of psychological denial. The individual benefits as an individual from his ability to deny the truth even though society as a whole, of which he is a part, suffers. Education can counteract the natural tendency to do the wrong thing, but the inexorable succession of generations requires that the basis for this knowledge be constantly refreshed.

In an approximate way, the logic of the commons has been understood for a long time, perhaps since the discovery of agriculture or the invention of private property in real estate. But it is understood mostly only in special cases which are not sufficiently generalized. Even at this late date, cattlemen leasing national land on the western ranges demonstrate no more than an ambivalent understanding, in constantly pressuring federal authorities to increase the head count to the point where overgrazing produces erosion and weed-dominance. Likewise, the oceans of the world continue to suffer from the survival of the philosophy of the commons. Maritime nations still respond automatically to the shibboleth of the "freedom of the seas." Professing to believe in the "inexhaustible resources of the oceans," they bring species after species of fish and whales closer to extinction.

The National Parks present another instance of the working out of the tragedy of the commons. At present, they are open to all, without limit. The parks themselves are limited in extent—there is only one Yosemite Valley—whereas population seems to grow without limit. The values that visitors seek in the parks are steadily eroded. Plainly, we must soon cease to treat the parks as commons or they will be of no value to anyone.

What shall we do? We have several options. We might sell them off as private property. We might keep them as public property, but allocate the right to enter them. The allocation might be on the basis of wealth, by the use of an auction system. It might be on the basis of merit, as defined by some agreed-upon standards. It might be by lottery. Or it might be on a first-come, first-served basis, administered to long queues. These, I think, are all the reasonable possibilities. They are all objectionable. But we must choose—or acquiesce in the destruction of the commons that we call our National Parks.

POLLUTION

In a reverse way, the tragedy of the commons reappears in problems of pollution. Here it is not a question of taking something out of the commons, but of putting something in—sewage, or chemical, radioactive, and heat wastes into water; noxious and dangerous fumes into the air; and distracting and unpleasant advertising signs into the line of sight. The calculations of utility are much the same as before. The rational man finds that his share of the cost of the wastes he discharges into the commons is less than the cost of purifying his wastes before releasing them. Since this is true for everyone, we are locked into a system of "fouling our own nest," so long as we behave only as independent, rational, free-enterprisers.

The tragedy of the commons as a food basket is averted by private property, or something formally like it. But the air and waters surrounding us cannot readily be fenced, and so the tragedy of the commons as a cesspool must be prevented by different means, by coercive laws or taxing devices that make it cheaper for the polluter to treat his pollutants than to discharge them untreated. We have not progressed as far with the solution of this problem as we have with the first. Indeed, our particular concept of private property, which deters us from exhausting the positive resources of the earth, favors pollution. The owner of a factory on the bank of a stream—whose property extends to the middle of the stream—often has difficulty seeing why it is not his natural right to muddy the waters flowing past his door. The law, always behind the times, requires elaborate stitching and fitting to adapt it to this newly perceived aspect of the commons.

The pollution problem is a consequence of population. It did not much matter how a lonely American frontiersman disposed of his waste. "Flowing water purifies itself every 10 miles," my grandfather used to say, and the myth was near enough to the truth when he was a boy, for there were not too many people. But as population became denser, the natural chemical and biological recycling processes became overloaded, calling for a redefinition of property rights.

MUTUAL COERCION MUTUALLY AGREED UPON

The social arrangements that produce responsibility are arrangements that create coercion, of some sort. Consider bank-robbing. The man who takes money from a bank acts as if the bank were a commons. How do we prevent such action? Certainly not by trying to control his behavior solely by a verbal appeal to his sense of responsibility. Rather than rely on propaganda we follow Frankel's lead and insist that a bank is not a commons; we seek the definite social arrangements that will keep it from becoming a commons. That we thereby infringe on the freedom of would-be robbers we neither deny nor regret.

The morality of bank-robbing is particularly easy to understand because we accept complete prohibition of this activity. We are willing to say "Thou shalt not rob banks," without providing for exceptions. But temperance also can be created by coercion. Taxing is a good coercive device. To keep downtown shoppers temperate in their use of parking space we introduce parking meters for short periods, and traffic fines for longer ones. We need not actually forbid a citizen to park as long as he wants to; we need merely make it increasingly expensive for him to do so. Not prohibition, but carefully biased options are what we offer him.

To say that we mutually agree to coercion is not to say that we are required to enjoy it, or even to pretend we enjoy it. Who enjoys taxes? We all grumble about them. But we accept compulsory taxes because we recognize that voluntary taxes would favor the conscienceless. We institute and (grumblingly) support taxes and other coercive devices to escape the horror of the commons.

An alternative to the commons need not be perfectly just to be preferable. With real estate and other material goods, the alternative we have chosen is the institution of private property coupled with legal inheritance. Is this system perfectly just? As a genetically trained biologist I deny that it is. It seems to me that, if there are to be differences in individual inheritance, legal possession should be perfectly correlated with biological inheritance—that those who are biologically more fit to be the custodians of property and power should legally inherit more. But genetic recombination continually makes a mockery of the doctrine of "like father, like son" implicit in our laws of legal inheritance. An idiot can inherit millions, and a trust fund can keep his estate intact. We must admit that our legal system of private property plus inheritance is unjust—but we put up with it because we are not convinced, at the moment, that anyone has invented a better system. The alternative of the commons is too horrifying to contemplate. Injustice is preferable to total ruin.

As nearly as I can make out, automatic rejection of proposed reforms is based on one of two unconscious assumptions: (i) that the status quo is perfect; or (ii) that the choice we face is between reform and no action; if the proposed reform is imperfect, we presumably should take no action at all, while we wait for a perfect proposal.

But we can never do nothing. That which we have done for thousands of years is also action. It also produces evils. Once we are aware that the status quo is action, we can then compare its discoverable advantages and disadvantages with the predicted advantages and disadvantages of the proposed reform, discounting as best we can for our lack of experience. On the basis of such a comparison, we can make a rational decision which will not involve the unworkable assumption that only perfect systems are tolerable.

RECOGNITION OF NECESSITY

Perhaps the simplest summary of this analysis of man's population problems is this: the commons, if justifiable at all, is justifiable only under conditions of low-population density. As the human population has increased, the commons has had to be abandoned in one aspect after another.

First we abandoned the commons in food gathering, enclosing farm land and restricting pastures and hunting and fishing areas. These restrictions are still not complete throughout the world.

Somewhat later we saw that the commons as a place for waste disposal would also have to be abandoned. Restrictions on the disposal of domestic sewage are widely accepted in the Western world; we are still struggling to close the commons to pollution by automobiles, factories, insecticide sprayers, fertilizing operations, and atomic energy installations.

In a still more embryonic state is our recognition of the evils of the commons in matters of pleasure. There is almost no restriction on the propagation of sound waves in the public medium. The shopping public is assaulted with mindless music, without its consent. Our government is paying out billions of dollars to create supersonic transport which will disturb 50,000 people for every one person who is whisked from coast to coast 3 hours faster. Advertisers muddy the airwaves of radio and television and pollute the view of travelers. We are a long way from outlawing the commons in matters of pleasure. Is this because our Puritan inheritance makes us view pleasure as something of a sin, and pain (that is, the pollution of advertising) as the sign of virtue?

Every new enclosure of the commons involves the infringement of somebody's personal liberty. Infringements made in the distant past are accepted because no contemporary complains of a loss. It is the newly proposed infringements that we vigorously oppose; cries of "rights" and "freedom" fill the air. But what does "freedom" mean? When men mutually agreed to pass laws against robbing, mankind became more free, not less so. Individuals locked into the logic of the commons are free only to bring on universal ruin; once they see the necessity of mutual coercion, they become free to pursue other goals. I believe it was Hegel who said, "Freedom is the recognition of necessity."

The most important aspect of necessity that we must now recognize, is the necessity of abandoning the commons in breeding. No technical solution can rescue us from the misery of overpopulation. Freedom to breed will bring ruin to all. At the moment, to avoid hard decisions many of us are tempted to propagandize for conscience and responsible parenthood. The temptation must be resisted, because an appeal to independently acting consciences selects for the disappearance of all conscience in the long run, and an increase in anxiety in the short.

The only way we can preserve and nurture other and more precious freedoms is by relinquishing the freedom to breed, and that very soon. "Freedom is the recognition of necessity"—and it is the role of education to reveal to all the necessity of abandoning the freedom to breed. Only so, can we put an end to this aspect of the tragedy of the commons.

27

SOLUTIONS,
NOT WINNERS

Dean G. Pruitt (1987)

Have you ever wondered why schooling in the United States includes the three
"essentials''—reading, writing, and 'rithmetic, but not the social skills that are
also almost universally needed? It is estimated that approximately 90 percent of
today's young adults will marry (at least once) and that most adults will have at
least one child. Most adults will also be working with and living near others with
whom they will have to get along. So why don't we learn the communication
skills that will enhance our intimate and working relations with others?

Myers, in Module 27, suggests four important skills: contact, cooperation,
communication, and conciliation. Anyone who has been around children two
years old or older can see these skills in the making, but all too often children are
taught only a few simple techniques and are able to observe only the most
primitive cooperative, communicative, and conciliatory attempts in the adult
conflicts occurring around them. And this is the extent of their training for life!
We all need to learn when to accept others' ideas and when to suggest one's own
brilliant contributions; when to acknowledge what another person is feeling
versus when to focus on problem solving; and when to be conciliatory versus
firm. These are all complex skills, yet this kind of knowledge helps individuals to
face the many challenges in life. Pruitt suggests some interesting group processes
that individuals can pursue when they are unable to successfully communicate
and resolve conflicts. Taking this one step further, mediation skills would be
helpful for all of us in most aspects of interpersonal lives.

The woman squirmed uncomfortably. Her husband, sitting next to her, glared across the table at a younger couple, who glared back. At the head of the table, a schoolteacher in her 30s was explaining what would happen next. "First Mr. and Mrs. Smith will tell their side of the story. Then you, Mr. and Mrs. Brown, will have your chance. After that, we'll discuss the situation and try to find a way to resolve it. I assure you that nothing you say will leave this room."

The two couples were feuding neighbors whose controversy had finally reached the courts, where a judge had referred them to a local dispute-settlement center. He felt that a skilled volunteer mediator such as the teacher would be better equipped than the courts to sort out intricate relationships between neighbors.

The Smiths said that Mr. Smith had been trapped in his garage twice because Mrs. Brown's sister had parked her car in a common driveway between the two houses. He had gone over to complain and received a chilly reception both times. Then the Browns' children had retrieved a ball from the Smiths' garden, trampling some flowers in the process. When Mr. Smith asked them to leave, Mr. Brown stormed over to complain about his speaking to them, leading to a shouting match. After that, the Browns' 6th- and 7th-graders had called the Smith teenagers names and ridden their bicycles on the Smith lawn. Finally, the Browns accused the Smiths' teenage son of setting the Brown family car on fire and had him arrested.

The Browns saw things a bit differently. They said that the wife's sister had blocked the driveway only once and that they had apologized and promised it would never happen again. The second car belonged to someone they didn't know. Mr. Brown had gone over to complain about Mr. Smith telling the children to "get the hell out of my garden." The Brown children had not called names or ridden bicycles on the lawn, but the Smith teenagers had often made obscene gestures and ridden their cars on the Brown lawn. The Smiths' boy had thrown a firecracker under the Browns' car, causing it to catch fire. They had seen him do it and had called the police.

While each side was telling its story, the other family kept interrupting with outbursts such as "that's not true" or "wait a minute," which were quieted by the mediator. After the families told their stories, the mediator led a discussion that kept circling back over the same material. Since the hearing was going nowhere, the mediator held a private caucus with each of the families during which she clarified the key issues and demands of each side. These became the agenda for the next joint session, which was considerably more productive. Finally, the mediator drew up a contract that was signed by all four disputants. It stipulated that the driveway would be kept open at all times; that the young people would be polite and stay in their own yards except when carefully retrieving balls; and most importantly, that future problems would be handled quietly in discussions between the adults. The Browns agreed to withdraw their legal complaint against the Smith teenager. Fortunately, their insurance company agreed to replace the car.

Sessions such as these are part of a mediation movement that has been growing rapidly since the Justice Department funded a demonstration project in 1977. The American Bar Association estimates that more than 300 dispute-resolution centers in the United States now process more than 230,000 cases a year. Some of these centers are funded by state and local governments, while others are operated by non-profit and community organizations.

The centers' main function is to assist people who are or have been in continuing relationships reach a mutually acceptable resolution of their disputes. They help neighbors settle noise problems, former spouses work out changes in visitation arrangements, mothers and daughters develop rules for help around the house, former friends settle a dispute about who should pay the hospital bills for injuries incurred during a fight, landlords and tenants decide who is to pay for repairs and former lovers divide up common property. Handling matters of this kind in dispute centers helps ease the pressure on already crowded court calendars.

Many of the centers also help resolve small-claims disputes between people who have not had continuing relationships, such as customers and storekeepers. Referrals come from many sources, including judges, district attorneys, legal aid, court clerks, police, social workers and consumer-protection agencies. The men and women who hear these cases are usually volunteers who have been trained by psychologists, lawyers or other professionals.

The past 10 years have also seen a rapid growth of mediation in other settings. Divorce mediation has become quite popular, with divorcing couples meeting in professional sessions to develop an agreement to submit to the court. Large public-resource issues, such as the building of a dam or the division of federal money among state agencies, are often mediated. Furthermore, judges are increasingly doing pretrial mediation of civil cases that come before them.

A growing number of researchers have begun studying these new forms of mediation and sharing their findings in journals, professional societies and conferences. Most of these efforts have been devoted to evaluating mediation programs. In reviewing this research, psychologists Janice Roehl and Royer Cook of the Institute for Social Analysis in Washington, D.C., have found a remarkable consistency in findings. Agreements reached in mediation are usually satisfactory to the disputants and hold up well over time. Relationships between the disputants often improve after the hearing. In addition, both sides tend to be pleased with the treatment they have received in the hearing and see the outcome as fair. A large majority of them say that they would return to the center if they had another problem and would recommend the service to a friend. Mediation generally receives higher ratings in all of these areas than do court hearings.

Psychologist Neil Vidmar of the University of Western Ontario has pointed out that the latter findings may result in part from the fact that when one or both sides of a dispute are willing to accept some responsibility for the problem, they are more likely to go to mediation and come up with a solution. When neither side admits any responsibility, the problem is more difficult and is likely to go to court. However, these differences don't seem strong enough to explain why mediation consistently works better than legal proceedings. The advantages of mediation persist when cases are randomly assigned to mediation and courtroom hearings.

Psychologists Gary Welton and William Rick Fry, graduate students Neil McGillicuddy, Josephine Zubek, Carol Ippolito, Lynn Castrianno and I have been studying the subject by observing mediation sessions and gathering further information through questionnaires and interviews with mediators and their clients.

We have conducted most of our research at the Dispute Settlement Center of the Better Business Bureau in Buffalo, New York, with the active collaboration of its vice president, Judith A. Peter. Our first study compared three procedures that are used if no agreement is reached during mediation. The first is straight mediation, in which the case is simply dropped. The second is med/arb(same), in which the mediator becomes an arbitrator and makes a binding decision. The third is med/arb(diff), in which a different person arbitrates the case.

Each of these procedures has its proponents and detractors in the field of dispute settlement. Supporters of straight mediation say that arbitration takes responsibility for the decision out of the hands of the disputants. They argue that since disputants know the issues better than an arbitrator does, they are better able to develop solutions that satisfy both sides. Supporters also say that making disputants completely responsible for an agreement makes compliance much more likely. They would rather have no decision, and hope that the disputants work things out later, than have an imposed decision.

Those who support med/arb(same) insist that it encourages the disputants to reach agreement during mediation, because they fear loss of control over the result if they must go to arbitration. Proponents also argue that having the latent power to arbitrate gives mediators enough authority to persuade reluctant disputants to make concessions and come up with solutions.

Proponents of med/arb(diff) agree that the threat of arbitration helps. But they question giving mediators the power to arbitrate because it might make them too forceful, resulting in agreements that reflect their views rather than those of the disputants. Med/arb(diff) supporters also maintain that mediation is a bad preparation for arbitration because mediators may become biased in favor of one solution. A different arbitrator avoids this danger.

We randomly assigned 36 cases passed along to the Dispute Settlement Center by the Buffalo City Court to the three procedures. The hearings were watched by two observers. One used an electronic recording device to classify everything each disputant said, using 26 categories such as "makes new proposals," "asks hostile question" and "criticizes other's behavior." The second observer recorded 28 categories of mediator behavior, such as "urges agreement," "argues for a particular proposal" and "mentions the cost of no agreement."

Our results supported med/arb(same) over the other two procedures. With it, the disputants showed less hostility toward each other and proposed many more new ideas to solve the problem. They seemed more anxious to reach agreement, showed greater respect for the mediator and reached agreement somewhat more often than with the other procedures.

Med/arb(diff) came in a poor second. Not only were disputants less creative, mediators also seemed less interested in the sessions, perhaps because the prospect of having someone else take over the case made them feel less involved. Straight mediation did worst of all. Without the prospect of arbitration to prod them, disputants were especially hostile. They swore, asked biting questions and complained endlessly about one another's behavior and character. They were also especially uncreative in coming up with solutions. It is hard to believe that many of them would have gone on to resolve their own problems.

THE CONTROVERSY OVER CAUCUSES

Mother and daughter sat across a table, eyeing each other warily. The mediator asked the daughter to begin, because she had called for the meeting. The daughter spoke about how hard she had to work at home—cleaning the house, washing the dishes, taking care of her younger brother—and the fact that the mother was always complaining about her daughter's work.

The mother disagreed strongly. The jobs were not unreasonable, she insisted, and the daughter's help was needed to keep the household going with both parents working. In any case, the daughter's responsibilities were not out of line with those of other teenagers. Furthermore, the girl was not doing a good job. Dishes sat in the sink. Dust accumulated under the beds.

After this confrontation, mother and daughter lapsed into an embarrassed silence, and the mediator could not get them to discuss the issues. Finally she suggested that they meet separately with her. In private, the daughter clarified her priorities. Her biggest problem was not the chores but the fact that her mother always yelled at her about them. The mediator asked permission to discuss this with the mother and the girl agreed. In private, the mother acknowledged that she often raised her voice and said that she felt bad about it. The problem was that her husband often complained about the girl's work and this made the mother nervous.

The mediator suggested she tell her daughter about this and also try to clarify just what she expected in the work. The succeeding joint session was much more fruitful. The daughter's responsibilities were defined, she agreed to try harder and the mother agreed to stop yelling. Mother and daughter left the room cheerfully, in an apparently affectionate mood.

This vignette illustrates the productive use of caucusing, meeting separately with each side in a dispute. Some mediators and dispute centers have rejected this procedure completely, believing that it creates more problems than it solves. They argue that disputants may mislead the mediator by making inaccurate statements while the other side is not present to dispute them.

Critics also point out that disputants may become suspicious of the mediator while he or she is caucusing with the other side or may spend the time meeting with friends, relatives or other supporters who strenghten their commitment to their positions. Another argument against caucusing is that joint problem-solving by the disputants is the best way to solve an immediate problem and to foster skills they can use in future controversies when a mediator is not available.

Our studies show that there is, in fact, more criticism of the opponent's behavior and more character assassination in caucuses than in joint sessions. We are still gathering evidence on the other allegations. Overall, however, our research suggests four reasons caucusing should help get unproductive meetings going. First, since the other side is not present, the disputant is normally less tense and defensive than in a joint session and thus more flexible and creative. Second, the disputant feels freer to speak openly, to suggest new solutions and to react frankly to ideas from the mediator.

Third, since the other party can't see or hear the mediator, he or she can be warm and supportive with one side without appearing partial, thus encouraging rapport and the sharing of information. The mediator is also free to make critical remarks to one side without seeming to curry favor with the other.

Fourth, it is more effective for the mediator to ask each party individually to develop solutions than to ask both parties at the same time. When both sides are challenged in the other's presence, each is likely to conclude that the other has more responsibility to come up with solutions, letting them both off the hook.

Our findings also supported the prediction that mediators in med/arb(same) would act forcefully. They threatened to end the session if there was no progress and advocated a particular position more often than mediators did in the other two conditions. However, they tended to use these pressure tactics only at the end of the sessions, suggesting a last-ditch effort to rescue a failing mediation rather than a consistent policy of forceful advocacy. Furthermore, the questionnaire showed that the disputants in med/arb(same) saw the mediator as less forceful and themselves as more involved in working out the agreement than they did in the other conditions.

The success of med/arb(same) indicates the value of mediator power in dispute resolution. The traditional view is that mediators should be powerless and totally neutral—"eunuchs from Mars," to borrow attorney Roger Fisher's colorful phrase. Yet mediator power works quite well in other situations, from mediation in family disputes to mediation between nations. Our results suggest that mediator power can encourage seriousness of purpose and hard work on the part of the disputants.

Mediator power can become a problem, however, if it tempts the mediator to dictate terms early in the session. We see several ways to help avoid this possibility. One is to train mediators to adopt a democratic orientation toward the disputants, urging the mediators to strive constantly for input and consent from them. Periodic refresher courses for mediators should also stress this theme. And there should always be enough time in each hearing to build the trust and willingness to compromise that is required for a lasting agreement.

It should be emphasized that the superiority of the med/arb(same) procedure in our study means only that it was more useful during the mediation phase. If a hearing must go to arbitration, having the same mediator act as arbitrator can present problems. The biggest is that mediators may become biased toward one side during caucus sessions (see "The Controversy Over Caucuses," this article).

The solution to this problem seems again to lie in training. Mediator-arbitrators should be taught to treat the accusations they hear in caucus as information about the speaker's views—allegations that are not to be accepted as fact until the accused party has had a chance to refute them.

My research and that of others have convinced me that mediation is an effective method for resolving many of the conflicts that create problems in our society. One major advantage mediation has over courtroom hearings is that mediation sessions are held more promptly. Another is that mediation sessions are usually longer, giving each side a better chance to tell its story and to explore the case in detail. The emphasis in mediation on finding win-win solutions for the future rather than establishing guilt or innocence also makes it possible for both sides to benefit.

In some cases, such as when there is a clear right and wrong or a serious crime has been committed, mediation isn't appropriate. Or if one side is much more powerful than the other, that side will almost surely win a procedure that calls for consent by both sides. Such cases should be arbitrated or decided in court.

28

GAIN AND LOSS OF ESTEEM AS DETERMINANTS OF INTERPERSONAL ATTRACTIVENESS

Elliot Aronson and Darwyn Linder (1965)

A simple reward theory of attraction suggests that the individuals who are reinforcing (those who send you chocolates or roses or lift your self-esteem) or are associated with rewarding events (those standing near you when you learn you won the lottery or attend the rock concert) are the relationships that you will want to continue. Aronson and Linder recognized that this model was simplistic in that it failed to account for changes in feelings in relationships. They hypothesized that we like people who come to like us over time more than people who like us from the start. Furthermore, when we fall from someone's favor, we dislike them *more* than someone who never liked us in the first place. Sound reasonable from the perspective of the hindsight bias? Perhaps, but when this article was published in 1965, it had a major impact on the way psychologists understood the process of coming to have affection for others.

And now a caveat about reading this selection—in 1965, psychologists were at the height of using jargon so there are a lot of awkward terms, like "P" for person and "O" for other. Reading this article slowly and calmly will help you to overcome the annoyance you might have with the terminology and will allow you to enjoy the creative method and interesting results. Note that the confederate who changes her mind in favor of the subject (negative-positive condition in Table 28-1) is liked significantly more than the confederate who says *twice* as many nice things about the subject and liked her all along (positive-positive condition in Table 28-1).

On a more personal level, think of the one nonrelative with whom you have been most in love in your life. Now go back in time and gauge your first impression of that person. I (SLE) do this in my social psychology class and usually half the students have a negative first impression of the "love of their life." The same holds true for the other end of the spectrum. When asked to give the first impression of the "hate of their life," even more than half describe their first impressions as positive. Often it is a former best friend or lover who somehow betrayed a person's trust. And for many of my students, it was the same person who was their main love and hate focus!

One of the major determinants of whether or not one person (P) will like another (O) is the nature of the other's behavior in relation to the person. Several investigators have predicted and found that if P finds O's behavior "rewarding," he will tend to like O (Newcomb, 1956, 1961; Thibaut and Kelley, 1959; Homans, 1961; Byrne, 1961; Byrne and Wong, 1962). One obvious source of reward for P is O's attitude regarding him. Thus, if O expresses invariably positive feelings and opinions about P, this constitutes a reward and will tend to increase P's liking for O.

Although this has been demonstrated to be true (Newcomb, 1956, 1961), it may be that a more complex relationship exists between being liked and liking others. It is conceivable that the sequence of O's behavior toward P might have more impact on P's liking for O than the total number of rewarding acts emitted by O toward P. Stated briefly, it is our contention that the feeling of gain or loss is extremely important— specifically, that a gain in esteem is a more potent reward than invariant esteem, and similarly, the loss of esteem is a more potent "punishment" than invariant negative esteem. Thus, if O's behavior toward P was initially negative but gradually became more positive, P would like O more than he would had O's behavior been uniformly positive. This would follow even if, in the second case, the sum total of rewarding acts emitted by O was less than in the first case.

This "gain-loss" effect may have two entirely different causes. One is largely affective, the other cognitive. First, when O expresses negative feelings toward P, P probably experiences some negative affect, e.g., anxiety, hurt, self-doubt, anger, etc. If O's behavior gradually becomes more positive, his behavior is not only rewarding for P in and of itself, but it also serves to reduce the existing negative drive state previously aroused by O. The total reward value of O's positive behavior is, therefore, greater. Thus, paradoxically, P will subsequently like O better *because* of O's early negative, punitive behavior. What we are suggesting is that the existence of a prior negative drive state will increase the attractiveness of an individual who has both created and reduced this drive state.

The same kind of reasoning (in reverse) underlies the "loss" part of our notion. Here, P will like O better if O's behavior toward P is invariably negative than if O's initial behavior had been positive and gradually became more negative. Although in the former case O's behavior may consist of a greater number of negative acts, the latter case constitutes a distinct loss of esteem and, therefore, would have a greater effect upon reducing P's liking for O. When negative behavior follows positive behavior, it is not only punishing in its own right but also eradicates the positive affect associated with the rewarding nature of O's earlier behavior. Therefore, P dislikes the positive-negative O more than the entirely negative O precisely because of the fact that, in the first case, O had previously rewarded him.

The predicted gain-loss effect may also have a more cognitive cause. By changing his opinion about *P, O* forces *P* to take his evaluation more seriously. If *O* expresses uniformly positive or uniformly negative feelings about *P, P* can dismiss this behavior as being a function of *O*'s style of response, i.e., that *O* likes everybody or dislikes everybody, and that is *his* problem. But if *O* begins by evaluating *P* negatively and then becomes more positive, *P* must consider the possibility that *O*'s evaluations are a function of *O*'s perception of him and not merely a style of responding. Because of this he is more apt to be impressed by *O* than if *O*'s evaluation had been invariably positive. It is probably not very meaningful to be liked by a person with no discernment or discrimination. *O*'s early negative evaluation proves that he has discernment and that he's paying attention to *P*—that he's neither blind nor bland. This renders his subsequent positive evaluation all the more meaningful and valuable.

By the same token, if *O*'s evaluation of *P* is entirely negative, *P* may be able to write *O* off as a misanthrope or a fool. But if *O*'s initial evaluation is positive and then becomes negative, *P* is forced to conclude that *O* can discriminate among people. This adds meaning (and sting) to *O*'s negative evaluation of *P* and, consequently, will decrease *P*'s liking for *O*.

The present experiment was designed to test the major prediction of our gain-loss notion, that is, the primary intent of this experiment was to determine whether or not *changes* in the feelings of *O* toward *P* have a greater effect on *P*'s liking for *O* than the total number of rewarding acts emitted by *O*. A secondary purpose was to shed some light on the possible reasons for this relationship. The specific hypotheses are (1) *P* will like *O* better if *O*'s initial attitude toward *P* is negative but gradually becomes more positive, than if his attitude is uniformly positive; (2) *P* will like *O* better if his attitude is uniformly negative than if his initial attitude toward *P* is positive and becomes increasingly negative.

METHOD

Subjects and Design

In order to provide a test of the hypotheses, it was necessary to design an experiment in which a subject interacts with a confederate over a series of discrete meetings. During these meetings the confederate should express either a uniformly positive attitude toward the subject, a uniformly negative attitude toward the subject, a negative attitude which gradually becomes positive, or a positive attitude which gradually becomes negative. It was essential that the interactions between subject and confederate be constant throughout experimental conditions except for the expression of attitude. At the close of the experiment, the subject's liking for the confederate could be assessed.

The subjects were 80 female students at the University of Minnesota. Virtually all of them were sophomores; they were volunteers from introductory classes in psychology, sociology, and child development. All subjects were randomly assigned to one of the four experimental conditions.

Procedure

The experimenter greeted the subject and led her to an observation room which was connected to the main experimental room by a one-way window and an audioamplification system. The experimenter told the subject that two students were scheduled for this hour, one would be the subject and the other would help the experimenter perform the experiment. He said that since she arrived first, she would be the helper. He asked her to wait while he left the room to see if the other girl had arrived yet. A few minutes later, through the one-way window, the subject was able to see the experimenter enter the experimental room with another female student (the paid confederate). The experimenter told the confederate to be seated for a moment and that he would return shortly to explain the experiment to her. The experimenter then returned to the observation room and began the instructions to the subject. The experimenter told the subject that she was going to assist him in performing a verbal conditioning experiment on the other student. The experimenter explained verbal conditioning briefly and told the subject that his particular interest was in the possible generalization of conditioned verbal responses from the person giving the reward to a person who did not reward the operant response. The experimenter explained that he would condition the other girl to say plural nouns to him by rewarding her with an "mmm hmmm" every time she said a plural noun. The experimenter told the subject that his procedure should increase the rate of plural nouns employed by the other girl. The subject was then told that her tasks were: (1) to listen in and record the number of plural nouns used by the other girl, and (2) to engage her in a series of conversations (not rewarding plural nouns) so that the experimenter could listen and determine whether generalization occurred. The experimenter told the subject that they would alternate in talking to the girl (first the subject, then the experimenter, then the subject) until each had spent seven sessions with her.

The experimenter made it clear to the subject that the other girl must not know the purpose of the experiment lest the results be contaminated. He explained that, in order to accomplish this, some deception must be used. The experimenter said that he was going to tell the girl that the purpose of the experiment was to determine how people form impressions of other people. He said that the other girl would be told that she was to carry on a series of seven short conversations with the subject, and that between each of these conversations both she and the subject would be interviewed, the other girl by the experimenter and the subject by an assistant in another room, to find out what impressions they had formed. The experimenter told the subject that this "cover story" would enable the experimenter and the subject to perform their experiment on verbal behavior since it provided the other girl with a credible explanation for the procedure they would follow. In actuality, this entire explanation was, in itself, a cover story which enabled the experimenter and his confederate to perform their experiment on the formation of impressions.

The independent variable was manipulated during the seven meetings that the experimenter had with the confederate. During their meetings the subject was in the observation room, listening to the conversation and dutifully counting the number of plural nouns used by the confederate. Since the subject had been led to believe that the confederate thought that the experiment involved impressions of people, it was quite natural for the experimenter to ask the confederate to express her feelings about the subject. Thus, without intending to, the subject heard herself evaluated by a fellow student on seven successive occasions.

There were four experimental conditions: (1) Negative-Positive, (2) Positive-Negative, (3) Negative-Negative, and (4) Positive-Positive. In the Negative-Positive condition the confederate expressed a negative impression of the subject during the first three interviews with the experimenter. Specifically, she described her as being a dull conversationalist, a rather ordinary person, not very intelligent, as probably not having many friends, etc. During the fourth session she began to change her opinion about her. The confederate's attitude became more favorable with each successive meeting until, in the seventh interview, it was entirely positive. In the Positive-Positive condition the confederate's stated opinions were invariably positive. During the seventh interview her statements were precisely the same as those in the seventh meeting of the Negative-Positive condition. In the Negative-Negative condition the confederate expressed invariably negative feelings about the subject throughout the seven interviews. The Positive-Negative condition was the mirror image of the Negative-Positive condition. The confederate began by stating that the subject seemed interesting, intelligent, and likeable, but by the seventh session she described the subject as being dull, ordinary, etc.

In the Positive-Positive condition the confederate made 28 favorable statements about the subject and zero unfavorable statements. In the Negative-Negative condition the confederate made 24 unfavorable statements about the subject and zero favorable ones. In both the Negative-Positive and Positive-Negative conditions the confederate made 14 favorable and 8 unfavorable statements about the subject.

At the opening of the first interview, the experimenter informed the confederate that she should be perfectly frank and honest and that the subject would never be told anything about her evaluation. This was done so that the subject, upon hearing favorable statements, could not readily believe that the confederate might be trying to flatter her.

Interactions between Subjects and Confederate

Prior to each interview with the experimenter, the confederate and the subject engaged in a 3-minute conversation. This provided a credible basis upon which the confederate might form and change her impression of the subject. During these sessions it was essential that the confederate's conversations with the subject be as uniform as possible throughout the four experimental conditions. This was accomplished by informing the subject, prior to the first session, of the kind of topics she should lead the confederate into. These included movies, teachers, courses, life goals, personal background information, etc. Once the subject brought up one of these topics, the confederate spewed forth a prepared set of facts, opinions, and anecdotes which were identical for all experimental subjects. Of course, since a social interation was involved, it was impossible for the confederate's conversations to be entirely uniform for all of the subjects.

Occasionally the confederate was forced to respond to a direct question which was idiosyncratic to a particular subject. However, any variations in the statements made by the confederate were minor and nonsystematic.

The subject and confederate met in the same room but they were separated at all times by a cardboard screen which prevented visual communication. This was done for two reasons. First, it made it easier for the confederate to play the role of the naive subject. We feared that the confederate, after saying negative things about the subject, might be reluctant to look her squarely in the eye and engage in casual conversation. In addition, the use of the screen allowed for a more precise control of the conversation of the confederate by enabling her to read her lines from a prepared script which was tacked to the screen. The use of the screen was easily explained to the subject (in terms of the verbal reinforcement cover story) as a necessary device for eliminating inadvertant nonverbal reinforcement, like nods and smiles.

The confederate carried on her end of the conversation in a rather bland, neutral tone of voice, expressing neither great enthusiasm nor monumental boredom. The same girl (an attractive 20-year-old senior) was used as the confederate throughout the experiment. In order to further convince the subject of the validity of the cover story, the confederate used increasingly more plural nouns throughout the course of the experiment.

The Dependent Variable

At the close of the experiment the experimenter told the subject that there was some additional information he needed from her, but that it was also necessary for him to see the other girl to explain the true nature of the experiment to her. He said that, since he was pressed for time, the subject would be interviewed by his research supervisor while he, the experimenter, explained the experiment to the other girl. The experimenter then led the subject into the interviewer's office, introduced them, and left.

A separate interviewer was used in order to avoid bias, the interviewer being ignorant of the subject's experimental condition. The purpose of the interview was to measure the subject's liking for the confederate; but this could not be done in any simple manner because the bare outlines of this experiment were extremely transparent: the confederate evaluated the subject, then the subject evaluated the confederate. Unless the interviewer could provide the subject with a credible rationale (consistent with the cover story) for asking her to evaluate the other girl, even the most naive of our subjects might have guessed the real purpose of the experiment. Therefore, the interviewer took a great deal of time and trouble to convince the subject that these data were essential for an understanding of the other girl's verbal behavior. The essence of his story was that the attitudes and feelings that the "helpers" in the experiment had for the "subjects" in the experiment often found expression in such subtle ways as tone of voice, enthusiasm, etc. "For example, if you thought a lot of the other girl you might unwittingly talk with warmth and enthusiasm. If you didn't like her you might unwittingly sound aloof and distant." The interviewer went on to explain that, much to his chagrin, he noticed that these subtle differences in inflection had a marked effect upon the gross verbal output of the other girls, that is, they talked more when they were conversing with people who seemed to like them than when they were conversing with people who seemed not to like them. The interviewer said that this source of variance was impossible to control but must be accounted for in the statistical analysis of the data. He explained that if he could get a precise indication of the "helpers'" feelings toward the "subjects," he could then "plug this into a mathematical formula as a correction term and thereby get a more or less unbiased estimate of what her gross verbal output would have been if your attitude toward her had been neutral."

The interviewer told the subject that, in order to accomplish this, he was going to ask her a number of questions aimed at getting at her feelings about the other girl. He emphasized that he wanted her *feeling,* her "gut response"; i.e., that it was essential that she give her frank impression of the other girl regardless of whether or not she had solid, rational reasons for it.

After the subject indicated that she understood, the interviewer asked her whether she liked the other girl or not. After she answered, the interviewer showed her a card on which was printed a 21-point scale, from -10 to $+10$. The interviewer asked her to indicate the magnitude of her feeling as precisely as possible. He verbally labeled the scale: " $+10$ would mean you like her extremely, -10 that you dislike her extremely. Zero means that you are completely indifferent. If you liked her a little, you'd answer $+1$, $+2$, or $+3$; if you liked her moderately well, you'd answer $+4$, $+5$, or $+6$; if you liked her quite a bit, you'd answer with a higher number. What point on the scale do you feel reflects your feeling toward the girl most accurately?"

This was the dependent measure. In addition, the interviewer asked the subjects to rate the confederate on 14 evaluative scales including intelligence, friendliness, warmth, frankness, etc. Most of these were asked in order to ascertain whether or not general liking would manifest itself in terms of higher ratings on specific attributes; a few were asked as possible checks on the manipulations.

Finally, the interviewer asked the subject if it bothered, embarrassed, annoyed, or upset her to hear the other girl evaluate her to the experimenter. After recording her answer, the interviewer probed to find out whether or not the subject suspected the real purpose of the experiment. He then explained, in full, the true nature of the experiment and the necessity for the deception. The subjects, especially those who had been negatively evaluated, were relieved to learn that it was not "for real." Although several of the girls admitted to having been quite shaken during the experiment, they felt that it was a worthwhile experience, inasmuch as they learned the extent to which a negative evaluation (even by a stranger) can affect them. They left the interview room in good spirits.

In most cases the interviewer remained ignorant of which of the four experimental conditions the subject was in until the conclusion of the interview. On a few occasions, however, a subject said something casually, in the midst of the interview, from which the interviewer could infer her experimental condition. It should be emphasized, however, that the dependent variable was the first question asked; in no case was the interviewer aware of a subject's experimental condition before she responded to that question.

RESULTS AND DISCUSSION

Our hypotheses were that the confederate would be liked better in the Negative-Positive condition than in the Positive-Positive condition and that she would be liked better in the Negative-Negative condition than in the Positive-Negative condition. To test these hypotheses we compared the subjects' ratings of their liking for the confederate across experimental conditions. The significance of the differences were determined by t-test. Table 28-1 shows the means, SDs, t-values, and significance levels. An examination of the table reveals that the means are ordered in the predicted direction. Moreover, it is clear that the confederate was liked significantly more in the Negative-Positive condition than in the Positive-Positive condition ($p < .02$, two-tailed). The difference between the Negative-Negative condition and the Positive-Negative condition showed a strong trend in the predicted direction, although it did not reach an acceptable level of significance ($p < .15$, two-tailed). There is a great deal of variability in these two conditions. This large variability may be partly a function of the well-known reluctance of college students to express negative feelings about their fellow students, even when the behavior of the latter is objectively negative (e.g., Aronson and Mills, 1959). Typically, in social psychological experiments, regardless of how obnoxiously a stooge behaves toward a subject, many subjects find it difficult to verbalize negative evaluations of the stooge. In these two conditions the behavior of the stimulus person would seem to have brought forth a negative evaluation; although most of the subjects were able to do this, several came out with highly positive evaluations.

Table 28-1 also indicates that there is a very large difference between those conditions in which the confederate ended by expressing a positive feeling for the subject and those in which she ended with a negative feeling for the subject. For example, a comparison of the Positive-Positive condition with the Negative-Negative condition yields a t of 7.12, significant at far less than the .001 level. As predicted, the widest mean difference occurs between the Negative-Positive condition ($M = +7.67$) and the Positive-Negative condition ($M = +0.87$). This is interesting in view of the fact that the confederate made the same number of positive and negative statements in these two conditions; only the sequence was different.

TABLE 28-1   MEANS AND STANDARD DEVIATIONS FOR LIKING OF THE CONFEDERATE

Experimental condition	Mean	SD	t-values	
1. Negative-Positive	+ 7.67	1.51	1 vs. 2	2.71**
2. Positive-Positive	+ 6.42	1.42	2 vs. 3	7.12***
3. Negative-Negative	+ 2.52	3.16	3 vs. 4	1.42*
4. Positive-Negative	+ 0.87	3.32		

*$p < .15$.
**$p < .02$.
***$p < .001$ (all p levels are two-tailed).

It will be recalled that the subjects were asked to rate the confederate on 14 evaluative scales in order to ascertain whether or not greater liking would manifest itself in terms of higher ratings on specific attributes. No evidence for this was found; e.g., although the subjects liked the confederate better in the Negative-Positive condition than in the Positive-Positive condition, they did not find her significantly more intelligent or less conceited. In fact, the only ratings that reached an acceptable level of significance showed a reverse effect: In the Positive-Positive condition the confederate was rated more friendly ($p < .01$), nicer ($p < .01$), and warmer ($p < .01$) than in the Negative-Positive condition. Our failure to predict this effect may be attributable to a naive belief in generalization which served to blind us to more obvious factors. Thus, although we did not predict this result, it is not startling if one considers the simple fact that in the Positive-Positive condition the confederate's evaluations of the subject, because they were entirely positive, *did* reflect greater friendliness, niceness, and warmth. That is, when forced to consider such things as friendliness, niceness, and warmth, the subjects in the Negative-Positive condition could not give the confederate a very high rating. The confederate, here, is not the kind of person who exudes niceness; by definition she is capable of saying negative things. Nevertheless, when asked for their "gut-response" regarding how much they liked the confederate, the subjects in the Negative-Positive condition tended to give her a high rating. To speculate, we might suggest the following: When one is asked to rate a person on a particular attribute, one tends to sum the person's relevant behavior in a rather cognitive, rational manner. On the other hand, when one is asked how much one likes a person, one tends to state a current feeling rather than to add and subtract various components of the person's past behavior.

In the Negative-Positive condition the subject has succeeded in showing the confederate that he (the subject) is not a dull clod but is, in fact, a bright and interesting person. This is no mean accomplishment and therefore might lead the subject to experience a feeling of competence or efficacy (White, 1959). Thus, in this condition, part of the reason for O's great attractiveness may be due to the fact that he has provided the subject with a success experience. Indeed, during the interview many subjects in this condition spontaneously mentioned that, after hearing O describe them as dull and stupid, they tried hard to make interesting and intelligent statements in subsequent encounters with O. It is reasonable to suspect that they were gratified to find that these efforts paid off by inducing a change in O's evaluations. This raises an interesting theoretical question; it may be that the feeling of competence is not only a contributing factor to the "gain" effect but may actually be a necessary condition. This possibility could be tested in future experimentation by manipulating the extent to which the subject feels that O's change in evaluation is contingent upon the subject's actual behavior.

Possible Implications

One of the implications of the gain-loss notion is that "you always hurt the one you love," i.e., once we have grown certain of the good will (rewarding behavior) of a person (e.g., a mother, a spouse, a close friend), that person may become less potent as a source of reward than a stranger. If we are correct in our assumption that a gain in esteem is a more potent reward than the absolute level of the esteem itself, then it follows that a close friend (by definition) is operating near ceiling level and therefore cannot provide us with a gain. To put it another way, since we have learned to expect love, favors, praise, etc. from a friend, such behavior cannot possibly represent a gain in his esteem for us. On the other hand, the constant friend and rewarder has great potential as a punisher. The closer the friend, the greater the past history of invariant esteem and reward, the more devastating is its withdrawal. Such withdrawal, by definition, constitutes a loss of esteem.

An example may help clarify this point. After 10 years of marriage, if a doting husband compliments his wife on her appearance, it may mean very little to her. She already knows that her husband thinks she's attractive. A sincere compliment from a relative stranger may be much more effective, however, since it constitutes a gain in esteem. On the other hand, if the doting husband (who used to think that his wife was attractive) were to tell his wife that he had decided that she was actually quite ugly, this would cause a great deal of pain since it represents a distinct loss of esteem.

This reasoning is consistent with previous experimental findings. Harvey (1962) found a tendency for subjects to react more positively to a stranger than a friend when they were listed as sources of a relatively positive evaluation of the subject. Moreover, subjects tended to react more negatively to a friend than a stranger when they were listed as sources of negative evaluations of the subject. Similarly, experiments with children indicate that strangers are more effective as agents of social reinforcement than parents, and that strangers are also more effective than more familiar people (Shallenberger and Zigler, 1961; Stevenson and Knights, 1962; Stevenson, Keen, and Knights, 1963). It is reasonable to assume that children are accustomed to receiving approval from parents and familiar people. Therefore, additional approval from them does not represent much of a gain. However, approval from a stranger *is* a gain and, according to the gain-loss notion, should result in a greater improvement in performance. These latter results add credence to our speculations regarding one of the underlying causes of the gain-loss effect. Specifically, children probably experience greater social anxiety in the presence of a stranger than a familiar person. Therefore, social approval from a stranger may be reducing a greater drive than social approval from a friend. As previously noted, this reasoning is identical to that of Walters and his colleagues regarding the effect of prior anxiety on subsequent performance (Walters and Ray, 1960; Walters and Foote, 1962).

SUMMARY

In a laboratory experiment, coeds interacted in two-person groups over a series of brief meetings. After each meeting the subjects were allowed to eavesdrop on a conversation between the experimenter and her partner in which the latter (actually a confederate) evaluated the subject. There were four major experimental conditions: (1) the evaluations were all highly positive; (2) the evaluations were all quite negative; (3) the first few evaluations were negative but gradually became positive; (4) the first few evaluations were positive but gradually became negative.

The major results showed that the subjects liked the confederate best when her evaluations moved from negative to positive and least when her evaluations moved from positive to negative. The results were predicted and discussed in terms of a "gain-loss" notion of interpersonal attractiveness.

29

EXCERPT FROM
INTIMATE RELATIONSHIPS

Sharon S. Brehm (1992)

It has been said that to poets, love is a mystery but to social psychologists, love is a dependent variable. Cynicism aside, consider these questions. Who do you like and why? Who do you love and why? Why is love sometimes enough and sometimes not? Can love last forever? Does the initial passion have to subside? These are questions that have concerned humans far beyond the relatively short history of social psychology. Songs, books, movies, even advice columns center on these affairs of the heart.

Many of our folk sayings display conflicting assumptions about attraction and love. Does absence make the heart grow fonder? Or is it out of sight, out of mind? Do birds of a feather flock together? Or do opposites attract? Do love and marriage go together like the proverbial horse and carriage? These are valid questions that require complex answers.

In this selection Brehm discusses two topics: the role of arousal in passionate love, and what happens after a divorce. We all like to study love, especially in our own lives; few of us like to think about when love fails. Projections, however, for first marriages ending in divorce are about 50 percent, and for second marriages are about 60 percent. And already, approximately one-quarter of children under 18 are living with only one parent. Thus, these issues are very real and require a great deal of thought, particularly in terms of the stresses that lead to an epidemic of divorce and the stresses that are the consequence of divorce. The work in addressing these issues is just beginning in psychology, and Brehm helps start us down that research path.

Source: Excerpted from *Intimate Relationships* (2d edition) by S. Brehm, 1992, New York: McGraw-Hill. Copyright © 1992 by McGraw-Hill. Reprinted by permission of the publisher and the author.

COMPANIONATE AND PASSIONATE LOVE

Many social scientists maintain that all love is divided into two parts: companionate and passionate (Hatfield, 1988; Peele, 1988). *Companionate love* is a secure, trusting attachment—similar in many ways to what Rubin called liking. *Passionate love* is a state of high arousal, filled with the ecstasy of being loved by the partner and the agony of being rejected. If you examine the Passionate Love Scale in Table 29-1, you can see that it describes a much more emotionally intense version of love than Rubin's Loving Scale (1970; or see Module 29).

TABLE 29-1 THE PASSIONATE LOVE SCALE (SHORT FORM)

This questionnaire asks you to describe how you feel when you are passionately in love. Some common terms for this feeling are: passionate love, infatuation, love sickness, or obsessive love. Please think of the person whom you love most passionately *right now*. If you are not in love right now, please think of the last person you loved passionately. If you have never been in love, think of the person whom you came closest to caring for in that way. Keep this person in mind as you complete this section of the questionnaire. (The person you choose should be of the opposite sex if you are heterosexual or of the same sex if you are homosexual.) Try to tell us how you felt at the time when your feelings were the most intense.

Answer each item in terms of this scale:

1	2	3	4	5	6	7	8	9
Not at all true				Moderately true				Definitely true

1. I would feel deep despair if _____ left me.
2. Sometimes I feel I can't control my thoughts; they are obsessively on _____.
3. I feel happy when I am doing something to make _____ happy.
4. I would rather be with _____ than anyone else.
5. I'd get jealous if I thought _____ were falling in love with someone else.
6. I yearn to know all about _____ .
7. I want _____ —physically, emotionally, mentally.
8. I have an endless appetite for affection from _____ .
9. For me, _____ is the perfect romantic partner.
10. I sense my body responding when _____ touches me.
11. _____ always seems to be on my mind.
12. I want _____ to know me—my thoughts, my fears, and my hopes.
13. I eagerly look for signs indicating _____ 's desire for me.
14. I possess a powerful attraction for _____.
15. I get extremely depressed when things don't go right in my relationship with _____ .

Higher scores on the PLS indicate greater passionate love.

Source: Hatfield & Rapson, 1987.

Arousal.   Because of its intensity, passionate love is the stuff of great drama. What would novelists, playwrights, poets, and scriptwriters do without it? Actually, were we not so accustomed to it—in fictional accounts and, perhaps, in our own lives—we would regard passionate love as a distinctly odd aspect of human behavior. Passionate love isn't always a state of pure pleasure. In fact, it is often shot through with anxiety and obsession (Hindy, Schwarz, & Brodsky, 1989). Yet the agony just seems to increase the ecstasy. How could this be?

According to Elaine Hatfield* and Ellen Berscheid, the answer lies in arousal (Berscheid & Walster, 1974a; Walster, 1971). Drawing on Schachter's (1964) two-factor theory of emotion, Hatfield and Berscheid characterize passionate love as consisting of (1) physiological arousal and (2) the belief that this arousal is caused by a reaction to the beloved. Sometimes, the connection between arousal and love is obvious. It isn't particularly surprising, for example, that sexually aroused men report more love for their romantic partners than do those who are not aroused (Dermer & Pyszczynski, 1978; Stephan, Berscheid, & Walster, 1971). But the two-factor theory of passionate love allows for an unexpected twist. Arousal can be attributed to the wrong source—*misattributed*—and, thereby, create all kinds of interesting complications.

According to Hatfield and Berscheid, passionate love is produced, or at least intensified, when feelings of arousal in the beloved's presence are explained solely by that presence. The actual, also arousing, effects of other aspects of the situation are ignored. This process has been called *excitation transfer* (Zillmann, 1978, 1984). Arousal caused by one stimulus is transferred and added to that elicited by a second stimulus. The combined arousal is then perceived as caused by only the second stimulus.

Suppose, for example, that Dan is afraid of flying, but his fear is not particularly extreme and he doesn't like to admit it to himself. This fear, however, does cause him to be physiologically aroused. Suppose further that Dan takes a flight and finds himself sitting next to Judy on the plane. With heart racing, palms sweating, and breathing labored, Dan chats with Judy as the plane takes off. Suddenly, Dan discovers that he finds Judy terribly attractive, and he begins to try to figure out ways that he can continue to see her after the flight is over. What accounts for Dan's sudden surge of interest in Judy? Is she really that appealing to him, or has he taken the physiological arousal of fear and mislabeled it as attraction?

This possibility that fear might be mislabeled as sexual attraction was first examined by Dutton and Aron (1974), who conducted their experiment near two bridges located in a scenic tourist spot. One bridge was suspended over a deep gorge; the bridge swayed from side to side, and walking across it would make most people quite nervous. The other bridge was more stable and not far off the ground; most people would be perfectly comfortable walking across it.

As unaccompanied males (limited to those between 19 and 35 years of age) walked across these bridges, they were met by a research assistant, who was either male or female. The research assistant would ask each person to participate in a brief experiment

*Earlier work by Professor Hatfield appears under the name E. Walster.

in which he answered a few questions and wrote a brief story in response to a picture he was shown. When this was completed, the research assistant noted that if the subject wanted more information about the study, he could give the assistant a call at home.

The picture that the male subjects in this experiment told a story about was from the Thematic Apperception Test (TAT), and it is possible to score these stories in terms of sexual imagery. Dutton and Aron found that those male subjects who were met on the supension bridge by a female research assistant had the highest sexual imagery scores for their stories. In addition, these subjects were more likely to call the assistant at her home. Fear had fueled attraction.

Or had it? Some researchers have argued that it is not necessary to rely on complicated processes like misattribution and excitation transfer to explain why romance blossoms in the midst of fear (Kenrick & Cialdini, 1977; Riordan & Tedeschi, 1983). Instead, they say, fondness for those who are with us in a time of distress comes from the comfort we take from their presence (Epley, 1974; Schachter, 1959). Because having them with us helps to reduce our distress, their presence is rewarding. Thus, the link between fear and love is just another example of how social rewards create attraction and strengthen attachment.

Subsequent research, however, indicated that a reward-based explanation could not provide an adequate explanation for the relationship between arousal and romance. In one study, male subjects ran in place for either 2 minutes or 15 seconds (White, Fishbein, & Rutstein, 1981). Subjects then saw a videotape of a young woman whom they expected to meet later in the experiment. Through the wonders of makeup, this young woman appeared either very attractive or very unattractive. When subjects gave their impressions of the woman they had seen on the videotape, it was found that both arousal and the characteristics of the female were important. For the attractive woman, high arousal led to greater attraction; for the unattractive woman, high arousal led to *less* attraction.

These results were replicated in a somewhat more elaborate second experiment. Here, White et al. had male subjects listen to one of three kinds of tape-recorded material:

- *Negatively arousing.* A description of the brutal mutilation and killing of a missionary while his family watched.
- *Positively arousing.* Selections from Steve Martin's album, *A Wild and Crazy Guy.*
- *Neutral.* A boring description of the circulatory system of a frog.

As in the first experiment, subjects then viewed a videotape of an attractive or unattractive female whom they expected to meet later, and indicated their impressions of how attractive she was. Once again, attraction was found to be affected by both arousal and the attractiveness of the woman. Subjects who were aroused (by positive, funny material as well as by the negative, horrible material) found the attractive woman more attractive than did subjects in the neutral condition. In contrast, aroused subjects perceived the unattractive woman to be less attractive than did the nonaroused subjects.

Taken together, these two studies demonstrate that the association between arousal and romance is not a simple matter of rewards. The men who participated in the first study did not experience any physical or emotional discomfort; there was no distress to be reduced by the woman's videotaped presence. In the second study, it did not matter whether arousal was created by a positive or a negative stimulus. In both studies, the same principle applied: Arousal intensified subjects' initial emotional reaction, positive *or* negative, to a member of the opposite sex.

The implications of this research are startling. Is love totally at the mercy of airplanes, bridges, exercise, and Steve Martin comedy routines? Fortunately, for our peace of mind, the answer is no. Misattribution and excitation transfer have their limits (Marshall & Zimbardo, 1979; Maslach, 1979; Reisenzein, 1983). One limit is imposed by the passing of time. A long delay between initial arousal and subsequent emotional response wipes out the possibility of excitation transfer. Initial arousal dissipates, and no leftover excitation is available for misattribution (Cantor, Zillmann, & Bryant, 1975; Zillmann, Johnson, & Day, 1974).

Another limit may be set by attributional clarity (White & Kight, 1984). If excitation transfer depends on *mis*attribution, knowing the real reason for our initial arousal will short-circuit the process. When Dan thinks, "Oh boy, here I go again, afraid of flying," he won't be able to mistake his fear as sexual attraction to Judy. Some researchers, however, question whether misattribution is necessary for one source of arousal to fuel another kind of emotional response (Allen, Kenrick, Linder, & McCall, 1989). Instead, they propose that what may be involved is a simple process of response facilitation. Whenever arousal is present, no matter what its source or the degree of our awareness of that source, our most likely response to the situation will be energized. According to this perspective, it does not matter whether Dan knows that his initial arousal was elicited by his fear of flying. In Judy's presence, his dominant response is sexual attraction, and this response will be automatically strengthened by any arousal added to it. In essence, then, the debate between the misattribution and response-facilitation explanations of arousal carryover effects centers on the issue of cognitive control. Further research is necessary before that debate can be fully resolved. In the meantime, think about its possible implications for your own life. When you walk out of a gym and encounter a most attractive person, will you dismiss your state of arousal as simply the result of a good workout and walk on by? Or might you fall in love anyway?

WHAT HAPPENS AFTER A DIVORCE?

To those involved, the end of a marriage can be a time of complete chaos and confusion. So much is happening that everything begins to blur together, and life becomes separated into two large chapters: before and after. In fact, however, there are some specific areas of change that are particularly important and can be particularly difficult to handle. Here, we examine three such areas: economic changes, parental relation-ships, and remarriage.

Economic Changes.   It may seem crass to say so, but some of the greatest prob-lems caused by divorce are a matter of money. Imagine, for instance, the following scenario:

> Bill and Ann were married for nine years. He is 36; she is 34. They have one child, Susan, who is 7 years old. Bill is a certified pubic accountant employed by a law firm; while Ann was married, she taught math at a church-run elementary school. Their joint financial assets consisted of two cars, a house and furnishings, and some savings. Under the terms of their separation agreement, these assets were divided equally. Each kept one car; they divided the savings equally; and they sold the house so that they could split the equity they had invested in it. Bill moved to a one-bedroom apartment close to where he works. Ann received custody of Susan, and they moved to a two-bedroom apartment some distance from where they used to live. Even though Bill contributes child support, Ann soon discovered that she could not support herself and Susan on her current salary. She took a job in the public schools for more money. Susan enrolled in a new school, closer to where she is now living. In just a few short months, all three changed their residence, Ann changed her job, and Susan changed schools.

Many people who have gone through a divorce, as adults or as children, will recognize parts of this scenario. It is not at all unusual, and the economics of divorce account for most of it. In her 1985 book *The Divorce Revolution,* Leonore Weitzman spells out the full financial impact of divorce.

First, why did Bill and Ann sell their house? If, for example, Ann and Susan had continued to live there, then they would have avoided the stress of moving to and liv-ing in a new place; Susan would have remained in the same school and kept her same friends. Yet, as Weitzman points out, selling the house is increasingly required in order to allow equal division of property held jointly by the spouses. And an equal division of "community property" is an increasingly common feature of "no-fault" divorce. Beginning in the 1970s, many states adopted no-fault divorce laws as a re-placement for, or alternative to, the former legal requirement to determine guilt in a di-vorce proceeding. A no-fault approach to divorce has much to recommend it—being less expensive, more honest, and less demeaning than the old divorce trials. What was not anticipated, however, was how much no-fault would influence the economic as-pects of divorce. Since, by definition, there is no guilty party in a no-fault divorce, it seems reasonable simply to split the family's assets. But you cannot split a house un-less you sell it and divide the proceeds. Thus, one of the unexpected consequences of no-fault divorce was the increasing tendency for court-approved divorce settlements to include the sale of the family's home, which, in turn, precipitates other major changes in family members' lives.

Another unexpected consequence was what Weitzman calls "the systematic impov-erishment of divorced women and children" (p. xiv). She estimates that, on average, divorced women suffer a 73 percent decline in their standard of living, while divorced men experience a 42 percent increase in their standard of living. Not surprisingly, the financial hardship experienced by many divorced women is associated with increased psychological distress for them and their children (Braver, Gonzalez, Wolchik, & Sandler, 1989; Emery, 1988). There are a number of reasons for the dramatic discrepancy between men's and women's postdivorce economic status. First, think back to our hypothetical couple, Ann and Bill. Like most married couples, Bill's income was greater than Ann's. As long as Ann was married, she didn't need to maximize her earnings because the two incomes combined were sufficient. On her own, however, Ann discovered that her salary would not cover her expenses, which were greater than Bill's because she had custody of Susan. In short, if women make less than men do, then women will have more financial problems after divorce than men do. Such problems are intensified when, as is usually the case, the children of divorce live with their mother instead of their father.

But this is nothing new. What is new is that the traditional way of compensating women for that income differential—alimony—has virtually disappeared. According to Weitzman, only about 17 percent of divorcing women are awarded alimony, and the average duration of the award is two years. It is very unlikely that a young, well-educated, employed woman like Ann would either ask for or receive alimony. And then there is child support. When Weitzman wrote her book on the financial consequences of no-fault divorce, child support was a national scandal. Studies indicated that a majority (around 53 percent) of women awarded court-ordered child support did not receive full payment, and a sizable minority (25 to 33 percent) did not receive a penny. In 1988, Congress attempted to rectify this situation by passing a law with much stricter provisions for the assessing and collecting of child-support payments. Employers will now be notified of court-awarded support payments and will be required to deduct the appropriate amount from the employee's paycheck. It is expected that these and other revisions in the Child-Support Enforcement Program will greatly improve the compliance rate with court orders (Rich, 1989). Since, however, court-ordered child-support payments are usually too low to cover the actual cost of raising a child (Peterson & Nord, 1990), then the financial strains faced by divorced mothers and the children who live with them will have been eased but not eliminated.

Even if the current levels of child-support payments stipulated in divorce agreements are not sufficient to meet the financial problems faced by many divorced mothers, such payments may have some important, and potentially beneficial, side effects. Increased child-support payments by noncustodial fathers are associated with more frequent visits with their children, raising the possibility that mandatory increases in one kind of involvement might result in increases in the other kind:

> Noncustodial parents who pay support may feel more uncomfortable about playing only part of the parent role than they do about avoiding parental responsibilities altogether, so if they pay child support they are more likely to visit as well (Seltzer, Schaeffer, & Charng, 1989, p. 1027).

Parental Relationships.   Continued contact with a noncustodial parent may, however, run into an interpersonal roadblock—continued conflict between the ex-spouses (Hetherington, Stanley-Hagan, & Anderson, 1989). If every visit involves a fight, why visit? In one of the saddest ironies of divorce, the end of the marriage does not necessarily mean the end of the acrimony. One study, for example, found that about half of the divorced couples with children who participated in the research had an angry, hostile relationship; only a small proportion could be regarded as friends (Ahrons & Wallisch, 1987). Upon finding a similar pattern, another researcher concluded that "post-marital harmony was a minority phenomenon" (Ambert, 1988, p. 327).

The psychological costs of a bad relationship between ex-spouses can be quite high for everyone involved. Conflict with the ex-spouse is associated with poor adjustment for both divorced men and women (Tschann, Johnston, & Wallerstein, 1989). Children, especially boys, exposed to continued conflict between their biological parents have more difficulty adjusting to divorce (Demo & Acock, 1988; Emery, 1988; Tschann, Johnston, Kline, & Wallerstein, 1989). Within nondivorced families, parental conflict also has negative effects on children (Grych & Fincham, 1990). Indeed, children have a better adjustment in a calm, harmonious single-parent family or stepfamily than they do in biological families of origin where conflict is high (Hetherington, Cox, & Cox, 1982; Lamb, 1977; Long & Forehand, 1987; Stolberg, Camplair, Currier, & Wells, 1987). The level of parental conflict has greater effects on children than does the structure of the family. Thus, the inability of many divorced couples to resolve their differences, even after they have dissolved their marriage, can make it much harder for them and their children to construct a rewarding new life.

Remarriage.   By far, the most popular way to construct that new life is to remarry: Half of all recent marriages involve at least one previously married individual (Bumpass, Sweet, & Castro Martin, 1990). Overall, some 80 percent of divorced individuals remarry (Norton, 1987). Men, however, are more likely to remarry than women. The rate of remarriage among men is around 83 percent, while women's remarriage rate may be as low as 70 percent (Norton & Moorman, 1987). In addition, remarriage appears to work better for men than for women: Remarried men report greater marital satisfaction than do remarried women (Vemer, Coleman, Ganong, & Cooper, 1989). Although most research has found that second marriages fail sooner and at a faster rate than do first ones (Cherlin, 1983; Furstenberg & Spanier, 1984), these differences may reflect the greater likelihood of remarriage for individuals who have an especially high rate of divorce (those who first married at a very young age and who have low levels of education). When age at first marriage and level of education are taken into account, remarriages appear to have no greater risk of disruption than first marriages (Castro Martin & Bumpass, 1989).

Some types of remarriage, however, may be easier to manage than others. Married couples involved in "simple" stepfamilies, in which only one of the adults brings children into the marriage, report greater marital satisfaction than do those in "complex" stepfamilies, in which both adults bring children into the marriage (Vemer et al., 1989). But all stepfamilies face some daunting problems. As noted in a *Newsweek* article entitled "Step by Step," just diagramming the family tree can be an advanced test in genealogy:

> The original plot goes like this: first comes love. Then comes marriage. Then comes Mary with a baby carriage. But now there's a sequel: John and Mary break up. John moves in with Sally and her two boys. Mary takes the baby Paul. A year later Mary

meets Jack, who is divorced with three children. They get married. Paul, barely 2 years old, now has a mother, a father, a stepmother, a stepfather, and five stepbrothers and stepsisters—as well as four sets of grandparents (biological and step) and countless aunts and uncles. And guess what? Mary's pregnant again. (Kantrowitz & Wingert, 1990, p. 24)

Besides the difficulty of simply keeping track of the characters, both adults and children often encounter problems adjusting to their new roles (Bray, 1988). Though family relationships tend to improve over time, stepparents usually remain less active as parents than biological parents who have custody (Hetherington et al., 1989). Stepmothers, however, may be more active than stepfathers (Santrock & Sitterle, 1987). And, whether as a cause or an effect of this more active involvement, stepmother families appear to encounter more difficulties than do stepfather families (Hetherington et al., 1989). But stepfathers do not necessarily have an easy time of it. Although stepsons usually adjust to the presence of a stepfather and benefit from their relationship with him, it is considerably harder for stepfathers to gain acceptance by a stepdaughter (Hetherington, 1987). Children in complex remarriages, where, as noted before, there are children in the home from the previous marriages of *both* spouses, have particularly high levels of behavior problems (Hetherington et al., 1989).

Remarriage, of course, is not limited to custodial parents, but the remarriage of noncustodial parents seems to have only slight effects on their involvement with their children (Furstenberg, 1988). By and large, those who had little involvement remain disengaged, while those who stayed in close contact continue to do so. And how does a close relationship with a noncustodial parent affect the child's relationship with his or her stepparent? Here, too, it appears that stepmothers may face more problems than stepfathers. Active involvement by a noncustodial father seems unlikely to damage, and may benefit, the relationship between a stepfather and a child (Maccoby, Depner, & Mnookin, 1990). In contrast, frequent visits by a noncustodial mother are associated with greater difficulties in the relationship between a stepmother and, especially, a stepdaughter (Brand, Clingempeel, & Bowen-Woodward, 1988). The child's own personal adjustment, however, may benefit from continued contact with the noncustodial mother (Zill, 1988).

Overall, then, current research describes a number of problems that stepfamilies may have to deal with. But such difficulties should not be exaggerated. According to Furstenberg (1987), stepfamily life is a "mixed picture." Relationships between stepchildren and stepparents may not be as close as those between biological parents and their children, but "the vast majority of stepfamilies appear to function quite well" (p. 56). On the whole, children in stepfamilies differ remarkably little from children who reside with both their biological parents (Ganong & Coleman, 1987). Moreover, the divorce rate for remarriages with children is no higher than that for remarriages without them (Castro Martin & Bumpass, 1989). Having children involved can make a remarriage both more complicated *and* more rewarding.

30

THE FEW, THE BRAVE, THE NOBLE

Eva Fogelman and Valerie Lewis Wiener (1985)

When do people help? Myers answers this question by focusing on the impressive body of work on helping behavior (altruism) generated by Latané and Darley in the 1960s and 1970s. Stimulated by the tragic murder of Kitty Genovese in 1964 (during which 38 people heard her screams for help but failed to come to her aid or even call the police), this line of research is a classic example of social psychological attempts to make sense of timely social phenomena. Other researchers such as Krebs and Miller (1985) developed conceptual schemes that describe the multiple influences on altruism.

Examining historical events is often a useful way of gaining insight into social behaviors. Perhaps no other instance in the recent history of the world invokes the notion of "help needed" more than the Holocaust carried out by Nazi Germany during World War II. Millions of Jews, gypsies, homosexuals, in fact, anyone the Third Reich thought should be exterminated, paid the ultimate price for their differentness before the firing squads and in the gas chambers. In 1993, The National Holocaust Memorial Museum opened in Washington, D.C. Its impact is not lost more than a half of a century after the closing of the concentration camps of Auschwitz, Maidanek, Plaszow, and Treblinka in Nazi-occupied Poland, Bergen-Belsen, Buchenwald, and Dachau in Germany. The museum is a troubling place but should be on any visitor's list of places to go in Washington, D.C.

As horrible as the Holocaust was, there were those under Hitler's rule who opposed his fanatic plans. Many Germans did not support the Nazi Party. Some actually put their own lives in jeopardy and became what have been called "rescuers." The reading by Fogelman and Wiener describes some of these

Source: Reprinted from *Psychology Today,* August, 1985, 60–65. Reprinted with permission from *Psychology Today* magazine. Copyright © 1985 (Sussex Publishers, Inc.).

remarkable people, rescuers who because of deeply held moral values; and/or emotional attachment to threatened individuals, risked death for subverting the Third Reich's plans. A recent Steven Spielberg movie, *Schindler's List,* tells the story of one such rescuer—a German businessman named Oskar Schindler—and in the telling provides us with hope for the future of humanity and hope for the effectiveness of one individual to make a difference in this world by sticking to higher moral principles.

In 1939, when Germany invaded Poland and segregated Warsaw Jews behind barbed wire, Stefania Podgórska was 16 years old. As reports of hunger, disease and death filtered out of the ghetto, Stefania, a Catholic girl also known as Fusia, became deeply concerned about her Jewish friends. Before long, she was making secret visits to the ghetto with gifts of food, clothing and medicine, putting her life in jeopardy each time she approached the people behind the walls.

One of Fusia's Jewish friends was Max, a medical student and the son of her former landlord and employer. When the Nazis began to ship the Jews out of the ghetto to concentration camps in 1942, Max made a daring escape in the middle of the night. After knocking on the doors of many friends and being refused shelter, he went to Fusia, who had been his mother's seamstress. She agreed to hide him in her apartment.

Such behavior was a rarity in the years of persecution throughout Poland and other European nations under Nazi control. Rescuers like Fusia were few, numbering only several thousand. Most citizens complied with the Nazi edicts and did not assist the Jews; to be caught meant arrest and possibly death. What made people like Fusia risk their lives for the sake of Jews? What qualities and characteristics did they have that others lacked?

In 1981 we began a study of non-Jewish rescuers and the Jewish survivors who probably would have died without their help. Two years later the project, directed by Stephen P. Cohen, a social psychologist at City University in New York, was combined with the work of Samuel Oliner of Humboldt State University in Arcata, California. Researchers for this international study, the Altruistic Personality Project, have interviewed 220 rescuers so far and plan to interview 300 more in the United States, Canada, Europe and Israel, if funds allow.

Our findings are based on interviews with 25 rescuers and 50 survivors, as well as on historical documents about other rescuers and the people they saved. In four cases, we were able to interview both a rescuer and the person he or she saved.

It was not easy to find these people. Many had died, some of them 40 or more years ago in the very act of rescuing. A number of rescuers did not want to be interviewed. Some were embarrassed to be recognized for doing something they considered unremarkable, some did not want to be reminded of their severe suffering. Others, particularly those still living in countries such as Poland and Germany, feared ostracism if their deeds became known.

All of the people we spoke with now live in the United States. Originally, they came from Belgium, Germany, Hungary, Poland and the Ukraine. Some had been forced to leave school as early as the fifth grade; others had completed several years of graduate school. They included farmers, factory workers, servants, clergymen and society matrons. Although they had diverse personalities, they shared one characteristic: They did not view themselves as heroes or heroines. Their behavior under the Nazis, they told us, was only natural. Up to the time of their heroic deeds, they lived ordinary lives and, on the surface, at least, were very similar to everyone else.

The motivations of rescuers cannot be reduced to a formula or explained by any single personality characteristic or type. However, there were some common trends.

We found that the rescuers fell into two groups, those motivated chiefly by deeply-held moral values and those whose motivation was mainly emotional and based on personal attachments or identification with the victim.

Rescuers of the first type felt ethically compelled to rescue Jews, while those of the second type usually personalized the situation between themselves and those they helped. They were less concerned about fulfilling abstract moral obligations than about trying to protect people from harm. This distinction between moral and emotional motivation is consistent with the findings of Harvard University social psychologist Carol Gilligan, who has noted that there are two styles of moral reasoning—one based on justice, the other on responsibility and care.

We could recognize value-oriented motivation immediately when we asked rescuers why they did it. Almost instinctively they would reply, "What do you mean?" as if there were no need to explain. Questioned further, such rescuers usually said matter-of-factly, "It was the right thing to do," or "I was only doing what a human being should for another human being."

This moral motivation was often coupled with intense anti-Nazi attitudes. Dorothy Ukalo, a Polish survivor, remembered asking her Christian rescuer, "Why are you so good to us?" The rescuer—known among Jews as the "Angel of Lvov" for her work heading an underground network that protected Jews—replied, "I resent strongly what the Germans are doing, and I curse them."

Some morally motivated rescuers had strong religious beliefs that influenced all areas of their lives. They educated their children religiously, were active church members and acted altruistically out of a religious duty to be "thy brother's keeper." In some cases, these rescuers were part of organized religious networks. Living in a community with a charismatic religious leader provided a spur to altruism. A network of Protestant church members rescued a German physician, Herman Pineas, after theologian Karl Barth exhorted them to help as many Jews as possible. These rescuers were also influenced by Dietrich Bonhoeffer, the Protestant theologian who was executed for plotting to assassinate Hitler.

Morally motivated rescuers, we found, helped people whether they liked or disliked them. Indeed, they often helped people they did not know at all. By contrast, the behavior of emotionally motivated rescuers often sprang from strong personal attachments. The intensity of such attachments was conveyed in the words of Gitta Bauer, a German journalist who sheltered Ilse Moslé, the 17-year-old daughter of Jewish friends: "It took me nine months to deliver her to freedom, so I consider Ilse my baby."

Inge Auerbacher, a survivor who has written poems and songs about her experiences as a child in Germany, described a similarly close relationship with the woman who had saved her: "My grandmother's maid for twenty-five years was like a member of the family. When we had to hide from the Nazis in the Jewish cemetery, she would come at night and put food out for us behind the tombstones."

A personal relationship was not always necessary to motivate a rescuer emotionally. Some helped people they barely knew but with whom they identified. Their empathy often stemmed from a belief that they, too, were vulnerable to persecution for their religious or political beliefs. In other instances a child, spouse or sibling of the rescuer had been persecuted.

This keen sense of identification was expressed by Edward Melnyczuk, a Ukrainian immigrant, whose wife's family hid Jews. "It is easy to understand what the Jews felt," he told us, "because the Jews and the Ukrainians were in similar positions everywhere." His wife's family, the Zahajkiewiczes, lived directly across the street from the Nazi police station in the western Ukrainian town of Peremyshl in Poland. They knew that if they were discovered harboring Jews in their pantry, they would all be executed.

The family was inspired by its patriarch, a theologian and teacher, who was called by Jewish newspapers a "Jewish Father." As a high school teacher in the Ukraine, he had shown a special affinity for poor students and often consoled Jews who were the butt of anti-Semitic incidents. His granddaughter, Halina Zahajkiewicz Melnyczuk, told us, "When Jewish kids were beaten up in school, he always came to their defense."

The Zahajkiewiczes had also lost a 17-year-old son, who disappeared when the Soviets took over their section of the Ukraine. Their success in sheltering Jews might have helped them master their feelings of helplessness over the loss.

Perhaps a similar psychological process was partially responsible for the rescue activities of the Angel of Lvov. During the war her son served as a pilot, and she worried about his safety. As she spoke of her own efforts to help Jews, she said, "Maybe someone will help him too."

With time, boundaries between moral and emotional motivation often blurred, and the relationship between rescuer and rescued became the sustaining element, whatever the original motivation. Years of long days and nights living under constant threat of exposure required something beyond moral conviction. This "something more" is best described in terms such as love, compassion and caring. In three of the cases we studied, rescuers eventually married the people they had helped. One of them was Fusia, who married the Jewish medical student she had hidden. They had known each other before the war, but their relationship had not been romantic.

Although the rescuers' motivations were different, they often shared certain characteristics. A family tradition of concern for others showed up in many rescuers, such as the Zahajkiewiczes and Fusia. When she was growing up, her Catholic parents were friendly with people of many religious backgrounds. They taught her, she said, "not to make differences between people. We all have one God. It doesn't matter how much money you have, or anything."

Many other rescuers said their behavior was strongly influenced by values exhibited by their parents. These parents not only talked about the importance of helping others and accepting human differences, but did things that exemplified these beliefs and encouraged their children to follow their example.

THE VILLAGE OF REFUGE

The first Jewish refugee from the Nazis to come to the southern French village of Le Chambon-sur-Lignon arrived in 1940. It was the winter following the fall of France, and the frightened woman knocked on the door of the Protestant pastor's house, looking for shelter. "She was in danger, and she heard that in Le Chambon somebody could help her," remembers Magda Trocmé, the pastor's wife. "Could she come into my house? I said, 'Naturally, come in.'"

During the next four years, the villagers of Le Chambon conducted one of the most remarkable rescue operations of World War II. Despite occupying Nazi SS forces and the collaborating French Vichy government, the village became a refuge for thousands of Jews, mostly children, who were fleeing arrest and death. The Chambonnais hid refugees in their homes, schools and churches and provided forged identity papers and escape routes.

"Their actions did not serve the self-interest of the little commune of Le Chambon-sur-Lignon," writes Philip Hallie, author of *Lest Innocent Blood Be Shed,* a book on the village. "On the contrary, those actions flew in the face of that self-interest: by resisting a power far greater than their own they put their village in grave danger of a massacre."

The origins of this altruism lie in the history of Le Chambon, a small Protestant village in a Catholic country. Many of the Chambonnais forebears had been persecuted by Catholic rulers from the time the Huguenots brought Prostestantism to France in the 16th century until the French Revolution in the late 18th century. Protestants had no rights; they were legally deprived of liberty, property and sometimes their lives, just as the Jews were under the Nazis. The Chambonnais hid many Protestant refugees in their isolated village during these centuries. The history of help given and received was very much in the minds of the villagers. Asked why she agreed to hide Jews, one woman told Hallie: "(It) was very much like what Protestants have done in France ever since the Reformation. . . . What we did was . . . the traces of what was being done here for centuries."

The man who transformed this sympathy into action was the village's Protestant pastor, André Trocmé, described by one refugee as "the soul of Le Chambon." Trocmé was born into a strict Huguenot family and learned the value of human life early, when his mother was killed in a car crash. He developed a philosophy of nonviolence during World War I, living in a German-occupied town, and also a firm belief that God required him to prevent others from doing harm, as well as to do none himself. A charismatic man, he inspired warmth, plans and activity in those around him. Magda Trocmé later explained that she believed first of all in her husband and everything he did, and second in never closing her door on someone in need. "This I think is my kind of religion," she said. "You see, it is a way of handling myself." The Trocmés mobilized the village in small actions of civil disobedience early in the occupation, which demonstrated that it was possible to resist the Nazis and set the stage for the rescue of the Jews.

"The great paradox of Le Chambon is that, although it was a collective action, people did not know exactly what their neighbors were doing," says Pierre Sauvage, who was born of refugee parents in the village in 1944 and has gathered historical material on it. Idle or incautious words overheard by the wrong person could bring disaster, so Magda Trocmé did not know who supplied the forged identity cards essential to the refugees' safety, although the forger turned out to be a refugee hiding in the village. The struggle of Le Chambon was a "kitchen struggle," a communal act of courage performed by individuals in the privacy of their homes, guided by their consciences.

In the end, the key to this struggle was its simplicity. "We fail to understand what happened in Le Chambon if we think *for them* their actions were complex and difficult," Hallie says. For the people of Le Chambon there was really only one choice to make, one course of action. For them, it was easier to open a door than to keep it closed—*Joshua Fischman.*

During the war, Elizabeth Bornstein ran a blouse-making business from her one-room apartment outside Berlin and hid a Jewish couple there. When we interviewed Bornstein she remembered that her mother was "always helping people," and told us how, as a young child, she would accompany her mother on outings to babysit, collect money for the poor and teach young mothers to cook.

Our findings contradict those of Freud and his followers, who claimed that those who undertake intensely dangerous acts are masochistic, seeking to fullfill neurotic needs or acting out grandiose fantasies. The rescuers we interviewed were not neurotic daredevils, although they all had an uncommon high tolerance for risk that allowed them to transcend the fear and anxiety inherent in life-and-death situations.

The rescuers also shared uncommon perseverance and a belief in their own competence that made them confident of success despite danger and adversity. Fusia said she had never been afraid despite all the risks she endured.

After she agreed to help Max, she and her sister built a false wall and ceiling in the attic of their small apartment with wood from abandoned apartments. Designed to hold seven people, the space eventually served as a hideaway for 13 Jews. For two and a half years, the 13 kept watch out of spy holes, spoke in whispers and survived on bread and onions. When one of the Jewish women became ill with typhus, Fusia secretly obtained lifesaving medicine for her.

The most traumatic event came in 1944 when the Germans demanded that she house two nurses in the apartment. The nurses and their boyfriends, who were German soldiers, lived in the apartment with Fusia until the Soviets liberated the town seven months later. They never learned of the 13 people in the attic.

Often, the rescuers had particular skills, contacts or opportunities. Those with knowledge of printing could provide false identification papers and ration cards. Others with access to extra food, lodging or jobs used these advantages to help out. In an unusual case, a doctor performed operations on Jewish men to remove signs of circumcision.

Some rescuers who possessed special talents or opportunities managed to save hundreds or thousands of Jews. Barna Kiss, a Hungarian who headed a battalion of Jewish soldiers, shepherded them through Nazi-imposed death marches by disobeying orders to kill them. Raoul Wallenberg, the Swedish diplomat and banker, used his negotiating and financial skills to obtain false identification papers and to find refuge for thousands of Jews in Hungary. Oskar Schindler, a German businessman with useful connections in both business and the criminal underworld, bought an enamelware factory in Poland and employed thousands of Jews, supplying them with the best food, clothing and shelter he could obtain on the black market.

The heroic acts of these rescuers have been greatly publicized, but there are many others who remain almost unknown. During the bleakest moments of World War II, average citizens in occupied nations never knew when they might be confronted on their doorstep by Nazi storm troopers or by fleeing refugees. Those who took the refugees in immediately endangered their own lives and the lives of their families. By the time we finished our interviews, we were filled with a great sense of admiration for these lesser-known heroes. Their willingness to risk their lives, to endure, to adhere to a higher principle in the midst of chaos and destruction inspired in us a renewed faith in humanity.

REFERENCES

(Number in brackets [ ] following reference refers to Reading number [1 through 30] or Reading introduction number [RI-1 through RI-30].)

Adorno, T. W., Frenkel-Brunswik, E., Levinson, D., & Sanford, R. N. (1950). *The authoritarian personality.* New York: Harper. [RI-14]

Ahrons, C. R., & Wallisch, L. S. (1987). The relationship between former spouses. In D. Perlman & S. Duck (Eds.), *Intimate relationships: Development, dynamics, and deterioration* (pp. 269–296). Newbury Park, CA: Sage. [29]

Ajzen, I., & Fishbein, M. (1977). Attitude behavior relations: A theoretical analysis and review of empirical research. *Psychological Bulletin, 84,* 888–918. [RI-9]

Allen, J. B., Kenrick, D. T., Linder, D. E., & McCall, M. A. (1989). Arousal and attribution: A response facilitation alternative to misattribution and negative-reinforcement models. *Journal of Personality and Social Psychology, 57,* 261–270. [29]

Allgeier, A. R. (1983). Informational barriers to contraception. In D. Byrne & W. A. Fisher (Eds.), *Adolescents, sex, and contraception* (pp.143–169). Hillsdale, NJ: Erlbaum. [7]

Allport, G. (1954). *The nature of prejudice.* New York: Addison-Wesley. [23]

Ambert, A. (1988). Relationship between ex-spouses: Individual and dyadic perspectives. *Journal of Social and Personal Relationships, 5,* 327–346. [29]

American Psychological Association. (1975). Minutes of the Council of Representatives. *American Psychologist, 30,* 633. [23]

American Psychological Association. (1983). *Publication manual of the American Psychological Association* (3rd ed.). Washington, DC: Author.

Amir, M. (1967). Forcible rape. *Federal Probation, 31.* [25]

Amir, M. (1971). *Patterns in forcible rape.* Chicago: University of Chicago Press. [6] [25]

Amir, Y. (1976). The role of intergroup contact in change of prejudice and intergroup relations. In P. Katz (ed.), *Toward the elimination of racism* (pp. 245–308). New York: Pergamon. [23]

Antonovsky, A. (1987). *Unravling the mystery of health: How people manage stress and stay well.* San Francisco: Jossey-Bass. [11]

Aron, A., Dutton, D. G., Aron, E. N., & Iverson, A. (1989). Experiences of falling in love. *Journal of Social and Personal Relationships, 6,* 243–257. [29]

Aronson, E., & Mills, J. (1959). The effect of severity of initiation on liking for a group. *Journal of Abnormal and Social Psychology, 59,* 177–181. [28]

Bales, R. F. (1958). Task notes and social roles in problem-solving groups. In E. E. Maccoby, T. M. Newcomb, & E. L. Hartley (Eds.). *Readings in social psychology* (3rd ed., pp. 437–447). New York: Holt, Rinehart & Winston. [20]

Bandura, A. (1971). *Social learning theory.* Morristown, NJ: General Learning Press. [8]

Barrett, K. (1982, September). Date rape: A campus epidemic? *Ms.,* p. 130. [25]

Barry, K. (1979). *Female sexual slavery.* New York: Avon. [25]

Bayer, R. (1987). *Homosexuality and American psychiatry: The politics of diagnosis* (2nd Ed.). Princeton, NJ: Princeton University Press. [23]

Beach, S. R. H., & Tesser, A. (1988). Love in marriage: A cognitive account. In R. J. Sternberg & M. L. Barnes (Eds.), *The psychology of love* (pp. 330–355). New Haven, CT: Yale University Press. [29]

Bem, D. J. (1972). Self-perception theory. In L. Berkowitz (Ed.), *Advances in experimental social psychology* (Vol. 6, pp. 1–62). New York: Academic Press. [7]

Bem, S. L., & Bem, D. J. (1970). Case study of a nonconscious ideology: Training the woman to know her place. In D. J. Bem (Ed.), *Beliefs, attitudes, and human affairs.* Belmont CA. Wadsworth. [RI-1] [RI-6]

Beneke, T. (1982a). *Men on rape.* New York: St. Martin's Press. [25]

Beneke, T. (1982b, July). Male rage: Four men talk about rape. *Mother Jones,* p. 13. [25]

Bentler, P. M., & Huba, G. J. (1979). Simple minitheories of love. *Journal of Personality and Social Psychology, 37,* 124–130. [29]

Berezin, M. (1972). Psychodynamic considerations of aging and the aged: An overview. *American Journal of Psychiatry, 128,* 1483–1491. [8]

Berkowitz, L. (1974). Some determinants of impulsive aggression: Role of mediated associations with reinforcements for aggression. *Psychological Review, 81,* 165–176. [19]

Bernard, J. (1969). *The sex game.* London: L. Frewin. [6]

Berscheid, E. & Walster, E. (1974). A little bit about love. In T. Huston (Ed.), *Foundations of interpersonal attraction* (pp. 355–381). New York: Academic Press. [29]

Biondo, J., & MacDonald, A. P. (1971). Internal-external locus of control and response to influence attempts. *Journal of Personality, 39,* 407–419. [21]

Blue, G. F. (1978). The ageing as portrayed in realistic fiction for children, 1945–1975. *Gerontologist, 18,* 187–192. [8]

Boswell, J. (1980). *Christianity, social tolerance, and homosexuality: Gay people in Western Europe from the beginning of the Christian era to the fourteenth century.* Chicago: University of Chicago Press. [23]

Bowers v. Hardwick, 478 U.S. 186 (1986). [23]

Brand, E., Clingempeel, W. G., & Bowen-Woodward, K. (1988). Family relationships and children's psychological adjustment in stepmother and stepfather families. In E. M. Hetherington & J. D. Arasteh (Eds.), *Impact of divorce, singleparenting, and stepparenting on children* (pp. 299–324) Hillsdale, NJ: Erlbaum. [29]

Braver, S. L., Gonzalez, N., Wolchik, S., & Sandler, I. N. (1989). Economic hardship and psychological distress in custodial mothers. *Journal of Divorce, 12,* 19–34. [29]

Bray, J. H. (1988). Children's development during early remarriage. In E. M. Hetherington & J. D. Arasteh (Eds.), *Impact of divorce, singleparenting, and stepparenting on children* (pp. 279–298) Hillsdale, NJ: Erlbaum. [29]

Brehm, J. W. (Ed.) (1966). *A theory of psychological reactance.* New York: Academic Press. [21]

Brehm, J. W., & Sensenig, J. (1966). Social influence as a function of attempted and implied usurpation of choice. *Journal of Personality and Social Psychology, 4,* 703–707. [21]

Brehm, J. W., Stires, L. K., Sensenig, J., & Shaban, J. (1966). The attractiveness of an eliminated choice alternative. *Journal of Experimental Social Psychology, 2,* 301–313. [21]

Brehm, S. S. (1988). Passionate love. In R. J. Sternberg & M. L. Barnes (Eds.), *The psychology of love* (pp. 232–263). New Haven, CT: Yale University Press. [29]

Brodyaga, L. (1975). Rape and its victims: *A report for citizens, health facilities, and criminal justice agencies.* Washington, DC: U.S. Government Printing Office. [25]

Brodyaga, L., Gates, M., Singer, S., Tucker, M., & White, R. (1975). *Rape and its victims: A report for citizens, health facilities, and criminal justice agencies* (National Institute of Law Enforcement and Criminal Justice, Law Enforcement Assistance Administration, U.S. Department of Justice). Washington, DC: U.S. Government Printing Office. [6]

Brotman, H. (1974). The fastest growing minority: The aging. *American Journal of Public Health, 64,* 249–252. [8]

Brown, R. (1965). *Social psychology.* New York: Free Press. [20]

Brownmiller, S. (1975). *Against our will: Men, women and rape.* New York: Simon & Schuster. [25]

Bryce, J. W. (1986). *Cries of children in Lebanon as voiced by their mothers.* Beirut: Express International. [11]

Buck, R., Miller, R., & Caul, W. F. (1974). Sex, personality, and physiological variables in the communication of affect via facial expression. *Journal of Personality and Social Psychology, 30,* 587–596. [6]

Bumpass, L., Sweet, J., & Castro Martin, T. (1990). Changing patterns of remarriage. *Journal of Marriage and the Family, 52,* 747–756. [29]

Burger, J. M., & Cooper, H. M. (1979). The desirability of control. *Motivation and Emotion, 3,* 381–393. [7]

Burger, J. M., & Inderbitzen, H. M. (1985). Predicting contraceptive behavior among college students: The role of communication, knowledge, sexual anxiety, and self-esteem. *Archives of Sexual Behavior, 14,* 343–350. [7]

Burgess, A. W., & Holmstrom, L. L. (1974). *Rape: Victims of crisis.* Bowie, MD: Robert J. Brady. [25]

Burnstein, E., & Vinokur, A. (1973). Testing two classes of theories about group induced shifts in individual choice. *Journal of Experimental Social Psychology, 9,* 123–137. [20]

Byrne, D. (1961). Interpersonal attraction and attitude similarity. *Jounal of Abnormal and Social Psychology, 62,* 713–715. [28]

Byrne, D., & Fisher, W. A. (1983). *Adolescents, sex, and contraception.* Hillsdale, NJ: Erlbaum. [7]

Byrne, D., & Wong, T. J. (1962). Racial prejudice, interpersonal attraction, and assumed dissimilarity of attitudes. *Journal of Abnormal and Social Psychology, 65,* 246–253. [28]

Cantor, J. R., Zillmann, D., & Bryant, J. (1975). Enhancement of experienced sexual arousal in response to erotic stimuli through misattribution of unrelated residual arousal. *Journal of Personality and Social Psychology, 32,* 69–75. [29]

Carter post-mortem: Debate hurts, but it wasn't only cause of defeat. (1980, November 9). *New York Times,* pp. 1, 18. [2]

Castro Martin, T. & Bumpass, L. L. (1989). Recent trends in marital disruption. *Demography, 26,* 37–51. [29]

Chappell, D. (1971). Forcible rape: A comparative study of offenses known to police in Boston and Los Angeles. In J. M. Henslin (Ed.), *Studies in the sociology of sex.* New York: Appleton-Century-Crofts. [25]

Cherlin, A. (1983). The trends: Marriage, divorce, remarriage. In A. S. Skolnick & J. H. Skolnick (Eds.), *Family in transition* (4th Ed., pp. 128–137). Boston: Little, Brown. [29]

Cleaver, E. (1968). *Soul on ice.* New York: Dell-Delta/Ramparts. [25]

Cohen, M. L., Garofalo, R., Boucher, R., & Seghorn, T. (1971). The psychology of rapists. *Seminars in Psychiatry, 3,* 317. [25]

Congregation for the Doctrine of the Faith. (1986). *Letter to the bishops of the Catholic church on the pastoral care of homosexual persons.* Vatican City: Author. [23]

Cvetkovich, G., & Grote, B. (1983). Adolescent development and teenage fertility. In D. Byrne & W. A. Fisher (Eds.), *Adolescents, sex, and contraception* (pp. 109–123). Hillsdale, NJ: Erlbaum. [7]

Davis, A. (1975, June). Joanne Little: The dialectics of rape. *Ms.,* p. 106. [25]

Davis, A. J. (1970). Sexual assaults in the Philadelphia prison system. In J. A. Gagnon & W. Simon (Eds.), *The sexual scene.* Chicago: Aldine. [25]

Davis, J. H. (1980). Group decision and procedural justice. In M. Fishbein (Ed.), *Progress in social psychology.* Hillsdale, NJ: Erlbaum. [20]

Davis, K. E., & Todd, M. J. (1982). Friendship and love relationships. In K. E. Davis & T. Mitchell (Eds.), *Advances in descriptive psychology* (Vol. 2, pp. 79–122). Greenwich, CT: JAI Press. [29]

Davis, L. J. (1977). Attitudes toward old age and aging as shown by humor. *Gerontologist, 17,* 220–226. [8]

Davis, M., & Eichhorn, R. (1963). Compliance with medical regimens: A panel study. *Journal of Health and Human Behavior, 4,* 240–249. [21]

Demo, D. H., & Acock, A. C. (1988). The impact of divorce on children. *Journal of Marriage and the Family, 50,* 619–648. [29]

Dermer, M., & Pyszczynski, T. A. (1978). Effects of erotica upon men's loving and liking responses for women they love. *Journal of Personality and Social Psychology, 36,* 1302–1309. [29]

Diamond, R. (1989, December 17). First gay Episcopal priest is ordained. *San Francisco Examiner,* p. A-6. [23]

Diener, E. (1979). Deindividuation, self-awareness, and disinhibition. *Journal of Personality and Social Psychology, 37,* 1160–1171. [19]

Dion, K. L., & Dion, K. K. (1976). Love, liking, and trust in heterosexual relationships. *Personality and Social Psychology Bulletin, 2,* 187–190. [29]

Dutton, D. G., & Aron, A. P. (1974). Some evidence for heightened sexual attraction under conditions of high anxiety. *Journal of Personality and Social Psychology, 30,* 510–517. [29]

Duval, S., & Wicklund, R. A. (1972). *A theory of objective self-awareness.* New York: Academic Press. [19]

Elms, A. (1972). *Social psychology and social relevance.* Boston: Little, Brown. [RI-14]

Emery, R. (1988). *Marriage, divorce and children's adjustment.* Newbury Park, CA: Sage. [29]

Epley, S. W. (1974). Reduction of the behavioral effects of aversive stimulation by the presence of companions. *Psychological Bulletin, 81,* 271–283. [29]

Falk, P. (1989). Lesbian mothers: Psychosocial assumptions in family law. *American Psychologist, 44,* 941–947. [23]

Farley, L. (1978). *Sexual shakedown.* New York: Warner. [25]

Federal Bureau of Investigation (1981). *Uniform crime reports for the United States.* Washington, DC: U.S. Government Printing Office. [25]

Fernandez, E, (1990, January 21). Gays ordained as ministers is an affront to ban. *San Francisco Examiner,* p. B-1. [23]

Festinger, L. (1957). *A theory of cognitive dissonance.* Stanford, CA: Stanford University Press. [7]

Festinger, L., Pepitone, S., & Newcomb, T. (1952). Some consequences of deindividuation in a group. *Journal of Abnormal and Social Psychology, 47,* 382–389. [19]

Fischoff, B. (1975a, April). The silly certainty of hindsight. *Psychology Today,* 71–76. [2]

Fischoff, B. (1975b). Hindsight is not equal to foresight: The effect of outcome knowledge on judgment under uncertainty. *Journal of Experimental Psychology: Human Perception and Performance, 1,* 288–299. [2]

Fischoff, B. (1977). Perceived informativeness of facts. *Journal of Experimental Psychology: Human Perception and Performance, 3,* 349–358. [2]

Fischoff, B., & Beyth, R. (1975). "I knew it would happen"—Remember probability of once-future things. *Organizational Behavior and Human Performance, 13,* 1–16. [2]

Fishbein, M. (1967). A behavior theory approach to the relations between beliefs about an object and the attitude toward the object. In M. Fishbein (Ed.), *Readings in attitude theory and measurement.* New York: Wiley. [21]

Footlick, J. K. (1975, November 10). Rape alert. *Newsweek,* pp. 71. [25]

Frazer, J. G. (Originally published in 1890; 1957). *The new golden bough: A study of magic and religion (abridged).* New York: Macmillan. [18]

French, J. R., & Raven, B. (1959). The bases of social power. In D. Cartwright (Ed.), *Studies in social power.* Ann Arbor, MI: University of Michigan Press. [8]

Furstenberg, F. F., Jr. (1988). Child care after divorce and remarriage. In E. M. Hetherington & J. D. Arasteh (Eds.), *Impact of divorce, singleparenting, and stepparenting on children* (pp. 245–261) Hillsdale, NJ: Erlbaum. [29]

Furstenberg, F. F., Jr., & Spanier, G. B. (1984). The risk of dissolution in remarriage: An examination of Cherlin's hypothesis of incomplete institutionalization. *Family Relations, 33,* 433–441. [29]

Ganong, L. H., & Coleman, M. (1987). Effects of parental remarriage on children. In K. Pasley & M. Ihinger-Tallman (Eds.), *Remarriage and Stepparenting* (pp. 94–140). New York: Guilford. [29]

Genet, J. (1963). *Our lady of the flowers* (translated by B. Frechtman). New York: Grove Press. [25]

Gergen, K. J., Gergen, M. M., & Barton, W. H. (1973). Deviance in the dark. *Psychology Today, 7,* 129–130. [19]

Gerrard, M. (1982). Sex, sex guilt, and contraceptive use. *Journal of Personality and Social Psychology, 42,* 153–158. [7]

Goethals, G. R., & Zanna, M. P. (1979). The role of social comparison in choice shifts. *Journal of Personality and Social Psychology, 37,* 1469–1476. [20]

Goffman, E. (1959). *The presentation of self in everyday life*. Garden City, NJ: Doubleday. [23]

Goffman, E. (1963). *Stigma: Notes on the management of spoiled identity*. Englewood Cliffs, NJ: Prentice-Hall. [23]

Goldman, A. L. (1989, June 27). Reform conference debates allowing homosexuals to become rabbis, *New York Times*, p. A8. [23]

Gonsiorek, J. C. (1982). Results of psychological testing on homosexual populations. *American Behavioral Scientist, 25*, 385–396. [23]

Gonsiorek, J. C., & Weinrich, J. D. (in press). *Homosexuality: Social, psychological, and biological issues* (2nd Ed.). Newbury Park, CA: Sage. [23]

Goodchilds, J. D. (1977). *Non-stranger rape: The role of sexual socialization*. Unpublished grant proposal, University of California, Los Angeles. [6]

Grabitz-Gniech, G. (1971). Some restrictive conditions for the occurence to psychological reactance. *Journal of Personality and Social Psychology, 19*, 188–196. [21]

Greendlinger, V., & Byrne, D. (1987). Coercive sexual fantasies of college men as predictors of self-reported likelihood to rape and overt sexual aggression. *Journal of Sex Research, 23*, 1–11. [RI-25]

Griffin, S. (1971, September). Rape: The all-American crime. *Ramparts, 10*. [25]

Gross, L. (1984). The cultivation of intolerance: Television, blacks and gays. In G. Melischek, K. E. Rosengrn, & J. Stappers (Eds.), *Cultural indicators: An international symposium* (pp. 345–363). Österreichischen Akademie der Wissenschaften. [23]

Groth, A. N., & Burgess, A. W. (1980). Male rape: Offenders and victims. *American Journal of Psychiatry, 137*, 806–810. [23]

Grych, J. H., & Fincham, F. D. (1990). Marital conflict and children's adjustment: A cognitive-contextual framework. *Psychological Bulletin, 108*, 267–290. [29]

Hall, J. A. (1978). Gender effects in decoding nonverbal cues. *Psychological Bulletin, 85*, 845–857. [6]

Hammock, T., & Brehm, J. W. (1966). The attractiveness of choice alternatives when freedom to choose is eliminated by a social agent. *Journal of Personality, 34*, 546–554. [21]

Harvey, O. J. (1962). Personality factors in resolution of perceptual incongruities. *Sociometry, 25*, 336–352. [28]

Hatfield, E. (1988). Passionate and companionate love. In R. J. Sternberg & M. L. Barnes (Eds.), *The psychology of love* (pp. 191–217). New Haven, CT: Yale University Press. [29]

Hatfield, E., & Rapson, R. L. (1987). Passionate love: New directions in research. In W. H. Jones & D. Perlman (Eds.), *Advances in personal relationships* (Vol. 1, pp. 109–139). Greenwich, CT: JAI Press. [29]

Hatfield, E., Traupmann, J., & Sprecher, S. (1984). Older women's perceptions of their intimate relationships. *Journal of Social and Clinical Psychology, 2*, 108–124. [29]

Helson, H. (1964). *Adaptation-level theory*. New York: Harper & Row. [21]

Hendrick, C. A. (1976). *Person perception and rape: An experimental approach*. Unpublished grant proposal, Kent State University. [6]

Herek, G. M. (1986b). The instrumentality of attitudes: Toward a neofunctional theory. *Journal of Social Issues, 42*, 99–114. [23]

Herek, G. M. (1987). Can functions be measured? A new perspective on the functional approach to attitudes. *Social Psychology Quarterly, 50*, 285–303. [23]

Herek, G. M. (in press). Stigma, prejudice, and violence against lesbians and gay men. In J. Gonsiorek & J. Weinrich (Eds.), *Homosexuality: Social, psychological, and biological issues* (2nd Ed.). Newbury Park, CA: Sage. [23]

Herek, G. M., & Glunt, E. K. (1988). An epidemic of stigma: Public reactions to AIDS. *American Psychologist, 43,* 886–891. [23]

Herskovits, M. J. (1955). *Cultural anthropology.* New York: Knopf. [18]

Hetherington, E. M. (1987). Family relations six years after divorce. In K. Pasley & M. Ihinger-Tallman (Eds.), *Remarriage and stepparenting* (pp. 185–205). New York: Guilford. [29]

Hetherington, E. M., Cox, M., & Cox, R. (1982). Effects of divorce on parents and children. In M. Lamb (Ed.), *Nontraditional families* (pp. 233–288). Hillsdale, NJ: Erlbaum. [29]

Hetherington, E. M., Stanley-Hagan, M. & Anderson, E. R. (1989). Marital transitions: A child's perspective. *American Psychologist, 44,* 303–312. [29]

Hindy, C. G., Schwarz, J. C., & Brodsky, A. (1989). *If this is love, why do I feel so insecure?* New York: Atlantic Monthly Press. [29]

Holmes, J. G., & Rempel, J. K. (1989). Trust in close relationships. In C. Hendrick (Ed.), *Review of personality and social psychology: Vol. 10: Close relationships* (pp. 187–220). Newbury Park, CA: Sage Publications. [29]

Homans, G. (1961). *Social behavior: Its elementary forms.* New York: Harcourt, Brace, and World. [28]

Hooker, E. (1957). The adjustment of the male overt homosexual. *Journal of Practice Techniques, 21,* 18–31. [23]

Horos, C. V. (1974). *Rape.* New Canaan, CT: Tobey. [25]

Horowitz, I. A. (1980). Juror selection: A comparison of two methods in several criminal cases. *Journal of Applied Social Psychology, 10,* 86–99. [20]

Hovland, C. I. (1951). Reconciling conflicting results derived from experimental and survey studies of attitude change. *American Psychologist, 14,* 8–17. [RI-15]

Hovland, C. I., Janis, I. L., & Kelley, H. H. (1953). *Communication and persuasion.* New Haven, CT: Yale University Press. [RI-15]

Hovland, C. I., Lumsdaine, A. A., & Sheffield, F. D. (1949). *Experiments on mass communication.* Princeton, NJ: Princeton University Press. [RI-15]

Iwao, S. (1988, August). Social psychology's models of man: Isn't it time for East to meet West? Invited address to the International Congress of Scientific Psychology, Sydney, Australia. [18]

Janis, I., & Rodin, J. (1979). Attitude, control, and decision-making: Social psychology and health care. In G. Stone, N. Adler, & F. Cohen (Eds.), *Health Psychology.* San Francisco: Jossey-Bass. [8]

Johnson-George, C., & Swap, W. (1982). Measurement of specific interpersonal trust: Construction and validation of a scale to assess trust in a specific order. *Journal of Personality and Social Psychology, 43,* 1306–1317. [29]

Johnston, L., O'Malley, P., & Bachman, J. (1988). *Illicit drug use, smoking, and drinking by America's high school students, college students, and young adults, 1975–1987.* National Institute on Drug Abuse, Rockville, MD. [16]

Kalven, H., & Zeisel, H. (1966). *The American jury.* Boston: Little, Brown. [20]

Kanin, E. J. (1957). Male aggression in dating-courtship relations. *American Journal of Sociology, 63,* 200. [6] [25]

Kanin, E. J. (1967). An examination of sexual aggression as a response to sexual frustration. *Journal of Marriage and the Family, 29,* 428–433. [6]

Kanin, E. J. (1969). Selected dyadic aspects of male sex aggression. *Journal of Sex Research, 5,* 12–28. [6]

Kanin, E. J., & Parcell, S. R. (1979). Sexual aggression: A second look at the offended female. *Archives of Sexual Behavior, 6,* 67–76. [6]

Kantrowitz, B., & Wingert, P. (1990, Winter/Spring). Step by step. *Newsweek Special Edition*, pp. 24–34. [29]

Kaplan, M. F., & Miller, C. E. (1987). Group decision making and normative versus informational influence: Effects of type of issue and assigned decision rule. *Journal of Personality and Social Psychology, 53,* 306–313. [20]

Karpman, B. (1954). *The sexual offender and his offenses.* New York: Julian Press. [25]

Katz, P. A. (1976). The acquisition of racial attitudes in children. In P. A. Katz (Ed.), *Towards the elimination of racism* (pp. 125–154). New York: Pergamon. [23]

Katz, S., & Mazur, M. (1979). *Understanding the rape victim: A synthesis of research findings.* New York: Wiley. [6]

Kelley, H. (1967). Attribution theory in social psychology. In D. Levine (Ed.), *Nebraska Symposium on Motivation.* Lincoln: University of Nebraska Press. [8]

Kenrick, D. T., & Cialdini, R. B. (1977). Romantic attraction: Misattribution versus reinforcement explanations. *Journal of Personality and Social Psychology, 35,* 381–391. [29]

Kidder, L. H. (1992). Requirements for being "Japanese": Stories of returnees. *International Journal of Intercultural Relations, 16,* 383–394. [18]

Kinsie, P. M. (1950). Sex crimes and the prostitution racket. *Journal of Social Hygiene, 36,* 250–252. [25]

Kirkham, G. L. (1971). Homosexuality in prison. In J. M. Henslin (Ed.), *Studies in the sociology of sex.* New York: Appleton-Century-Crofts. [25]

Kirkpatrick, C., & Kanin, E. (1975). Male sex aggression on a university campus. *American Sociological Review, 22,* 52–58. [6] [25]

Kluckhohn, C. (1954). Culture and behavior. In G. Lindzey (Ed.), *Handbook of social psychology* (Vol. 2, pp. 921–976). Cambridge, MA: Addison-Wesley. [18]

Komisar, L. (no date). *Violence and the masculine mystique.* Pittsburgh: KNOW. [25]

Koss, M. P., Gidycz, C. A., & Wisniewski, N. (1987). The scope of rape: Incidence and prevalence of sexual aggression and victimization in a national sample of higher education students. *Journal of Consulting and Clinical Psychology, 55,* 162–170. [RI-25]

Krebs, D. L., & Miller, D. T. (1985). Altruism and aggression. In G. Lindsay & E. Aronson (Eds.), *Handbook of social psychology,* 3rd ed. (vol. 2, pp. 1–71). New York: Random House. [RI-30]

La France, M., & Mayo, C. (1976). Racial differences in gaze behavior during conversations: Two systematic observational studies. *Journal of Personality and Social Psychology, 33,* 547–552. [6]

La France, M., & Mayo, C. (1978a). Cultural aspects of nonverbal communication. *International Journal of Intercultural Relations, 2,* 71–89. [6]

La France, M., & Mayo, C. (1978b). Gaze direction in interracial dyadic communication. *Ethnicity, 5,* 167–173. [6]

LaFree, G. (1981). Official reactions to social problems: Police decisions in sexual assault cases. *Social Problems, 28,* 592. [25]

LaFree, G. D. (1980). The effect of sexual stratification by race on official reactions to rape. *American Sociological Review, 45,* 842. [25]

Lamb, M. (1977). The effects of divorce on children's personality development. *Journal of Divorce, 1,* 163–174. [29]

Langer, E. (1979a). Old age: An artifact? *Biology, Behavior and Aging.* Washington, DC: National Research Council publication. [8]

Langer, E. (1979b). The illusion of incompetence. In L. Perlmutter & R. Monty (Eds.), *Choice and perceived control.* Hillsdale, NJ: Erlbaum. [8]

Langer, E., & Benevento, A. (1978). Self-induced dependence. *Journal of Personality and Social Psychology, 36,* 886–893. [8]

Langer, E., & Mulvey, A. (1980). Unpublished data. Harvard University, Department of Psychology. Cambridge, MA. [8]

Langer, E., & Rodin, J. (1976). The effects of choice and enhanced personal responsibility for the aged: A field experiment in an institutional setting. *Journal of Personality and Social Psychology, 34,* 191–198. [8]

Langer, E., Rodin, J., Beck, P., Weinman, C., & Spitzer, L. (1979). Environmental determinants of memory improvement in late adulthood. *Journal of Personality and Social Psychology, 37,* 2003–2013. [8]

Lattin, D. (1988, October 26). Episcopalians endorse gay "marriages." *San Francisco Chronicle,* p. A8. [23]

Laws, J. L., & Schwartz, P. (1977). *Sexual scripts.* Hinsdale, IL: Dryden Press. [25]

Leary, M. R. (1981). The distorted nature of hindsight. *Journal of Social Psychology, 115,* 25–29. [2]

LeGrand, C. E. (1973). Rape and rape laws: Sexism in society and law. *California Law Review, 61,* 922. [25]

Long, N., & Forehand, R. (1987). The effects of parental divorce and marital conflict on children: An overview. *Journal of Developmental and Behavioral Pediatrics, 8,* 292–296. [29]

Maccoby, E. E., Depner, C. E., & Mnookin, R. H. (1990). Coparenting in the second year after divorce. *Journal of Marriage and the Family, 52,* 141–155. [29]

Marshall, G. D., & Zimbardo, P. G. (1979). Affective consequences of an inadequately explained physiological arousal. *Journal of Personality and Social Psychology, 37,* 970–988. [29]

Maslach, C. (1979). Negative emotional biasing of explained arousal. *Journal of Personality and Social Psychology, 37,* 953–969. [29]

McCaldon, R. J. (1967). Rape. *Canadian Journal of Corrections, 9,* 47. [25]

McKinney, K., Sprecher, S., & DeLamater, J. (1984). Self-image and contraceptive behavior. *Basic and Applied Social Psychology, 5,* 37–57. [7]

Mead, M. (1968). *Sex and temperament in three primitive societies.* New York: Dell. [25]

Medea, A., & Thompson, K. (1974). *Against rape.* New York: Farrar, Straus & Giroux. [6] [25]

Melton, G. B. (1989). Public policy and private prejudice: Psychology and law on gay rights. *American Psychologist, 44,* 933–940. [23]

Merton, R. K. (1948). The self-fulfilling prophecy. *Antioch Review, 8,* 193–210. [RI-4]

Mitchell, H. E. (1979). *Informational and affective determinants of juror decision making.* Unpublished doctoral dissertation, Purdue University. [20]

Moscovici, S., & Zavalloni, M. (1969). The group as a polarizer of attitudes. *Journal of Personality and Social Psychology, 12,* 125–135. [20]

Myers, D. G. (1994). *Exploring Social Psychology.* New York: McGraw-Hill.

Myers, D. G., & Kaplan, M. F. (1976). Group induced polarization in simulated juries. *Personality and Social Psychology Bulletin, 2,* 63–66. [20]

Myers, D. G., & Lamm, H. (1975). The group polarization phenomenon. *Psychological Bulletin, 83,* 602–627. [20]

National Institute of Law Enforcement and Criminal Justice. (1977). *Forcible rape: A national survey of the response by prosecutors* (Vol. 1). Washington, DC: U.S. Government Printing Office. [25]

Negroes accuse Maryland bench: Double standard is charged in report on rape case. (1967, September 18). *New York Times,* p. 33. [25]

Newcomb, T. M. (1956). The prediction of interpersonal attraction. *American Psychologist, 11,* 575–586. [28]

Newcomb, T. M. (1961). *The acquaintance process.* New York: Holt, Rinehart, and Winston. [28]

Norton, A. J. (1987, July/August). Families and children in the year 2000. *Children Today,* pp. 6–9. [29]

Norton, A. J., & Moorman, J. E. (1987). Current trends in marriage and divorce among American women. *Journal of Marriage and the Family, 49,* 3–14. [29]

Pallack, M. S., & Heller, J. F. (1970). Interactive effects of commitment to future interaction and threat to attitudinal freedom. *Journal of Personality and Social Psychology, 14,* 39–45. [21]

Pam, A., Plutchik, R., & Conte, H. R. (1975). Love: A psychometric approach. *Psychological Reports, 37,* 83–88. [29]

Pearlin, L. I. (1989). The sociological study of stress. *Journal of Health and Social Behavior, 30,* 241–256. [11]

Peele, S. (1988). Fools for love: The romantic ideal, psychological theory, and addictive love. In R. J. Sternberg & M. L. Barnes (Eds.), *The psychology of love* (pp. 159–188). New Haven, CT: Yale University Press. [29]

Peele, S. (1989). *The diseasing of America: Addiction treatment out of control.* Lexington, MA: Lexington Books. [11]

Pennebaker, J. W., & Skelton, J. A. (1978). Psychological parameters of physical symptoms. *Personality and Social Psychology Bulletin, 4,* 524–530. [8]

Perloff, L. S. (1983). Perceptions of vulnerability to victimization. *Journal of Social Issues, 39,* 41–61. [7]

Perloff, L. S., & Fetzer, B. K. (1986). Self-other judgments and perceived vulnerability to victimization. *Journal of Personality and Social Psychology, 50,* 502–510. [7]

Person, E. S. (1988). *Dreams of love and fateful encounters.* New York: Norton.

Peterson, D. A., & Karnes, E. L. (1976). Older people in adolescent literature. *Gerontologist, 16,* 252–231. [8]

Peterson, J. L., & Nord, C. W. (1990). The regular receipt of child support: A multistage process. *Journal of Marriage and the Family, 52,* 539–551. [29]

Phillips, H. P. (1965). *Thai peasant personality: The patterning of interpersonal behavior in the village of Bang Chan.* Berkeley: University of California Press. [18]

Pogrebin, L. C. (1974, November). Do women make men violent? *Ms.,* p. 9. [25]

Reisenzein, R. (1983).The Schachter theory of emotion: Two decades later. *Psychological Bulletin, 94,* 239–264. [29]

Rich, S. (1989, December 8). Child-support collections jump in '88. *The Washington Post,* p. A13. [29]

Richman, J. (1977). The foolishness and wisdom of age: Attitudes toward the elderly as reflected in jokes. *Gerontologist, 17,* 219–229. [8]

Riddle, J. M. & Estes, J. W. (1992). Oral contraceptives in ancient and medieval times. *American Scientist, 80,* 226–233. [18]

Riordan, C. A., & Tedeschi, J. T. (1983). Attraction in aversive environments: Some evidence for classical conditioning and negative reinforcement. *Journal of Personality and Social Psychology, 44,* 683–692. [29]

Rodin, J. (1978). Somatophysics and attribution. *Personality and Social Psychology Bulletin, 4,* 531–540. [8]

Rodin, J. (1980). Managing the stress of aging: The role of control and coping. In S. Levine & H. Ursin (Eds.), *NATO Conference on Coping and Health.* New York: Academic Press. [8]

Rodin, J., & Janis, I. (1979). The social power of health-care practitioners as agents of change. *Journal of Social Issues, 35,* 60–81. [8]

Rodin, J., & Langer, E. (1977). Long-term effects of a control-relevant intervention with the institutionalized aged. *Journal of Personality and Social Psychology, 35,* 897–902. [8]

Rosen, G. M. (1987). Self-help treatment books and the commercialization of psychotherapy. *American Psychologist, 42,* 46–51. [11]

Rosenthal, R. (1971). Pygmalion reaffirmed. In J. Elashoff & R. Snow (Eds.), *Pygmalion reconsidered.* Worthington, OH: C. A. Jones. [8]

Rosenthal, R., Hall, J. A., DiMatteo, M. R., Rogers, P. L., & Archer, D. (1979). *Sensitivity to nonverbal communication: The PONS test.* Baltimore: Johns Hopkins University Press. [6]

Rosenthal, R. & Jacobson, L. (1968). *Pygmalion in the classroom: Teacher expectation and intellectual development.* New York: Holt, Rinehart & Winston. [RI-4]

Rothbaum, F., Weisz, J. R., & Snyder, S. S. (1982). Changing the world versus changing the self: A two-process model of perceived control. *Journal of Personality and Social Psychology, 42,* 5–37. [11]

Rozin, P., Millman, L., & Nemeroff, C. (1986). Operation of the laws of sympathetic magic in disgust and other domains. *Journal of Personality and Social Psychology, 50,* 703–712. [18]

Rubin, Z. (1973). *Liking and loving.* New York: Holt, Rinehart & Winston. [29]

Russell, D. E. H. (1975). *The politics of rape.* New York: Stein & Day. [6]

Russo, V. (1981). *The celluloid closet: Homosexuality in the movies.* New York: Harper & Row. [23]

Russo, V. (1989, June). *Nelly toons: A look at animated sissies.* Introduction to a program at the 13th Lesbian and Gay Film Festival, Castro Theater, San Francisco. [23]

Saks, M. J., & Hastie, R. (1978). *Social psychology in court.* New York: Van Nostrand Reinhold. [20]

Santrock, J. W., & Sitterle, K. A. (1987). Parent-child relationships in stepmother families. In K. Pasley & M. Ihinger-Tallman (Eds.), *Remarriage and stepparenting* (pp. 273–299). New York: Guilford. [29]

Schachter, S. (1959). *The psychology of affiliation: Experimental studies of the sources of gregariousness.* Stanford, CA: Stanford University Press. [29]

Schachter, S. (1964). The interaction of cognitive and physiological determinants of emotional state. In L. Berkowitz (Ed.), *Advances in experimental social psychology* (Vol. 1, pp. 49–80). New York: Academic Press. [29]

Schlenker, B. R. (1980). *Impression management: The self-concept, social identity, and interpersonal relations.* Belmont, CA: Brooks/Cole. [2]

Schneider, W., & Lewis, I. A. (1984, February). The straight story on homosexuality and gay rights. *Public Opinion, 16–20,* 59–60. [23]

Schulman, J., Shaver, P., Colman, D., Emrich, B., & Christie, R. (1973, May). Recipe for a jury. *Psychology Today,* pp. 37–44, 77–84. [20]

Schultz, L. (1960). Interviewing the sex offender's victim. *Journal of Criminal Law, Criminology and Police Science, 50,* 451. [25]

Schwendinger, J. R., & Schwendinger, H. (1974). Rape myths: In legal, theoretical, and everyday practice. *Crime and Social Justice, 1,* 19. [25]

Segrest, M., & Zeskind, L. (1989). *Quarantines and death: The Far Right's homophobic agenda.* (Available from Center for Democratic Renewal, PO Box 50469, Atlanta, GA 30302). [23]

Seligman, M. E. P. (1988). *Why is there so much depression today? The waxing of individual and the waning of the commons.* Invited lecture at the Annual Convention of the American Psychological Association, Atlanta. [11]

Seltzer, J. A., Schaeffer, N. C., & Charng, H. (1989). Family ties after divorce: The relationship between visiting and paying child support. *Journal of Marriage and the Family, 51,* 1013–1031. [29]

Shallenberger, P., & Zigler, E. (1961). Rigidity, negative reaction tendencies and cosatiation effects in normal and feebleminded children. *Journal of Abnormal and Social Psychology, 63,* 20–26. [28]

Shaw, M. E., & Sulzer, J. L. (1964). An empirical test of Heider's levels in attribution of responsibility. *Journal of Abnormal and Social Psychology, 69,* 39–46. [2]

Singer, J. E., Brush, C. A., Lublin, S. C. (1965). Some aspects of deindividuation identification and conformity. *Journal of Experimental Social Psychology, 1,* 356–378. [19]

Smith, E. R. (1978). Specifications and estimation of causal models in psychology: Comment on Tesser and Paulus. *Journal of Personality and Social Psychology, 36,* 34–38. [29]

Snyder, M., & Swann, W. (1978). Behavioral confirmation in social interaction: From social perception to social psychology. *Journal of Experimental Social Psychology, 14,* 148–162. [8]

Sohngen, M. (1977). The experiences of old age as depicted in contemporary novels. *Gerontologist, 17,* 70–78. [8]

Sohngen, M., & Smith, R. J. (1978). Images of old age in poetry. *Gerontologist, 18,* 181–186. [8]

Staff. (1968). Police discretion and the judgment that a crime has been committed: Rape in Philadelphia. *University of Pennsylvania Law Review, 117,* 318. [25]

Staff. (1980). The rape corroboration requirement: Repeal not reform. *Yale Law Journal, 81,* 1366. [25]

Staff. (1982). The corroboration rule and crimes accompanying a rape. *University of Pennsylvania Law Review, 118,* 461. [25]

Stasser, G., Kerr, N. L., & Bray, R. M. (1982). The social psychology of jury deliberations: Structure, process, and products. In N. L. Kerr and R. M. Bray (Eds.), *The psychology of the courtroom* (pp. 221–256). New York: Academic Press. [20]

Stasser, G., Kerr, N. L., & Davis, J. H. (1989). Influence processes and consensus models in decision-making groups. In P. B. Paulus (Ed.), *Psychology of group influence* (2nd ed., pp. 279–326). Hillsdale, NJ: Erlbaum. [20]

Steck, L., Levitan, D., McLane, D., & Kelley, H. H. (1982). Care, need, and conceptions of love. *Journal of Personality and Social Psychology, 43,* 481–491. [29]

Stephan, W., Berscheid, E., & Walster, E. (1971). Sexual arousal and heterosexual perception. *Journal of Personality and Social Psychology, 20,* 93–101. [29]

Stevenson, H. W., Keen, R., & Knights, R. M. (1963). Parents and strangers as reinforcing agents for children's performance. *Journal of Abnormal and Social Psychology, 67,* 183–185. [28]

Stevenson, H. W., & Knights, R. M. (1962). Social reinforcement with normal and retarded children as a function of pretraining, sex of E, and sex of S. *American Journal of Mental Deficiency, 66,* 866–871. [28]

Stolberg, L. A., Camplair, C., Currier, K., & Wells, M. J. (1987). Individual, familial, and environmental determinants of children's post-divorce adjustment and maladjustment. *Journal of Divorce, 11,* 51–70. [29]

Stoner, J. A. (1961). *A comparison of individual and group decisions involving risk.*

Unpublished master's thesis. School of Industrial Management, Massachusetts Institute of Technology. [20]

Strodtbeck, F. L., & Hook, L. H. (1961). The social dimensions of a twelve-man jury table. *Sociometry, 24,* 397–415. [20]

Strodtbeck, F. L., James, R. M., & Hawkins, D. (1957). Social status in jury deliberations. *American Sociological Review, 22,* 713–719. [20]

Sue S., Smith, R. E., & Caldwell, C. (1973). Effects of inadmissable evidence on the decisions of simulated jurors: A moral dilemma. *Journal of Applied Social Psychology, 3,* 345–353. [20]

Tennov, D. (1979). *Love and limerence: The experience of being in love.* New York: Stein & Day. [29]

Tesser, A. (1978). Toward a self-evaluation maintenance model of social behavior. In L. Berkowitz (Ed.), *Advances in experimental social psychology* (Vol. 21, pp. 181–227). New York: Academic Press. [29]

Tesser, A., & Paulus, D. L. (1976). Toward a causal model of love. *Journal of Personality and Social Psychology, 34,* 1095–1105. [29]

Tesser, A., & Paulus, D. L. (1978). On models and assumptions: A reply to Smith. *Journal of Personality and Social Psychology, 36,* 40–42. [29]

Thibault, J., & Kelley, H. H. (1959). *The social psychology of groups.* New York: Wiley.

Thorton, B., Robbin, M. A., & Johnson, J. A. (1981). Social perception of the rape victim's culpability: The influence of respondent's personal environmental causal attributional tendencies. *Human Relations, 34,* 233. [25]

Torrey, E. F. (1986). *Witchdoctors and psychiatrists: The common roots of psychotherapy and its future.* New York: Harper. [18]

Triandis, H. C. (1972). *The analysis of subjective culture.* New York: Wiley. [18]

Tschann, J. M., Johnston, J. R., Kline, M., & Wallerstein, J. S. (1989). Family process and children's functioning during divorce. *Journal of Marriage and the Family, 51,* 431–444. [29]

Tschann, J. M., Johnston, J. R., & Wallerstein, J. S. (1989). Resources, stressors, and attachment as predictors of adult adjustment after divorce: A longitudinal study. *Journal of Marriage and the Family. 51,* 1033–1046. [29]

Turnbull, C. M. (1961). *The forest people.* New York: Simon & Schuster. [RI-12]

Tversky, A., & Kahneman, D. (1974). Judgment under uncertainty: Heuristics and biases. *Science, 185,* 1124–1131. [2]

Unger, R. K., Draper, R. C., & Pendergrass, M. L. (1986). Personal epistemology and personal experience. *Journal of Social Issues, 42,* 67–79. [RI-3]

Vemer, E., Coleman, M., Ganong, L. H., & Cooper, H. (1989). Marital satisfaction in remarriage: A meta-analysis. *Journal of Marriage and the Family, 51,* 713–725. [29]

Visher, C. A. (1987). Juror decision making: The importance of evidence. *Law and Human Behavior, 11,* 1–17. [20]

Vontress, C. E. (1991). Traditional healing in Africa: Implications for cross-cultural counseling. *Counseling and Development, 70,* 242–249. [18]

Wack, J., & Rodin, J. (1978). Nursing homes for the aged: The human consequences of legislation-shaped environments. *Journal of Social Issues, 34*(4), 6–21. [8]

Walster, E. (1967). Second-guessing important events. *Human Relations, 20,* 239–249. [2]

Walster, E. (1971). Passionate love. In B. Murstein (Ed.), *Theories of attraction and love* (pp. 85–99). New York: Springer. [29]

Walters, R. H., & Foote, A. (1962). A study of reinforcer effectiveness with children. *Merrill-Palmer Quarterly: Behavioral Development, 8,* 149–157. [28]

Walters, R. H., & Ray, E. (1960). Anxiety, social isolation, and reinforcer effectiveness. *Journal of Personality, 28,* 258–267. [28]

Weinstein, N. D. (1980). Unrealistic optimism about future life events. *Journal of Personality and Social Psychology, 39,* 806–820. [7]

Weis, K., & Borges, S. S. (1973). Victimology and rape: The case of the legitimate victim. *Issues in Criminology, 8,* 71–115. [6] [25]

Weissman, E. (1978, August). Kids who attack gays. *Christopher Street,* pp. 9–13. [23]

Weitzman, L. J. (1985). *The divorce revolution: The unexpected social and economic consequences for women and children in America.* New York: The Free Press. [29]

White, G. L., Fishbein, M., & Rutstein, J. (1981). Passionate love: The misattribution of arousal. *Journal of Personality and Social Psychology, 41,* 56–62. [29]

White, G. L., & Kight, T. D. (1984). Misattribution of arousal and attraction: Effects of salience of explanation of arousal. *Journal of Experimental Social Psychology, 20,* 55–64. [29]

White, R. W. (1959). Motivation reconsidered: The concept of competence. *Psychological Review, 66,* 297-334. [28]

Wicklund, R. A., & Brehm, J. W. (1968). Attitude change as a function of felt competence and threat to attitudinal freedom. *Journal of Experimental Social Psychology, 4,* 64–75. [21]

Wilson, T. D., & Linville, P. W. (1985). Improving the performance of college freshmen with attributional techniques. *Journal of Experimental Social Psychology, 49,* 283–293. [RI-6]

Wolf, S., & Montgomery, D. A. (1977). Effects of inadmissible evidence and level of judicial admonishment. *Journal of Applied Social Psychology, 7,* 205–219. [20]

Wood, G. (1978). The knew-it-all-along effect. *Journal of Experimental Psychology: Human Perception and Performance, 4,* 345–353. [2]

Wood, P. L. (1973). The victim in a forcible rape: A feminist view. *American Criminal Law Review, 7,* 348. [25]

Wooley, S., & Wooley, O. W. (1977). *Obesity and women, I: A closer look at the facts.* Paper presented at the Second International Congress on Obesity, Washington, DC. [8]

Worchel, S., & Brehm, J. W. (1971). Direct and implied social restoration of freedom. *Journal of Personality and Social Psychology, 18,* 294–304. [21]

Wrightsman, L. S. (1987). *Psychology and the legal system.* Monterey, CA: Brooks/Cole. [20]

Yetman, N. R. (1970). *Voices from slavery.* New York: Holt, Rinehart, & Winston. [11]

Zill, N. (1988). Behavior, achievement and health problems among children in stepfamilies. In E. M. Hetherington & J. D. Arasteh (Eds.), *Impact of divorce, singleparenting, and stepparenting on children* (pp. 325–368). Hillsdale, NJ: Erlbaum. [29]

Zillmann, D. (1978). Attribution and misattribution of excitatory reactions. In J. H. Harvey, W. Ickes, & R. F. Kidd (Eds.), *New directions in attribution research* (Vol. 2, pp. 335–368). Hillsdale, NJ: Erlbaum. [29]

Zillmann, D. (1984). *Connections between sex and aggression.* Hillsdale, NJ: Erlbaum. [29]

Zillmann, D., Johnson, R. C., & Day, K. D. (1974). Attribution of apparent arousal and proficiency of recovery from sympathetic activation affecting excitation transfer to aggressive behavior. *Journal of Experimental Social Psychology, 10,* 503–515. [29]

Zimbardo, P. G. (1970). The human choice: Individuation, reason and order versus deindividuation, impulse and chaos. In W. J. Arnold & D. Levine (Eds.), *Nebraska Symposium on Motivation* (Vol. 18), Lincoln: University of Nebraska Press. [19]

Name Index

Abbey, A., 47
Acock, A. C., 229, 240
Adorno, T. W., 108, 237
Ahrons, C. R., 229, 237
Ajzen, I., 71, 237
Allen, J. B., 226, 237
Allen, W., 78
Allgeier, A. R., 237
Allport, G., 31, 183, 237
Ambert, A., 229, 237
Amir, M., 237
Amir, Y., 183, 237
Ananda, A. C., 8
Anderson, E. R., 243
Anderson, J., 14, 17, 18, 228
Anderson, R. D., 195
Anderson, S., 32
Andrews, D. S., 23
Antonovsky, A., 85, 238
Archer, D., 50, 247
Arendt, H., 109
Aristole, 133
Aron, A. P., 224, 225, 238, 240
Aron, E. N., 224, 225, 238
Aronson, E., 211, 218, 238
Asch, S., 42
Auerbacher, I., 233

Bachman, J., 131, 243
Bales, R. F., 160, 238
Bandura, A., 64, 238
Banks, W. C., 113
Barrett, K., 238
Barry, K., 238
Bart, P., 195
Barth, K., 233
Barton, W. H., 147, 149, 241
Bauer, G., 233
Bayer, R., 180, 238
Beach, S. R. H., 238
Beck, P., 68, 245
Bell, R. M., 122
Bem, D. J., 4, 23, 48, 61, 238
Bem, S. L., 4, 23, 32, 48, 238
Benedict, R., 38
Beneke, T., 238
Benevento, A., 70, 245
Bentler, P. M., 238
Berezin, M., 64, 238
Berkowitz, L., 149, 238

Bernard, J., 49, 238
Berscheid, E., 31, 224, 238, 248
Beyth, R., 15, 18
Biondo, J., 163, 238
Blue, G. F., 64, 238
Bobbitt, L., 155
Bond, J., 192
Bonhoeffer, D., 233
Borges, S. S., 49, 250
Bornstein, E., 236
Bossio, L. M., 83
Boswell, J., 180, 238
Boucher, R., 240
Bowe, F., 171
Bowen-Woodward, K., 230, 238
Brand, E., 230, 238
Braver, S. L., 228, 238
Bray, J. H., 230, 239
Bray, R. M., 248
Brehm, J. W., 163, 164, 239, 242, 250
Brehm, S. S., 222, 239
Briere, A., 194
Brodsky, A., 224, 243
Brodyaga, L., 49, 239
Brotman, H., 64, 239
Brown, R., 159, 239
Brownmiller, S., 239
Brush, C. A., 147, 148, 248
Bryant, J., 226, 240
Bryce, J. W., 85, 86, 239
Buck, R., 50, 239
Bumpass, L. L., 229, 230, 239, 240
Bunker, A., 69
Burger, J. M., 57, 58, 59, 239
Burgess, A. W., 182, 196, 239, 242
Burns, L., 57
Burnstein, E., 159, 239
Bush, G. H. W., 14
Butler, L., 64
Byrne, D., 58, 190, 212, 239, 242

Cacioppo, J. T., 116
Caldwell, C., 25
Camplair, C., 229, 248
Cantor, J. R., 226, 240
Cantril, H., 33
Carter, J. E., 15, 17
Castrianno, L., 207
Castro Martin, T., 229, 230, 239, 240
Caul, W. F., 50, 239

Russo, V., 180, 181, 247
Rutstein, J., 225, 250

Saks, M. J., 156, 247
Sanday, P., 191
Sandler, I. N., 228, 238
Sanford, R. N., 108, 237
Santrock, J. W., 230, 247
Sauvage, P., 235
Schachter, S., 224, 225, 247
Schaeffer, N. C., 228, 248
Schindler, O., 232, 236
Schlenker, B. R., 46, 247
Schneider, W., 181, 183, 247
Schulman, J., 161, 244
Schultz, L., 247
Schwartz, P., 245
Schwarz, J. C., 224, 243
Schwendinger, H., 247
Schwendinger, J. R., 247
Seghorn, T., 240
Segrest, M., 182, 183, 247
Seligman, M. E. P., 84, 248
Seltzer, J. A., 228, 248
Sensenig, J., 163, 239
Shaban, J., 163, 239
Shallenberger, P., 220, 248
Shanmugam, A. V., 143
Shaver, P., 247
Shaw, M. E., 19, 248
Sheffield, F. D., 116, 243
Sherk, D., 33
Siller, J., 174
Singer, J. E., 147, 148, 149, 153, 248
Singer, S., 49, 239
Sitterle, K. A., 230, 247
Skelton, J. A., 67, 246
Skrypnek, B., 32
Smith, D., 198
Smith, E. R., 248
Smith, R. E., 249
Smith, R. J., 64, 248
Snyder, M., 30, 38, 64, 248
Snyder, S. S., 84, 247
Sohngen, M., 64, 248
Spanier, G. B., 229, 241
Spielberg, S., 232
Spitzer, L., 68, 245
Sprecher, S., 58, 242, 245
Stanley-Hagan, M., 228, 243
Stasser, G., 156, 157, 160, 248
Steck, L., 248
Stephan, W., 224, 248
Stevenson, H. W., 220, 248

Stires, L. K., 163, 239
Stolberg, L. A., 229, 248
Stoner, J. A., 158, 248
Strodtbeck, F. L., 160, 249
Sue, S., 159 249
Sulzer, J. L., 19, 248
Swann, W., 64, 248
Swap, W., 243
Sweet, J., 229, 239

Tanke, E. D., 31
Tedeschi, J. T., 225, 246
Tennov, D., 249
Tesser, A., 238, 249
Thibault, J., 212, 249
Thomas, W. I., 30
Thompson, K., 49, 196, 245
Thorton, B., 249
Timerman, J., 109
Todd, M. J., 240
Torrey, E. F., 146, 249
Traupmann, J., 242
Triandis, H C., 141, 142, 143, 249
Triplett, N., 133, 141
Trocmé, A., 235
Trocmé, M., 235
Tschann, J. M., 229, 249
Tucker, M., 49, 239
Turnbull, C. M., 91, 141, 249
Tversky, A., 16, 249

Ukalo, D., 233
Unger, R. K., 24, 249
Uranowitz, S., 34

Vemer, E., 229, 249
Vidmar, N., 207
Vinokur, A., 159, 239
Visher, C. A., 156, 249
vonBaeyer, C., 33
Vontress, C. E., 145, 249

Wack, J., 69, 249
Wallenberg, R., 236
Wallerstein, J. S., 229, 249
Wallisch, L. S., 229, 237
Walster, E., 16, 224, 238, 248, 249
Walters, R. H., 220, 249, 250
Weiner, V. L., 109, 231
Weinman, C., 68, 245
Weinrich, J. D., 180, 242
Weinstein, N. D., 250
Weis, K., 49, 250
Weissman, E., 182, 250

Subject Index

see that I am wrong in treating it as a greater imposition. At bottom it is the same thing.[1]

I think I can now hear a dignified voice admonishing me: 'It is precisely because your neighbour is not worthy of love, and is on the contrary your enemy, that you should love him as yourself.'

Now it is very probable that my neighbour, when he is enjoined to love me as himself, will answer exactly as I have done and will repel me for the same reasons. I hope he will not have the same objective grounds for doing so, but he will have the same idea as I have. Even so, the behaviour of human beings shows differences, which ethics, disregarding the fact that such differences are determined, classifies as 'good' or 'bad'. So long as these undeniable differences have not been removed, obedience to high ethical demands entails damage to the aims of civilization, for it puts a positive premium on being bad.

The element of truth behind all this, which people are so ready to disavow, is that men are not gentle creatures who want to be loved, and who at the most can defend themselves if they are attacked; they are, on the contrary, creatures among whose instinctual endowments is to be reckoned a powerful share of aggressiveness. As a result, their neighbour is for them not only a potential helper or sexual object, but also someone who tempts them to satisfy their aggressiveness on him, to exploit his capacity for work without compensation, to use him sexually without his consent, to seize his possessions, to humiliate him, to cause him pain, to torture and to kill him. Who, in the face of all of his experience of life and of history, will have the courage to dispute this assertion? As a rule this cruel aggressiveness waits for some provocation or puts itself at the service of some other purpose, whose goal might also have been reached by milder measures. In circumstances that are favourable to it, when the mental counter-forces which ordinarily inhibit it are out of action, it also manifests itself spontaneously and reveals man as a savage beast to whom consideration towards his own kind is something alien. Anyone who calls to mind the atrocities committed during [human recorded history] will have to bow humbly before the truth of this view.

The existence of this inclination to aggression, which we can detect in ourselves and justly assume to be present in others, is the factor which disturbs our relations with our neighbour and which forces civilization into such a high expenditure [of energy]. In consequence of this primary mutual hostility of human beings, civilized society is perpetually threatened with disintegration. The interest of work in common would not hold it together; instinctual passions are stronger than reasonable interests. Civilization has to use its utmost efforts in order to set limits to man's aggressive instincts and to hold the manifestations of them in check by psychical reaction-

---

[1] A great imaginative writer may permit himself to give expression—jokingly, at all events—to psychological truths that are severely proscribed. Thus Heine confesses: 'Mine is a most peaceable disposition. My wishes are: a humble cottage with a thatched roof, but a good bed, good food, the freshest milk and butter, flowers before my window, and a few fine trees before my door; and if God wants to make my happiness complete, he will grant me the joy of seeing some six or seven of my enemies' hanging from those trees. Before their death I shall, moved in my heart, forgive them all the wrong they did me in their lifetime. One must, it is true, forgive one's enemies—but not before they have been hanged.' (*Gedanken Und Einfälle* [section I].)

formations. Hence, therefore, the use of methods to incite people into identifications and aim-inhibited relationships of love, hence the restriction upon sexual life, and hence too the ideal's commandment to love one's neighbour as oneself—a commandment which is really justified by the fact that nothing else runs so strongly counter to the original nature of man. In spite of every effort, these endeavours of civilization have not so far achieved very much. It hopes to prevent the crudest excesses of brutal violence by itself assuming the right to use violence against criminals, but the law is not able to lay hold of the more cautious and refined manifestations of human aggressiveness. The time comes when each one of us has to give up as illusions the expectations which, in his youth, he pinned upon his fellowmen, and when he may learn how much difficulty and pain has been added to his life by their ill-will. At the same time, it would be unfair to reproach civilization with trying to eliminate strife and competition from human activity. These things are undoubtedly indispensable. But opposition is not necessarily enmity; it is merely misused and made an *occasion* for enmity.

The communists believe that they have found the path to deliverance from our evils. According to them, man is wholly good and is well-disposed to his neighbour; but the institution of private property has corrupted his nature. The ownership of private wealth gives the individual power, and with it the temptation to ill-treat his neighbour; while the man who is excluded from possession is bound to rebel in hostility against his oppressor. If private property were abolished, all wealth held in common, and everyone allowed to share in the enjoyment of it, ill-will and hostility would disappear among men. Since everyone's needs would be satisfied, no one would have any reason to regard another as his enemy; all would willingly undertake the work that was necessary. I have no concern with any economic criticisms of the communist system; I cannot enquire into whether the abolition of private property is expedient or advantageous. But I am able to recognize that the psychological premises on which the system is based are an untenable illusion. In abolishing private property we deprive the human love of aggression of one of its instruments, certainly a strong one, though certainly not the strongest; but we have in no way altered the differences in power and influence which are misused by aggressiveness, nor have we altered anything in its nature. Aggressiveness was not created by property. It reigned almost without limit in primitive times, when property was still very scanty, and it already shows itself in the nursery almost before property has given up its primal, anal form; it forms the basis of every relation of affection and love among people (with the single exception, perhaps, of the mother's relation to her male child). If we do away with personal rights over material wealth, there still remains prerogative in the field of sexual relationships, which is bound to become the source of the strongest dislike and the most violent hostility among men who in other respects are on an equal footing. If we were to remove this factor, too, by allowing complete freedom of sexual life and thus abolishing the family, the germ-cell of civilization, we cannot, it is true, easily foresee what new paths the development of civilization could take; but one thing we can expect, and that is that this indestructible feature of human nature will follow it there.

It is clearly not easy for men to give up the satisfaction of this inclination to aggression. They do not feel comfortable without it. It is always possible to bind together a considerable number of people in love, so long as there are other people left over to re-